DATE			
		SEP 1 2 1988	

The Study of Temperament:
Changes, Continuities and Challenges

THE STUDY OF TEMPERAMENT: CHANGES, CONTINUITIES AND CHALLENGES

Edited by

ROBERT PLOMIN
University of Colorado, Boulder

JUDITH DUNN
University of Cambridge, Cambridge, England

LEA LAWRENCE ERLBAUM ASSOCIATES, PUBLISHERS
1986   Hillsdale, New Jersey   London

60 37184

Lawrence Erlbaum Associates, Inc., Publishers
365 Broadway
Hillsdale, New Jersey 07642

Library of Congress Cataloging in Publication Data
Main entry under title:

The Study of temperament.

Includes bibliographies and index.
1. Temperament in children—Research.   2. Temperament
—Research.   I. Plomin, Robert, 1948–   . II. Dunn,
Judy, 1939–   . [DNLM: 1. Personality—in fancy &
childhood.   BF 798 S933]
BF723.T53S78   1986   155.2   85-27556
ISBN 0-89859-670-X

Printed in the United States of America
10   9   8   7   6   5   4   3   2   1

Contents

Introduction

Robert Plomin

The modern history of temperament research began in the late 1950s with the New York Longitudinal Study conducted by Alexander Thomas, Stella Chess, and their colleagues. Twenty-five years later, temperament has become a major focus of research on early-developing emotional and social traits. For example, a computer search of *Psychological Abstracts* shows that since 1970 the number of articles on temperament has increased by 50% each 5 years. From 1970 through 1974, 26 articles with the word *temperament* in the title or abstract were published per year on the average. During the second half of that decade, approximately 42 articles appeared each year. The rising trend continues in the 1980s: From 1980 to 1983, 62 articles on temperament were published on average each year.

The impetus for this growth in temperament research stems from the merging of several shifts in child development research: from a view of the child as passive to a model of the child as an active, transacting partner with the environment; increasing interest in individual differences in development; an expansion of research on emotional and social development; and a clear change from an exclusive reliance on environmental explanations of developmental differences to a more balanced perspective that recognizes the possibility of biological as well as environmental influences. Most stimulating is the multidisciplinary flavor of temperament research—clinicians, infancy researchers, cultural anthropologists, and behavioral geneticists have, each for their own reasons, been drawn to the study of temperament.

Each of these fields is represented in the present volume, which provides the first overview of the growing field of temperament. Our goal was to summarize the main currents in the field today. For this reason, some of the chapters provide overviews of what is known about such issues as measurement, continuity and discontinuity, genetic influences, contextual influences, and clinical applications. Other chapters describe current theories of temperament and still others summarize major research programs. Together, they represent temperament today and should provide a useful introduction to the field for novitiates as well as a broadening experience for those who know temperament from only one of the multidisciplinary perspectives on temperament.

In the first chapter, Jack Bates discusses problems of measurement and makes the point that many of these issues hinge upon definitions of temperament and "constituencies" for temperament research. Sean McDevitt reviews data on the issue of continuity in the development of temperament, a review that highlights what is now generally accepted by temperament researchers: There is at least as much discontinuity as continuity in the development of temperament. Robert McCall emphasizes the need to consider discontinuity as well as continuity and normative developmental functions as well as individual differences, two themes for which he is well known in the field of mental development. The emphasis on change woven throughout this volume reflects a major shift in temperament theory and research. The MacArthur Research Network on the Transition from Infancy to Early Childhood provided financial support for a meeting in the mountains of Colorado at which the authors of this volume discussed their papers, and then revised them on the basis of three days' discussion, and revised them again on the basis of subsequent reviews. In addition to financial support, the MacArthur Transition Network provided the intellectual impetus to consider temperament in the context of transitions from infancy to childhood.

An important source of data on continuity and discontinuity is the New York Longitudinal Study (NYLS) which, as mentioned earlier, laid the foundation for the modern study of temperament. It is timely and most fitting that Alexander Thomas and Stella Chess provide an overview of their recent book which describes the follow-up of the NYLS probands as young adults (Chess & Thomas, 1984). This new emphasis on discontinuity in development should not obscure the fact that some temperamental continuity does exist, at least within major developmental periods, as seen most strikingly in the recent research by Jerome Kagan and his colleagues on the dimension of behavioral inhibition which is described in the chapter by Kagan, Reznick, and Snidman.

An energetic branch of temperament research is behavioral genetics. Arnold Buss and I provide an overview of our EAS approach to temperament which focuses on emotionality, activity, and sociability as the three most heritable early-developing personality traits (Buss & Plomin, 1984). Ronald Wilson and Adam Matheny describe their work on temperament in the unique longitudinal Louisville Twin Study. They note the mounting evidence for genetic influence on temperament even in infancy, document the research shift from dependence on parental ratings to the use of laboratory observations, and indicate the conceptual shift towards recognition of genetic sources of change as well as continuity in development.

In addition to increasing interest in developmental change and genetic change, another new emphasis in temperament research is contextual change, and the next three chapters focus on this topic. Concerns with contextual issues prompted the systematic program of research by Richard and Jacqueline Lerner, who, with their colleagues, discuss the results of their research on the concept of goodness of fit. Joan Stevenson-Hinde and Robert Hinde, distinguished for their ethological approach to the study of birds and nonhuman primates, have recently begun to focus their research on the study of temperament in humans. They emphasize the importance of social contexts such as those in the home and in school. Temperament research in different cultures has yielded interesting comparisons that implicate the importance of context, as described in the chapter by Charles Super and Sara Harkness.

A major stimulus for temperament research has come from its obvious clinical relevance which, for example, was the major reason for the initiation of the NYLS. William Carey's review of clinical applications indicates the relevance of temperament interactions to clinical issues and the need for much more research on this topic.

The coeditor of this volume, Judy Dunn, has been most interested in social relationships in the family, particularly triadic interactions among siblings and their mother (e.g., Dunn & Kendrick, 1982). Ethological observations of siblings interacting with each other and their mother in the home make it impossible to ignore temperament. Her interests and expertise are especially relevant to the study of temperament because the family—siblings as well as parents—provides a rich context in which to study developmental transactions between temperament and environment. Moreover, she represents an ethological orientation sorely needed in temperament research, an area in which most data have come from questionnaires and interviews and, more recently, laboratory observations. Her concluding commentary admirably distills the issues raised in this volume, the changes and continuities in temperament research and, especially, the challenges that point to directions for future research.

REFERENCES

Buss, A. H., & Plomin, R. (1984). *Temperament: Early developing personality traits.* Hillsdale, NJ: Lawrence Erlbaum Associates.

Chess, S., & Thomas, A. (1984). *Origins and evolution of behavior disorders.* New York: Brunner/Mazel.

Dunn, J., & Kendrick, C. (1982). *Siblings: Love, envy, & understanding.* London: Grant McIntyre.

1 The Measurement of Temperament

John E. Bates
Indiana University

The use of temperament concepts has been increasing exponentially. Temperament research on children is coming from the fields of clinical and developmental psychology, psychiatry, pediatrics, and education. In doing a computer search of abstracts, I found 162 articles concerning children and using the term temperament in the title or abstract between 1967 and mid-1983. Of these, 101, or 62% have been published since 1980, and 86% of them have been published since 1977. The history is similar for doctoral dissertations listed in the Dissertation Abstracts. Of the 78 concerning temperament since 1967, 60% have appeared since 1980, and 94% since 1977. When a concept is increasing so rapidly in usage as temperament is, it is important to consider how the concept is being measured. Several writers in the past few years have considered measurement issues (e.g., Bates, 1980; Goldsmith & Campos, 1982; Hubert, Wachs, Peters-Martin, & Gandour, 1982; MacPhee, 1983; Plomin, 1982). Much of what needs to be said in a "state of the art" paper on measurement has already been well said, so in this paper, my primary goal is to highlight some of the major points that have been made. However, I would also like to bring out a general point about assessment that may have been underemphasized in the past. This point is that one's evaluation of measurement depends to a large extent on which of the temperament area's various constituencies one comes from.

The constituency is defined by the primary purpose for an operationalization of the abstract concept of temperament. Some users of temperament are primarily interested in discovering basic, constitutional substrates to a child's personality. They are looking for behavioral characteristics marking basic psychophysiological and genetic processes. Others are less concerned with finding behavioral indicators of biological processes, but still are interested in basic

1

description of the individuality of very young children. For them, temperament concepts stand in for the personality concepts used with older children and adults, and it is not crucial to know the precise origin of the behavior characteristics. Still others are interested mainly in how temperament concepts help them to understand the development of socially relevant child characteristics, such as behavior disorders or intellectual competencies. Such workers tend to be clinically oriented, more interested in the practical yield of a measure than in the way in which the measure represents a step toward a better theory of child development. Of course, many researchers using temperament concepts belong to each of these kinds of constituency at different times. However, the main point is that what one is trying to do with an assessment should determine the particular concepts one measures and how they are measured.

The starting point for considering measurement issues is definitions. I will consider both general and specific definitions.

GENERAL DEFINITION

Considering the general meanings first, the widest unanimity in the definition seems to be that it concerns behavior traits which appear early and can be seen consistently, at least within a major class of situations. However, even this aspect of a general definition is not perfectly clear. There is some hedging on the trans-situationality issue, with number of writers suggesting that there must be theoretical and empirical flexibility. Goldsmith and Campos (1982) argue that it is worthwhile to think that some shifts in individual temperament characteristics occur, perhaps in lawful covariation with general developmental transitions. Thomas & Chess (1977) have argued that changes in the social environment could cause changes in temperament. It is easy to agree with Plomin (1983) that we must be able to demonstrate some form of stability if we are to invoke the concept of temperament. However, it is harder to say with certainty just exactly what kind of continuity ought to be shown, whether heterotypic or homotypic (Kagan & Moss, 1962), and how strong it should be before one is safe in regarding a construct to be a representative of the domain temperament.

We are also uncertain about how biology figures in temperament. Some feel that temperament traits ought to have a directly traceable root in genetic inheritance, or at least in earliest constitution (Plomin, 1983). Others (e.g., Goldsmith & Campos, 1982) do not see genetic inheritance as essential for all temperament traits. I myself agree that things we call temperament should have some conceptual roots in biology. These roots will probably have to be due to some sort of variation in the individual's constitution, as Plomin (1983) has said, and will probably have to pertain to processes we often see as emotional and attentional, as Goldsmith & Campos (1982) and Rothbart & Derryberry (1981) have said.

However, I come primarily from the clinical constituency. So it will not disappoint me, if in the process of searching for the roots of socially relevant individual differences we find a concept which meets the developmental continuity criterion, but fails the criterion of constitutional basis. The area of temperament can be of value in simply pointing the way to meaningful descriptions of early developmental characteristics, even if we eventually choose not to include a given measure in the concept of temperament.

SPECIFIC DEFINITIONS

I now consider specific definitions. One gets the impression that some users of temperament concepts have been mainly attracted to the *general* notion of temperament. They report correlations between the scales of some well-known temperament instrument and other variables of interest, with very little attention to the meanings of the specific scales. This kind of work may eventually serve as a useful data bank, but I do not feel it needs to be emphasized right now. Other users of temperament put more directed effort into their measures and interpretations. They are aiming at meaningful measurement of *specific* concepts, such as negative emotionality or sociability toward strangers. In the process, they have questioned what it is that their temperament scales measure. Recent validational research has given some answers to this question, but it has also pointed to the need to continue searching for better measures.

Several temperament concepts are represented in a number of different assessment methods and have a relatively broad base of empirical support. They are seen as relevant to important developmental issues. And they meet at least some of the definitional criteria. They seem the most likely to produce a useful dialogue between theoretical conceptions of temperament and empirical measures of real behavior. Here I discuss two such concepts. This emphasis on the specific over the general is made possible in part by the prior work of Hubert et al. (1982) and others in reviewing the adequacy of the various assessment devices as general methods.

There are several measurement considerations applicable to a wide range of specific temperament concepts. They include (1) clarity of theoretical definition, (2) basic psychometric properties of the measure, including (a) the extent to which items representing the theoretical construct cluster together, distinct from items representing other constructs, and (b) reliability across closely spaced administrations of the same test, and (3) validity, including (a) convergence between a temperament scale and another measure of the same concept, preferably dissimilar in measurement method, as well as (b) nonconvergence between measures of dissimilar concepts, (c) stability across development, and (d) predictive power, i.e., the ability to forecast the development of important characteristics, e.g., behavior problems.

Difficult Temperament.   The most widely used concept in the temperament literature is difficultness. At this point the concept is measured almost entirely through parental report. Observer ratings and laboratory measures have been used as approximations of the concept, but only as indexes for validating parent report, not with the intent of their becoming viable instruments on their own. One reason for this may be that the construct is most important to the clinical constituency. Clinicians tend to be the most motivated to find economical, widely applicable modes of assessment. What could be more appropriate for these goals than a parent-report questionnaire or interview?

In considering the measurement of difficultness or any other temperament construct, one must first consider the definition of the construct. Difficult temperament is rather unique in the temperament area. It is not a simple descriptor of what we usually think of as a temperament trait, in the sense of being primarily a monolithic dimension of a quality of behavior. Rather, it is primarily a concept that encapsulates the challenges of the child's characteristic emotional patterns for parents and other caregivers (Thomas, Chess, & Birch, 1968). In fact, Webster's New World Dictionary gives as its second meaning of difficult, "hard to satisfy, persuade, etc.: as, she is a *difficult* person." Thomas and Chess succeeded in translating this concept into a complex of five of their nine temperament scales.

One line of measurement work on difficultness has been to simplify the original Thomas and Chess concept. Factor analyses of the Carey Infant Temperament Questionnaire and other instruments in the Thomas and Chess tradition have typically shown that 3 of the 5 defining scales, Mood, Approach, and Adaptability tend to cluster independently of the other scales (e.g., MacPhee, 1983), although different studies differ on whether other scales may also be associated with the cluster. We developed our own operationalization of the concept through factor analysis, finding that the core of what parents of infants and toddlers mean when they rate a child as difficult is frequent and intense expression of negative emotion. We have found adaptability concepts relatively independent of our index of difficultness (e.g., Bates & Bayles, 1984). Thus, the Thomas–Chess definition of difficultness and our own are related, but not identical. There are also scales in other parent questionnaires that measure similar concepts of negative emotionality, specifically Plomin's EASI and Rothbart's Infant Behavior Questionnaire, although these are not referred to as difficultness. Despite the factor analysis work and the nearly universal inclusion of negative emotionality concepts in lists of temperament traits, however, on the basis of our own research we have come to the hypothesis that a simple, negative emotionality definition of difficultness is *not* sufficient. Logically, a child may frequently fuss and cry for different reasons, and these reasons may be relevant to the personality development of the child.

A second kind of measurement concern, aside from definition or location in the multivariate space of parental concepts, is how the measures of difficultness meet standard psychometric tests. These include internal consistency, i.e., the extent to which the items on the difficultness scale are correlated with one another, test-retest reliability, i.e., the extent to which the parent rates difficultness similarly on two occasions a few days or weeks apart, and susceptibility to irrelevant biases, e.g., a yes-saying response set. Since Hubert et al. (1982) have carefully reviewed the evidence on these issues recently, and as the differences between instruments in psychometric properties are not so major as to be crucial in the present context, I will merely make a few general comments. First, Hubert et al. (1982) have been critical of the main psychometric properties of existing instruments. I think that the interpretation of the psychometric data depends on one's perspective. From the perspective of a clinician, e.g., someone who wants an accurate screening device, the psychometric properties are problematic. However, from the perspective of a researcher, especially one who recognizes, as Plomin (1983), that we are at an early stage in temperament research, the picture is not so bad. We do not have a temperament instrument to compare to the WISC or Stanford-Binet tests of intelligence, but we do have some toeholds. We have some measures of difficult temperament, for example, which meet minimal psychometric standards. This is acceptable for now, especially considering that a longer scale tends to be more reliable, according to psychometric theory and experience, and many temperament scales are quite short. Scale-length is an old consideration in individual differences research (e.g., Wiggins, 1973), but has recently been discussed anew under the rubric of "aggregation" (Rushton, Brainerd, & Pressley, 1983). Attempts to develop high reliability in measures is good as an ideal. However, given a moderate level of reliability, I would suggest that the search for validity should take priority. When promisingly meaningful concepts are found, the reliability of their measures can be improved later.

The third kind of measurement concern, then, is validity. One facet of validity is stability. According to the general definition of temperament, difficultness ought to show stability over rather long periods of development. There is some evidence that this is true to a moderate degree, at least for our own operationalization of difficultness. We find a correlation of nearly .6 between mother perceptions of difficultness from 6- to 24-months-of-age, despite short scales and changes in item content to reflect developmental change (Lee & Bates, in press).

Another facet of validity is the issue of whether people who know the child will agree in their perceptions of the temperament of a child. It tends to be the case for difficultness as well as other temperament concepts that mothers and fathers agree to a moderate extent (Bates & Bayles, 1984; Plomin, 1983).

Agreement between parents and people who know the child less well is harder to find, although in the past 5 years findings of modest correlation between parent and observer perceptions of difficultness have steadily accumulated (e.g., see Bates, 1983). The convergence between the perceptions of parents and other raters is low, however, even allowing for the limited reliability of both the parent report and observer measures. Part of the problem here is that it is impractical to duplicate the parent's extensive experiences with the individual child. However, in addition, a number of workers have searched for characteristics of parents which might systematically bias their reports, thus lowering validity coefficients. We need not regard such characteristics as mere contaminants, but rather can see them as another facet of the meaning of the measure. Such characteristics have been found related to difficultness as defined in the NYLS style, e.g., self-reported anxiety (Vaughn, Taraldson, Crichton, Egeland, 1981) or race and social class (MacPhee, 1983; Sameroff, Seifer, & Elias, 1982). However, in our own research, the objective component of the perceptions of child characteristics remains after removing variance due to bias factors. Furthermore, bias factors such as social desirability are even less important in the case of our difficult temperament scales than with other kinds of rating (Bates & Bayles, 1984). Thus, my conclusion for the time being is that parents are telling us about difficultness at least somewhat objectively. Subjectivity cannot be ruled out on either logical or empirical grounds, but subjective influences are apparently not overwhelming.

Even more important to me in my role as a clinical researcher is a fourth facet of the validity of measures of difficult temperament. This is predictive validity, or the degree to which the measure forecasts a later variable of importance. Recent evidence, both from our own longitudinal study and others', supports the Thomas–Chess hypothesis that the difficult infant is at risk for behavior problems (e.g., Bates, Maslin, & Frankel, 1985; Pettit & Bates, 1984; Wolkind & DeSalis, 1982). For example, our own work suggests that difficult infants are likely to be higher than easier infants on both acting-out and internalizing kinds of behavior problems as seen by the mother at ages 3 and 4 years. The predictiveness is not so strong as to make difficult temperament immediately useful for preventive screening, however. Further work needs to be done to discover what it is that carries the prediction, leading to refinements in the concept and measurement of difficultness. The avenue that we are pursuing is to assume that our measure of difficult temperament represents two or more components relevant to the development of behavior problems. The leading candidates, based on theory and the work we have already done (Bates, Miller, & Bayles, 1984; Miller & Bates, 1984), are (1) a component of irritability, conceptually related to a tendency toward anxiety, and (2) a component of coercive demand of stimulation, conceptually related to acting-out disorders. Both of these components are plausible as constitutional variables (e.g., Eysenck & Eysenck, 1978). There is not much empirical evidence, however, and we are unsure of the role of environmental shaping.

Sociability Toward Strangers.   A second successful measurement story can be told about the concept of sociability. Some infants approach unfamiliar people readily, while others hang back, and still others show acute distress. There appears to be a genetic component in this variable, according to evidence reviewed by Lamb (1982) and Plomin (1983). I will discuss sociability as a single dimension, ranging from fear responses to unfamiliar people to positive, approaching responses. This makes some sense, and is in accord with other writers (e.g., Garcia-Coll, Kagan, & Resnick, 1984; Lamb, 1982). However, it is also possible that the single-dimension concept applies better to the behavior of very young children than older ones. It is possible that an older child could possess both a high degree of interest in people in general and a fearful response to them when they are unfamiliar. Perhaps further work will clear up this definitional issue.

The approach vs. fear dimension is represented in a number of different parent-report scales, including those based on the NYLS approach, the Plomin scales, Rothbart's scales, as well as our own. In our second-order factor analysis, we have found that mothers consistently distinguish adaptation to new people and places from other dimensions of temperament throughout the first two years of their children's development (Bates & Bayles, 1984), thus giving evidence that this concept is distinct from other temperament concepts, an important step in establishing the psychometric credibility of a measure.

A distinctive feature in measurement of the sociability concept is that much of it has been observational. By its nature, the concept suggests a structured situation that is easy to arrange. A number of researchers have confronted the infant with a stranger and recorded the responses, e.g., when the infant is given the Bayley test. These records have taken the form of items from the Bayley Infant Behavior Record (e.g., Bates & Bayles, 1984; Goldsmith & Gottesman, 1981), specially constructed rating scales (Lamb, 1982), ratings of the infant in response to an unfamiliar person visiting the home (Bates & Bayles, 1984), and even psychophysiological measures (Garcia-Coll et al., 1984).

To consider psychometric properties of the various forms of assessment, there is some evidence for test-retest reliability of an average level for temperament measures, even for the laboratory measures (Bates & Bayles, 1984; Garcia-Coll et al., 1984; Lamb, 1982). Parent-parent and observer-observer agreement has been acceptable, too.

Long-term stability is more apparent with the parent report indexes of sociability (Bates & Bayles, 1984) than with the laboratory measures (Lamb, 1982), although Garcia-Coll et al. (1984) did find stability in laboratory indexes among young children who scored at the extremes of the dimension. It is possible that with appropriate aggregation of behavior observations, the stability of laboratory measures will become more evident.

The validation of sociability is as good as in any other area of temperament. The laboratory and parent-report measures correlate to a modest-to-moderate level (Bates & Bayles, 1984; Garcia-Coll et al., 1984). Furthermore, indexes of sociability correlate with other theoretically interesting variables. Lamb (1982) concludes that a substantial component of the variability of young children's performance on cognitive development tests overlaps with sociability. It is unresolved how much this is due to sociable children actually being smarter because they elicit more stimulation from the environment; it may also be due to outgoing children merely performing better for the unfamiliar examiner (Lamb, 1982). Sociability might also have implications for behavior problems. We have found that negative adaptation to new people and situations in infancy predicts, to a modest degree, perceived anxiety-type problems at age 3 years, consistent with the interpretation that unsociability indicates a form of anxiety (Bates & Bayles, 1984; Bates et al., 1985). Appropriately, the adaptability measures do not predict acting-out problems.

A final validational issue is the relationship between sociability and attachment behavior. Some feel that temperament, especially sociability, ought to influence responses in the Ainsworth paradigm (e.g., Goldsmith & Campos, 1982). However, in research to date, parent-report measures of sociability have not been associated with the most important attachment concept, attachment security (Bates et al., 1985; Sroufe & Waters, 1982). On the other hand, Lamb (1982) has demonstrated that laboratory measures of sociability do correlate with attachment classification. However, in keeping with the dominant interpretation of attachment security as an index of the quality of the parent-infant relationship, Lamb sees the correlations as reflecting the influence of environment upon sociability. Further research on the issue should be interesting.

GOALS FOR IMPROVING TEMPERAMENT ASSESSMENT

The measurement considerations I have discussed in connection with difficult temperament and sociability could have been applied to many other specific temperament concepts. However, for the most part, the other concepts have not received as much empirical attention as these two. Previous writing about the measurement of temperament has convincingly stated the need for improved measurement of temperament in general. My point is that this improvement will occur not so much as the result of a general effort, but rather as the result of attempts to measure specific concepts. The general concepts of temperament must be kept in mind, and it will often be an advantage to work on more than one specific concept at a time (Bates & Bayles, 1984), but the real progress will come from researchers who care about measuring specific concepts.

I would like to reemphasize Plomin's (1983) point that the temperament area is at an early stage of development. We should not expect that we will have an exceedingly complex concept such as temperament theoretically and empirically defined in a short time. We have made notable progress in the past 20 years, but the theoretical and methodological problems are large. In the process of improving our measurement of temperament, we must at the same time improve our theory. A number of writers have called for a multivariate approach to temperament research (e.g., Bates et al., 1979; Goldsmith & Campos, 1982; Plomin, 1983). By assessing the same temperament construct in several ways, e.g., parent-report, home observation, and laboratory observation, and relating these measures to one another and to measures of theoretically different constructs, we will gain the information we need to refine both the measures and the theoretical concepts. This is essentially the point that Cronbach and Meehl (1955) made so many years ago. Because of advances in computer and statistical technology, we are increasingly able to put this principle into action.

Ultimately, as we understand better what it is that we are attempting to measure, we will find better and better assessment methods. We can follow the advice of Hubert et al. (1982) and learn more specifically the qualities in young children's behavior that are most salient to parents, and then assess these more systematically. We can try to learn more about the perceptual process of our most important instruments for assessing temperament, the child's caregivers, for example by trying to identify consistent biases that can be used as correction factors (Bates, 1983). And we can follow the approach of Goldsmith and Rieser-Danner (1984), Rothbart (1984), and others and try to develop laboratory situations which bring out behavior which generalizes to the characteristics of the child in natural situations. However, we will also have to try to deal with the intertwining of child characteristics, even theoretically innate ones, with the characteristics of the environment.

It is when I face this problem of indeterminacy, the likelihood that we will never have a "pure" measure of temperament, at least in our own species, that I find myself turning most to the goal of description. For me, temperament concepts are useful, along with other kinds of concepts, in providing a structure for description, a way of simplifying how I describe individual differences in development. If I keep this in mind, I am better able to tolerate the ambiguity in the concepts and measures of temperament. Certainly theory sometimes drives observation. However, what is learned through good, comprehensive descriptions of the social development of individual children will also drive theories. To the extent that our measures of temperament describe meaningful phenomena they will be useful. These meaningful phenomena may or may not correspond closely to our current concepts of temperament.

REFERENCES

Bates, J. E. (1980). The concept of difficult temperament. *Merrill-Palmer Quarterly, 26*, 299–319.
Bates, J. E. (1983). Issues in the assessment of difficult temperament: A reply to Thomas, Chess, and Korn. *Merrill-Palmer Quarterly, 29*, 89–97.
Bates, J. E., & Bayles, K. (1984). Objective and subjective components in mothers' perceptions of their children from age 6 months to 3 years. *Merrill-Palmer Quarterly, 30*, 111–130.

Bates, J. E., Freeland, C. A. B., & Lounsbury, M. L. (1979). Measurement of infant difficultness. *Child Development, 50,* 794–803.

Bates, J. E., Maslin, C. A., & Frankel, K. A. (1985). Attachment security, mother-child interaction and temperament as predictors of behavior problem ratings at age three years. In I. Bretherton & E. Waters (Eds.), Growing points in attachment theory and research. *Monographs of the Society for Research in Child Development.*

Bates, J. E., Miller, E., & Bayles, K. (1984, April). *Understanding the link between difficult temperament and behavior problems: toward identifying subtypes of difficultness.* Paper presented as part of symposium ''Difficult temperament: Toward an integration of parental, clinical and research perspectives,'' organized by I. St. James-Roberts & D. Wolke, at International Conference on Infant Studies. New York.

Cronbach, L. J., & Meehl, P. (1955). Construct validity in psychological tests. *Psychological Bulletin, 52,* 281–302.

Eysenck, H. J., & Eysenck, S. B. G. (1978). Psychopathy, personality, and genetics. In R. D. Hare & D. Schalling (Eds.), *Psychopathic behavior: Approaches to research.* New York: Wiley.

Garcia-Coll, C., Kagan, J., & Reznick, J. L. (1984). Behavioral inhibition in young children. *Child Development, 55,* 1005–1019.

Goldsmith, H. H., & Campos, J. J. (1982). Toward a theory of infant temperament. In R. N. Emde & R. J. Harmon (Eds.), *The development of attachment and affiliative systems.* New York: Plenum.

Goldsmith, H. H., & Gottesman, I. I. (1981). Origins of variation in behavioral style: A longitudinal study of temperament in young twins. *Child Development, 52,* 91–103.

Goldsmith, H. H., & Rieser-Danner, L. (1984, April). *The objective assessment of temperament: LAB-TAB and VIDEO-TAB.* Paper presented as part of symposium ''Developmental perspectives on infant temperament,'' organized by M. K. Rothbart, at International Conference on Infant Studies, New York.

Hubert, N. C., Wachs, T. D., Peters-Martin, P., & Gandour, M. J. (1982). The study of early temperament: Measurement and conceptual issues. *Child Development, 53,* 571–600.

Kagan, J., & Moss, H. A. (1962). *Birth to maturity: A study in psychological development.* New York: Wiley.

Lamb, M. (1982). The individual differences in infant sociability: Their origins and implications for cognitive development. In H. W. Reese & L. Lipsett (Ed.), *Advances in child development and behavior* (Vol. 16, pp. 213–239). New York: Academic Press.

Lee, C., & Bates, J. (in press). Mother-child interaction at age two years and perceived difficult temperament. *Child Development.*

MacPhee, D. (1983, March). *What do ratings of infant temperament really mean?* Presented at convention of Society for Research in Child Development, Detroit.

Miller, E. M., & Bates, J. E. (1984, April). *Infant difficultness and interactional style.* Presented at International Conference on Infant Studies, New York.

Pettit, G. S., & Bates, J. E. (1984, April). *An age four year follow-up of infants and their families.* Paper presented at the International Conference of Infant Studies, New York.

Plomin, R. (1983). Childhood temperament. In B. Lahey & A. Kazdin (Eds.), *Advances in clinical child psychology* (Vol. 6). New York: Plenum.

Rothbart, M. K. (1984, April). *Temperament and the development of behavioral inhibition.* Paper presented in symposium ''Developmental perspectives on infant temperament,'' at International Conference on Infant Studies, New York.

Rothbart, M. K., & Derryberry, D. (1981). Development of individual differences in temperament. In M. E. Lamb (Ed.) *Advances in developmental psychology* (Vol. 1). Hillsdale, NJ: Lawrence Erlbaum Associates.

Rushton, J. P., Brainerd, C. J., & Pressley, M. (1983). Behavioral development and construct validity: The principle of aggregation. *Psychological Bulletin, 94,* 18–38.

Sameroff, A. J., Seifer, R., & Elias, P. K. (1982). Sociocultural variability in infant temperament ratings. *Child Development, 53,* 164–173.

Sroufe, L. A., & Waters, E. (1982). Issues of temperament and attachment. *American Journal of Orthopsychiatry, 52,* 743–746.

Thomas, A., & Chess, S. (1977) *Temperament and development.* New York: Brunner/Mazel.

Thomas, A., Chess, S., & Birch, H. G. (1968). *Temperament and behavior disorders in children.* New York: New York University Press.

Vaughn, B., Taraldson, B., Crichton, L., & Egeland, B. (1981). The assessment of infant temperament: A critique of the Carey Infant Temperament Questionnaire. *Infant Behavior and Development, 4,* 1–18.

Wiggins, J. S. (1973). *Personality and prediction.* Reading, MA: Addison.

Wolkind, S. N., & DeSalis, W. (1982). Infant temperament, maternal mental health and child behavioural problems. In R. Porter & G. Collins (Eds.), *Temperamental differences in infants and young children: Ciba Foundation symposium 89.* London: Pitman.

2 Issues of Stability and Continuity in Temperament Research

Robert B. McCall
Boys Town Center, Boys Town, Nebraska

I have been asked to step out of my usual context of mental development to discuss issues of stability and continuity in temperament research. The hope is, I suppose, that I am free of whatever conceptual and methodological allegiances and investments may characterize those who toil in the field of temperament and that I can provide some objective perspective on these issues.

It is a laudable purpose, but one riding on shaky premises. Are we really wiser after 7 decades of studying mental behavior? In some respects, we are; in a shocking number of other respects, we are not. And will a vagrant from another field, one unfamiliar with most of the written literature and all of the unwritten lore about temperament, not look like a kibitzing duck out of water? Undoubtedly.

Therefore, I offer these perspectives gleaned from the study of mental development in the spirit of the concept "if the shoe fits, put it on." If it doesn't fit, accept it as an offering of a naive, well-meaning interloper, and throw it out.

THE TWO REALMS OF DEVELOPMENT

It will help to make a distinction and to establish some vocabulary at the outset. Specifically, research in psychology in general (Cronbach, 1957) and in developmental psychology in particular (McCall, 1981a; Wohlwill, 1973) tends to fall into one of two spheres that are so isolated they are almost separate disciplines.

One sphere is of that of individual differences. This is the focus on the consistency of the relative rank ordering of individuals from one age to another or across different variables. The other realm of study focuses on group differences—differences between the mean performance of a single group across ages or contexts, the mean difference between two comparable groups subjected to different treatment conditions, or the mean difference between two naturally occurring, contrasting groups.

To be sure, investigators sometimes explore both spheres, but not often and not much.

Application to Development

Applied to behavioral development, these two realms translate into a concern with developmental functions versus individual differences.

Developmental Function.   A developmental function (Wohlwill, 1973) is the average behavior for a group or individual over age. Piaget (1954) described the developmental function for sensorimotor intelligence, for example. In his case, it was the *species-general developmental function,* because he intended it to apply to all human infants. But developmental functions can exist for more specific groups, even individuals. If the developmental function reflects the same qualitative characteristic at each age, the function is *continuous;* if it changes qualitatively, it is *discontinuous.* [1]

Individual Differences.   Individual differences in a behavior are usually reflected in the relative rank ordering of subjects on a measure, and this is typically related to a relative rank ordering of the same subjects on the same variable at another age or on a different variable. If these orderings are similar (i.e., the correlation is significant), the individual differences are *stable;* otherwise they are *not stable.*

Potential Independence.   The crucial point is that developmental functions and individual differences are potentially independent. This means that the developmental function may increase, decrease, remain constant, or be discontinuous over age, while at the same time individual differences may be stable or not stable. This is so, at least potentially, because the correlation coefficient, for example, is independent of the means of the distributions entering its calculation (if those distributions are symmetrical).

We have not always kept the potential independence of these realms in mind, and we frequently generalize inappropriately from one domain to the other. For example, Bloom's (1964) classic statement that one-half of adult intelligence is established by age four is based on the fact that the correlation between IQ at age four and IQ at 18 years is approximately 0.71 which represents 50% of the

---

[1]Continuous vs. discontinuous development is a conceptual distinction. Whether the plot over age is continuous or discontinuous depends on how the characteristic is measured.

variance. However, this sweeping conclusion, based entirely on individual differences, ignores the fact that mental age will more than quadruple (in some sense) during this period of time. Analogously, would we say that the development of giant Sequoia trees is half accomplished after 2 years if the relative heights of 2-year seedlings (which may stand less than a few feet tall) correlated with differences in the heights of those trees a century later when they were 300 feet tall?

Similarly, conclusions about the heritability of IQ, based solely on individual differences, are often applied to intelligence in general. Individual differences in mental performance in childhood or adulthood may be 40–70% heritable, but this says nothing about the relative contributions of heredity and environment to the species-general developmental function which has not been, and cannot be, studied by conventional behavioral genetic techniques (one must sample different species to determine the heritability of a species-general developmental function).

Finally, the potential independence of means and individual differences suggests that factors that produce individual differences within a group may be different from those factors that produce differences between groups. This point has been raised frequently with respect to racial differences in intelligence, but it might also apply to environmental and biological factors that influence temperament within and between families, racial or social groups, and cultures.

STABILITY AND CONTINUITY OF TEMPERAMENT

With this distinction in mind, I want to look at some of the major issues of continuity and stability in temperament research, occasionally drawing parallels with the mental development literature.

The Focus on Individual Differences

Plomin (1983) suggested that one reason for the contemporary interest in temperament is the desire to focus on the description and explanation of individual differences in development rather than on average or normative development, which strategy has characterized the recent study of cognition.

But a look at the history of mental development suggests a similar origin. If modern interest in the development of intelligence began with Binet, then the first 4 or 5 decades of its history represented a concern with individual differences. It was Piaget, whose influence was not felt in America until the early 1960s, who was totally disinterested in individual differences and who led the movement toward studying the species-general developmental function for intelligence.

Apparently, a similar historical progression characterizes the field of socialization. Maccoby (1983) argues that the development of social behavior and personality is almost entirely focused on individual differences, and she calls for greater study of both species-general developmental functions (i.e., qualitative sequences that characterize all children) and individual differences in developmental functions (i.e., qualitative sequences characterizing some but not other children).

Study Both Realms.   I urge researchers of temperament not to limit themselves to studying individual differences but to study developmental functions as well. Otherwise, you would focus on only one of the two realms of development, and you would probably not study the *development* of temperament in the full sense of that term.

Specifically, the conceptual and statistical strategies typically used to study individual differences are designed to detect *lack* of change or development—how *similar* is the relative rank ordering of subjects at one versus another age? In its simplest form, a nonsignificant correlation (presumably indicating that change has occurred in this relative rank ordering) is not an interpretable finding. It is a failure to reject the null hypothesis and an uninteresting and disappointing result. In contrast, the conceptual and statistical strategies typically invoked to study developmental functions are designed to detect change—increases, decreases, and perhaps discontinuities in developmental functions. A flat developmental function is uninteresting and disappointing. Therefore, a focus on individual differences is likely associated with the search for stability (not lack of stability) and completely ignores continuity or discontinuity of developmental function.

Researchers need to study change in both realms. Indeed, some of us have argued that change is the essence of developmental disciplines (Maccoby, 1983; McCall, 1977; Wohlwill, 1973), and that we should be just as vigorous in describing change, whether in individual differences or developmental functions and whether in mental development or temperament, as we are in the search for stability and continuity.

Definitions and Development

I understand researchers are having difficulty defining temperament to everyone's satisfaction. That disagreement does not bother me much. We don't have a very satisfactory definition of intelligence, although people seem to agree to a workable extent on which behaviors are "intelligent" and which are not. I am told the physicists do not have a very good definition of gravity, although they seem to agree on its measurement. As long as there is at least some agreement about which behaviors are "temperamental" and which are not, research can proceed and perhaps a definition will emerge empirically.

Temperament Versus Other Qualities. But that is precisely what bothers me about the definitional debate. Very little attention is being paid to what distinguishes behaviors that are temperamental from those that are not temperamental—that are mental, social, and pathological, for example. And how is temperament different from personality?

Instead, temperament researchers seem more interested in prescribing, by definition, some general characteristics (e.g., stability, heritability) of such unspecified "temperamental" behaviors. This does not tell me what temperament is; it tells nature what researchers want temperament—whatever temperament is—to be like. Certainly, any behavior that is stable and inherited is not temperamental (e.g., childhood intelligence), and, I suspect, some behaviors that people would call temperamental will not turn out to be stable or inherited. Therefore, I suggest scholars of temperament concentrate on defining the characteristics of behaviors that are temperamental as opposed to mental or social. Then, researchers can study those behaviors, permitting nature to tell us if they are stable and inherited, for example.

To illustrate this and a related concern, consider the definition of temperament accorded "considerable consensus" (Plomin, 1983) by the 1980 Temperament Research Symposium in New Haven:

Temperament involves those dimensions of personality that are largely genetic or constitutional in origin, exist in most ages and most societies, show some consistency across situations, and are relatively stable, at least within major developmental eras (Plomin, 1981, p. 269).

In short, temperament is relatively stable, continuous, pervasive, and inherited. I recall another definition:

By intelligence, the psychologist understands inborn, all-round, intellectual ability. It is inherited, or at least innate, not due to teaching or training; it is intellectual, not emotional or moral, and remains uninfluenced by industry or zeal; it is general, not specific, i.e., it is not limited to any particular work, but enters into all we do or say or think. Of all our mental qualities, it is the most far reaching. . . (Burt, Jones, Miller, & Moodie, 1934).

In short, intelligence is relatively stable, continuous, pervasive, and inherited. To be sure, both definitions are subject to considerable debate. But accepting them for the moment, note that all we know about what behaviors are temperamental is that they are the stable, continuous, inherited, and pervasive aspects of personality. Is temperament simply a subset of personality characteristics? What's personality? And all we know about intelligence is that it is all-round intellectual ability, not emotional or moral—statements that beg the question.

Certainly, temperament is not intelligence, but these definitions do not tell us how they are different.

Simplistic Concepts. Even if the characteristics that distinguish tempera- ment, intelligence, personality, and sociability were added to their definitions, what would we have? We would have a handful of stable, continuous, pervasive, inherited characteristics that would persumably account for the vast majority of individual differences in most of human behavior at most ages. In a moment of cynical musing, I can imagine a four- or five-term polynominal equation ac- counting for 80% (to pick a number) of human existence. If accepted at full strength, such definitions are fantasies. They are the simplest characterization of human behavior—one variable does all things for all people at all ages. Notice also that these definitions are not developmental. Change is not involved. Per- haps it is this simplicity that lures us to initially define a concept in this way. Nature is often poetically simple—but not that simple. Sometimes the lack of parsimony exists in nature.

One can argue, of course, that defining temperament in this way has heuristic value—people will investigate its stability, continuity, pervasiveness, and heritability. Certainly some heuristic benefit will accrue, but such definitions also have a biasing effect. We do not, for example, readily alter the definition in the face of negative evidence. The notion that intelligence was relatively continu- ous and stable across the lifespan received considerable empirical support from the early longitudinal studies. So much support existed, that few researchers sought to describe change in intelligence. For example, while the year-to-year correlations are near 0.90 after age 6, meaningful change in relative mental performance can occur for a substantial subgroup of individuals (McCall, Ap- pelbaum, & Hogarty, 1973). Specifically, the average middle-class child changes 28.5 IQ points, one in seven changes as much as 40 points, and a few individuals change more than 70 points between $2\frac{1}{2}$ and 17-years-of-age. These changes are not simply random fluctuations about a constant value, but they are relatively simple, progressive patterns of change (McCall et al., 1973). But very few people looked for these changes; and if they looked, no one paid much heed until recently.

This bias against studying change was somewhat understandable given the high year-to-year correlations during childhood and beyond, but the persistent search for stability in individual differences from infancy to later life was less excusable. More than 5 decades of research consistently showed essentially no correlation to later IQ from test performance during the first 18 months and only modest and clinically useless levels of prediction thereafter until approximately 3-years-of-age, depending on sample, sex, and other factors (McCall, 1979; McCall, Hogarty, & Hurlburt, 1972). Sometimes, I suggest, it is necessary to "accept" the null hypothesis. But instead of vigorously studying what produced this lack of stability, we clung to the definition that intelligence was really constant even during infancy. It must be mysteriously hiding within the infant, we felt, if we could only find a way to measure it. Some advocated throwing out the infant tests since they obviously were not valid, attributing more validity to the original definition of intelligence than to 5 decades of research. And the search for an infant intelligence that predicts later IQ still continues, now in the realm of brain responses to simple stimuli or patterns of attentional deployment to familiar and novel stimuli (e.g., Fagan & McGrath, 1981; Lewis & Brooks-Gunn, 1981; McCall, 1981b).

John Stuart Mill reportedly warned us that this has happened before. He said, I am told, something like:

The tendency has always been strong to believe that whatever receives a name must be an entity of being, having an independent existence of its own. And if no real entity answering to the name could be found, men did not for that reason suppose that none existed, but imagined that it was peculiarly abstruse and mysterious.

My point is that definitions direct and bias scientific attempts to describe nature, and the more prescriptive the definitions, the more biasing they are. It is fine to ask if temperament is stable over age; it is prejudicial to say that temperament *is* stable, otherwise "it" is not temperament. Old definitions die hard, even in the face of negative evidence. What if "temperament" is not stable, not continuous, not pervasive, and not very heritable, at least during some major period of the lifespan? If this turns out to be the case, what will you call "it?" Or will "temperament" not exist during those ages? Your colleagues in mental development are facing this issue with respect to "intelligence" in infancy.

Measurement

A consensus measurement of temperament does not exist, although the Carey Scales (Carey & McDevitt, 1978) are used frequently. The measurement problem will not be solved until somebody attacks it directly in a comprehensive, longitudinal fashion with considerable attention to psychometric detail. Despite the professional rewards for having a test bearing your name, most researchers do not want to put it in the time and nuts-and-bolts effort required to create a psychometrically sound, comprehensive, developmental instrument. But I suspect progress in the study of temperament will be slow until this is done.

Creating such a measurement of temperament requires more perspiration than inspiration. The first step is creating an item pool at each age. Plomin (1983) lists 33 stylistic characteristics that have already been used on temperament questionnaires. One would begin by creating small sets of items for each stylistic feature at each appropriate age. A compromise must be forged between having items that possess face validity and appropriateness at a given age and having as much item overlap across age as possible so that patterns of consistency and change in developmental function and individual differences can be assessed. If all the items change from one age to the next, for example, lack of stability may be confounded with a discontinuity produced deliberately by the test construction; if all the items are the same across age, instability is confounded with development in the organism to which the test is insensitive.

Once representative item pools are established at each age, an enormous amount of psychometric dirty work is needed to boil down the set of items, determine internal and external psychometric properties, and so forth. But without this labor of love, progress will be limited, I believe.

Heritability

In this realm, I have more encouragement for what you are already doing than suggestions for different approaches. Your task is more complicated that it has been for mental development, because you will have several dimensions of temperament rather than a single score (although "intelligence" should also be assessed as a multidimensional concept).

Obviously, you need to look at the heritabilities of separate dimensions of temperament within an age, but I also suggest you seek heritabilities for patterns of dimensions (Matheny, 1980)—types or syndromes of temperaments within an age, for example. Statistically, it is possible that the heritabilities of patterns of dimensions will be much higher (or lower) than the heritabilities of any single dimension, in the same way that it is possible to have a highly significant multivariate result even when no univariate result is individually significant. This is so, because the multivariate procedures take into account the relationships among the separate dimensions, whereas the univariate procedures do not.

In addition, the genetics of temperament should be examined from a developmental standpoint. It is an axiom of behavior genetics that not all genetic characteristics are manifest at birth; some emerge later and some change at various points during the lifetime. Yet we rarely study the heritability of developmental changes.

One reason to do so is that different factors may govern individual differences within an age than across age. For example, in a study of sibling and parent-child similarity in pattern of IQ performance over age, individual differences in subjects' *average* IQs across age showed the typical pattern of similarity between kinship pairs. But there was no significant similarity among kinship pairs relative to matched unrelated pairs for the *pattern of change* in IQ across age (McCall, 1970, 1972). Wilson (1972, 1974, 1978; Wilson & Harpring, 1972) did find greater similarity for MZ than DZ twins for pattern of IQ over age, but the heritabilities for developmental pattern were less than for single-age comparisons (McCall, Eichorn, & Hogarty, 1977).

The same may be true of temperament. I note, for example, that at least one study found adult neuroticsm to be heritable within an age, but changes over a 2-

year period for this scale were not (Eaves & Eysenck, 1976). Also, the pattern over age of certain temperamental characteristics show heritabilities as high or higher than heritabilities for individual differences within an age (Matheny, 1980; Matheny & Dolan, 1975), and a substantial portion of the developmental variability in a "reactivity" factor assessed identically at ages four and seven was associated with genetics (Goldsmith & McArdle, 1982).

Finally, Plomin (1983) has encouraged colleagues to use behavioral genetic methods to study environmental influences. One of the more important consequences of this strategy is the discovery for mental performance (McCall, 1983; Rowe & Plomin, 1981), temperament, and some personality dimensions (Goldsmith, 1983; Rowe & Plomin, 1981) that within-family, not just between-family, environmental circumstances contribute substantially to those characteristics. Moreover, within-family environmental factors seem to contribute to differences between siblings, not to similarities, and this area deserves more study.

Types of Continuity and Stability

Generally, developmentalists prefer rather simple patterns of continuity and stability. As indicated above, the working definition of temperament represents the simplest possible model—a continuous developmental function, possibly of a relatively constant magnitude, with rather stable individual differences across age. Mental development in infancy, however, may be neither continuous nor stable. Might temperament be the same?

What on earth would we do theoretically or methodologically with a concept that changed its qualitative as well as its quantitative characteristics over age and individual differences were not stable? Those are characteristics we typically associate with random error. But discontinuity and instability do not necessarily imply randomness; instead, they may signal the quintessence of development—sytematic change in developmental function and in patterns of individual differences. If development means change, then this is what we are here to study.

Temperament researchers may arrive at this crossroads more quickly than those who studied mental development, because current evidence indicates less cross-age stability for temperament (Plomin, 1983) than for mental development (McCall, 1979), and because certain dimensions of temperament may be much more salient at one age than at another (e.g., physical activity, persistence). As a result, you may have the opportunity, if you perceive it as an opportunity rather than as a roadblock, to be really developmental and to advance the entire developmental discipline by investigating a variety of models of continuity and stability.

Models. Numerous authors have described a long list of possible developmental progressions (Buss & Royce, 1975; Flavell, 1972; Maccoby, 1969; McCall, Eichorn, & Hogarty, 1977; Van den Daele, 1969, 1974; Wohlwill, 1973), and some have deliberately attempted to describe developmental patterns that are combinations of continuity-discontinuity on the one hand and stability-instability on the other (McCall, 1981a; McCall et al., 1977). But when it comes to empiricism, most of the models actually tested are relatively simple.

I speculate, however, that temperament researchers may need more complicated models to demonstrate some important functions of temperament in development. For example, your definitional emphasis on the style rather than the content of behavior means that temperament will probably be multivariate and conceptual as opposed to directly observable. It may function more as a moderator variable, interacting with other conditions to produce certain outcomes, than as a main line in the developmental progression. For example, Wachs and Gandour's (1983) study suggests that certain types of parental stimulation may have different, perhaps opposite, effects on infants as a function of their temperament. This suggests a branching developmental progression. It also suggests that it may be necessary to seriously study the transactional model of development (Sameroff & Chandler, 1975), because it is likely that the infant's response will modify the parent, perhaps as a function of the parent's temperament. This can get complicated very quickly.

Statistics.   Finally, the multivariate nature of temperament and the likelihood that, despite its current definition, change may predominate over stability and continuity, suggests that temperament research will be an ideal context for the use of path analysis, structural equations, and a variety of techniques based on similar statistical principles. These are powerful, valuable methods of analysis that can contribute greatly to our discipline—if they are used appropriately. But at least one journal editor (Hetherington, personal communication, 1984) has observed that structural equations has become a fad, and that it is being used in contexts that exceed its purpose and limitations. I urge researchers to become familar with the purposes, assumptions, and limits of path analysis, structural equations, and other multivariate longitudinal statistical techniques before designing their experiments, to say nothing of analyzing them (e.g., Appelbaum & McCall, 1983).

Specifically, path analysis and structural equations are primarily designed to test the relative merits of two or more hypotheses about a multivariate longitudinal data set. This means they are hypothesis-testing, not descriptive, techniques, and they are best suited to decide between two specific hypotheses, not to test the plausibility of a single hypothesis. Further, the more specific the hypotheses, the more likely the technique will be able to determine whether the data conform to one better than to the other hypothesis. Unfortunately, especially in the early stages of a field, we do not have specific hypotheses and we require descriptive rather than hypothesis-testing techniques. Although all statistical approaches make certain assumptions and impose certain criteria to achieve a solution, three-mode factor analysis (Tucker, 1963) may be more suited to a descriptive task than is structural equations.

CONCLUSIONS

I urge researchers of temperament to:

1. study the developmental function as much as you study individual differences in temperament;
2. search after change at least as vigorously as you pursue continuity and stability;
3. distinguish temperament from other behaviors and avoid prescribing it to be stable, continuous, pervasive, and inherited—decide these issues empirically;
4. concentrate on creating a multidimensional, developmental assessment instrument and do the nuts-and-bolts psychometric work;
5. investigate the heritabilities of a multivariate concept of temperament, not just individual dimensions, and do so both within an age and across age; and
6. explore complicated patterns of developmental consistency and change, especially the potential role of temperament as a moderator variable.

Godspeed—speedier than those of us in mental development have learned these lessons. In fact, we have not yet learned many of them very well.

REFERENCES

Appelbaum, M. I., & McCall, R. B. (1983). Design and analysis in developmental psychology. W. Kessen (Ed.), *Handbook of child psychology* (Vol. I). *Fourth Edition.* New York: Wiley.
Bloom, B. S. (1964). *Stability and change in human characteristics.* New York: Wiley.
Burt, C., Jones, E., Miller, E., & Moodie, W. (1934). *How the mind works.* New York: Appleton-Century-Crofts.
Buss, A. H., & Royce, J. R. (1975). Ontogenetic change in cognitive structure from a multivariate perspective. *Developmental Psychology, 11,* 87–101.
Carey, W. B., & McDevitt, S. C. (1978). Revision of the Infant Temperament Questionnaire. *Pediatrics, 61,* 735–739.
Cronbach, L. J. (1957). The two disciplines of scientific psychology. *American Psychologist, 12,* 671–684.
Eaves, L. J., & Eysenck, H. J. (1976). Genetic and environmental components of inconsistency and unrepeatability in twins' responses to a neuroticism questionnaire. *Behavior Genetics, 6,* 145–160.
Fagan, J. F. III, & McGrath, S. K. (1981). Infant recognition memory and later intelligence. *Intelligence, 5,* 121–130.
Flavell, J. H. (1972). An analysis of cognitive-developmental sequences. *Genetic Psychology Monographs, 86,* 279–350.

Goldsmith, H. H. (1983). Genetic influences on personality from infancy to adulthood. *Child Development, 54,* 331–355.

Goldsmith, H. H., & McArdle, J. J. (1982). *A structural modeling approach to the analysis of the longitudinal stability of childhood temperament.* Unpublished manuscript, University of Texas, Austin.

Lewis, M., & Brooks-Gunn, J. (1981). Visual attention at three months as a predictor of cognitive functioning at two years of age. *Intelligence, 5,* 131–140.

Maccoby, E. E. (1969, April). *Tracing individuality within age-related change.* Paper presented at the meetings of The Society for Research in Child Development, Santa Monica, California.

Maccoby, E. E. (1983, April). *Socialization and developmental change.* Presidential Address to the Society for Research in Child Development, Detroit.

Matheny, A. P. (1980). Bayley's Infant Behavior Record: Behavioral components and twin analyses. *Child Development, 51,* 1157–1167.

Matheny, A. P., & Dolan, A. N. (1975). Persons, situations, and time: A genetic view of behavioral change in children. *Journal of Personality and Social Psychology, 35,* 1106–1110.

McCall, R. B. (1970). IQ pattern over age: Comparisons among siblings and parent-child pairs. *Science, 170,* 644–648.

McCall, R. B. (1972). Similarity in developmental profile among related pairs of human infants. *Science, 178,* 1004–1005.

McCall, R. B. (1977). Challenges to a science of developmental psychology. *Child Development, 48,* 333–344.

McCall, R. B. (1979). The development of intellectual functioning in infancy and the prediction of later IQ. In J. D. Osofsky (Ed.), *Handbook of infant development* (pp. 707–741). New York: Wiley.

McCall, R. B. (1981a). Nature-nurture and the two realms of development: A proposed integration with respect to mental development. *Child Development, 52,* 1–12.

McCall, R. B. (1981b). Early predictors of later IQ: The search continues. *Intelligence, 5,* 141–147.

McCall, R. B. (1983). Environmental effects on intelligence: The forgotten realm of discontinuous non-shared within-family factors. *Child Development, 54,* 408–415.

McCall, R. B., Appelbaum, M. I., & Hogarty, P. S. (1973). Developmental changes in mental performance. *Monographs of the Society for Research in Child Development, 38* (Serial No. 150).

McCall, R. B., Eichorn, D. H., & Hogarty, P. S. (1977). Transitions in early mental development. *Monographs of the Society for Research in Child Development, 42* (No. 171).

McCall, R. B., Hogarty, P. S., & Hurlburt, N. (1972). Transitions in infant sensorimotor development and the prediction of childhood IQ. *American Psychologist, 27,* 728–748.

Piaget, J. (1954). *The construction of reality in the child* (M. Cook, trans.). New York: Basic Books.

Plomin, R. (1981). Heredity and temperament: A comparison of twin data for self-report questionnaires, parental ratings, and objectively assessed behavior. In L. Gedda, P. Parisi, & W. E. Nance (Eds.), *Progress in clinical and biological research: Twin research III, Part B. Intelligence, personality, and development* (Vol. 69B). New York: Alan R. Liss.

Plomin, R. (1983). Childhood temperament. In B. B. Lahey & A. E. Cazdin (Eds.), *Advances in clinical child psychology, Vol. 6.* New York: Plenum.

Rowe, D. C., & Plomin, R. (1981). The importance of non-shared (E_1) environmental influences in behavioral development. *Developmental Psychology, 17,* 517–531.

Sameroff, A. J., & Chandler, M. J. (1975). Reproductive risk and the continuum of caretaking casualty. In F. D. Horowitz (Ed.), *Review of child development research, Vol. 4.* Chicago: University of Chicago Press.

Tucker, L. R. (1963). Implications of factor analysis of three-way matrices for measurement of change. In C. W. Harris (Ed.), *Problems in measuring change* (pp. 122–137). Madison: University of Wisconsin Press.

Van den Daele, L. D. (1969). Qualitative models in developmental analysis. *Developmental Psychology, 1,* 303–310.

Van den Daele, L. D. (1974). Infrastructure and transition in developmental analysis. *Human Development, 17,* 1–23.

Wachs, T. D., & Gandour, N. J. (1983). Temperament, environment, and six-month cognitive-intellectual development: A test of the organismic specificity hypothesis. *International Journal of Behavioral Development, 6,* 135–152.

Wilson, R. S. (1972). Twins: Early mental development. *Science, 175,* 914–917.

Wilson, R. S. (1974). Twins: Mental development in the preschool years. *Developmental Psychology, 10,* 580–588.

Wilson, R. S. (1978). Synchronies in mental development: An epigenetic perpective. *Science, 202,* 939–948.

Wilson, R. S., & Harpring, E. B. (1972). Mental and motor development in infant twins. *Developmental Psychology, 7,* 277–287.

Wohlwill, J. F. (1973). *The study of behavioral development.* New York: Academic Press.

Continuity and Discontinuity of Temperament in Infancy and Early Childhood: A Psychometric Perspective

3

Sean C. McDevitt
Devereux Center in Arizona

It is generally agreed that the demonstration of consistency over time is an important element in temperament research. The inclusion of relative stability as a definitional criterion of temperament (Buss & Plomin, 1975, 1984) differentiates it from other behavioral or personality variables. Finding links between early individual differences in temperament and later temperament assessment tends to validate the uniqueness of the construct. The presumed connection between temperament and biological or constitutional factors is strengthened by studies showing early stability, suggesting that these differences in behavior are not primarily determined by environmental events. Clinically, longitudinal stability is important if temperament is to be considered a predisposing factor for later behavior disorder, at least if the interactionist position on how behavior disorders emerge is to be accepted (Thomas & Chess, 1977). Continuity of temperament from early infancy onward suggests that temperament may be the basis from which later, more complex, personality characteristics emerge. Finally, stability between measures of temperament developed for different age periods supports the argument that similar characteristics are being measured at distinctly different periods of development (McDevitt & Carey, 1981).

Reviews of the issues in research on temperamental consistency (Carey, 1981; Plomin, 1983; Rutter, 1982; Thomas & Chess, 1977) invariably address the multiple difficulties in demonstrating the continuity or stability of the construct. A cursory look at the literature reveals a plethora of studies using differing concepts, variables, methods (questionnaire, interview, lab assessment, observations, etc.), and time intervals to demonstrate that temperament remains constant over some period of development. Nearly all, however, utilize the stability correlation to summarize the degree of consistency found and this common link

27

provides a meaningful point of comparison. But correlation coefficients are not directly comparable when there are significant differences in the reliabilities of the measures from which the correlations are obtained. A critical review of temperament measures (Hubert, Wachs, Peters-Martin, & Gandour, 1982) has made this point and suggested that such psychometric considerations tend to confound the theoretical and conceptual development of temperament research. Therefore the strategy adopted for this review was to examine reported stability in the context of the reliability of the measures that produced them. Stability can then be seen as a portion of total reliable variation. An additional benefit of this procedure was that it also allowed an estimate of the reliable variation associated with change. Thus, stability, change, and error were estimated for each study where reliability was reported. It is possible that a large percentage of variation can be attributed to each of these three components in a single study.

Reliable covariation is the product of the retest reliabilities of the two measures. Variation due to error is found by subtracting reliable variance from 100%. Observed stability (e.g., the stability coefficient) squared is the percentage of the total variance that is stable; the difference between the two can be used as an estimate of reliable change. Although this partitioning of total variance assumes that the observed stability coefficient accurately samples from the total reliable variance, the fact that most studies use multiple variables allows the median r to be used as a general estimate that will be less influenced by sampling error than a single coefficient. Whatever the biologic, genetic, or environmental factors at work in producing stability or change in temperament, these must be differentiated from changes associated with measurement error to obtain a clearer picture of their importance. Given this approach, the developmentally interesting question is, "What relative proportions of stability and change in temperament are associated with changes over time?" In addition, "Which variables or procedures influence patterns of stability and change?"

Any review of longitudinal temperament studies must acknowledge two limitations: (1) Studies have only begun to fill in the course of developmental stability and change and there are many gaps where few or no data exist on temperamental consistency; (2) When studies have been conducted across similar age ranges there has rarely been conceptual or methodological equivalence of data. This chapter acknowledges a third limitation related to its focus, namely, that it ignores to a large extent the specific content of the dimensions studied. An essentially atheoretical review of empirical findings such as this one looks at patterns of stability data and detailed tracing of the performance of specific constructs or variables cannot be considered within its scope. Given the controversy over the definition of temperament and the disagreement about which variables or how many variables represent the domain of behavioral style, it may be useful to examine these longitudinal data apart from the sophistication of the various conceptual frameworks and the eloquence of the authors who represent them. Thus the present review cannot be considered definitive or complete;

rather it is intended to evaluate the empirical status of stability studies and identify trends and issues in the current literature, highlight the areas where additional data are needed.

DEVELOPMENTAL TRENDS IN CONTINUITY AND STABILITY OF TEMPERAMENT

Examination of the data on temperamental stability from birth onward seems to indicate one major finding: Age of assessment for the predictor variable determines the degree of stability observed and the length of time for which significant stability can be obtained. The review of studies is therefore organized according to age at the initial assessment. Table 3.1 summarizes the studies reviewed and indicates percentage of reliable variance and proportion of stable variance associated with each interval. For purposes of discussion the age groups are separated roughly according to the level of predictive power characteristic of the findings.

BIRTH TO THREE MONTHS

The most common predictor of later temperament used in the neonatal/early infancy period has been the Brazelton Neonatal Assessment Scale. Stabilities to later temperament assessment have tended to be low, scattered and inconsistent between studies. No matter what measure is used no study was found to show good stability from less than 3 months of age to beyond 6 months. Perhaps the most promising study of early stability comes from the Louisville Twin Study (Wilson, 1982), which showed a number of moderate correlations between neonatal behavior and 6-month temperament, and the relationships found seem to have at least some face validity. As seen in Table 3.1, however, the median r in the correlation matrix still does not reach significance. Factors cited as possible reasons for the lack of observed stability have been interuterine effects and maturational factors. However, these aspects seem secondary to the issue of unreliability of the assessments since this alone could account for the poor overall stability. Only about 22% of the total variance between measures is reliable. Retest reliability for the Brazelton has been estimated at about .30 (see Plomin, 1983). Sullivan, Horrowitz, and Pannabecker (1982) found even lower 3–28 day stability for the BNAS-K. Kaye (1978) has suggested that about 5 Brazelton assessments would be needed to achieve overall reliability adequate for long term prediction. Stability is evident in specific links between neonatal and early infant behavior, though the continuities demonstrated thus far have not been numerous or strong (Peters-Martin & Wachs, in press).

TABLE 3.1
Longitudinal Data of Temperamental Consistency by Age Period

Age of Predictor	Source	Interval	Total Reliable Variance	Stability r	Stability Var. (%)	Change Var. (%)
Birth to 3 Months	Sullivan et al. (1982)	3 days to 28 days	NA	.18	3.24	NA
	Wilson (1982)	3-4 days to 6 mos	NA	.25	6.25	NA
	Peters-Martin & Wachs (in press)	1-6 mos	22.5%	.24	5.76	16.74
4 to 11 Months	Hagekull & Bohlin (1981)	4-13 mos	55.5%	.31	9.61	45.87
	Peters-Martin & Wachs (1984)	6-12 mos	61%	.32	10.24	50.76
	McDevitt & Carey (1981)	6 mos to 1-3 yrs	61%	.38	14.40	45.60
	Persson-Blennow & McNeil (1980)	6-13 mos	53.9%	.31	9.60	44.30
	Bates (1982)	6-13 mos	49%	.63	39.69	9.31
	Bates (1982)	6-24 mos	49%	.57	32.49	16.51
	McDevitt (1976)	6 mos to 3-5 yrs	68%	.29	8.41	59.49
	Huttunen & Nyman (1982)	7 mos to 5 yrs	NA	.24	5.76	NA
1 Year	Thomas & Chess (1977)	12-24 mos	NA	.38	14.40	NA
	Plomin & DeFries (1985)	12-24 mos	53.3%	.54	29.70	23.59
	Matheny et al. (1984)	12-18 mos	65.6%	.44	19.36	46.25

	Study	Age	%	r		
	Matheny et al. (1984)	18-24 mos	65.6%	.65	42.25	23.36
	Kagan et al. (1984)	21 mos to 4 yrs	NA	.50	25.00	NA
2 Years	Thomas & Chess (1977)	2-3 yrs	NA	.28	7.84	NA
3 Years	Thomas & Chess (1977)	3-4 yrs	NA	.26	6.76	NA
	Matheny (1984)	3-4 yrs	66%	.57	32.49	33.51
	Fox (1979)	3-4 yrs	66%	.67	44.89	21.11
3 Years	Hegvik et al. (1981)	3-7 to 8-12 yrs	71.3%	.42	17.64	53.64
3 Years	Stevenson-Hinde & Simpson (1982)	42-50 mos	64%	.53	28.09	35.91
4 Years	Thomas & Chess (1977)	4-5 yrs	NA	.31	9.61	NA
	Matheny (1984)	4-5 yrs	66%	.60	36.00	30.00
	Fox (1979)	4-5 yrs	66%	.63	39.69	26.31
5 Years	Matheny (1984)	5-6 yrs	66%	.66	43.56	22.44
	Fox (1979)	5-6 yrs	66%	.67	44.89	21.11
6 Years	Fox (1979)	6-7 yrs	66%	.70	49.00	17.00

NA = Not available
____ indicates that the stability r is not a median figure.

A major difficulty of this age period is whether anything approaching the later concept of temperament is being measured during the neonatal and early infant periods. The Brazelton scales are observational ratings obtained in the course of an examination; variables such as state modulation, response to stress and social interactions do not correspond in content to later assessment of temperament. Additional factors of low reliability and the discrepancies between measurement settings militate further against strong continuities. Theoreticians may identify processes that account for these discontinuities or point out specific dimensions of behavioral style that may show stability. Current empirical evidence is clear that no stable cluster of temperament constructs has emerged at this developmental period.

FOUR TO ELEVEN MONTHS PREDICTION

A number of studies have been conducted using predictor assessments of 4 to 8 months. This is the first age for which questionnaires are standardized, though laboratory investigations have also been completed. Questionnaire studies based on the NYLS uniformly find statistically significant median correlations in the .30–.38 range beyond the age of 12 months up to about 5 years of age. No study was found showing significant stability beyond this point. The magnitude of the correlations themselves do not show a linear decline in predictive power as a function of interval; corrected for reliability, however, a linear trend is evident. Using a 4–8 month predictor about 50–60% of the total variance is reliable and 20% of the reliable variance is stable into the second year, 12% is stable to 3 to 5 years.

In contrast, data reported by Bates using the ICQ at 6 months with later assessments at 13 and 24 months show a different pattern. Based on reliabilities and stability coefficients reported, most of the reliable variance assessed at 6 months remains stable at both 13 and 24 months. This apparently means that the social perceptions concept of difficult temperament (a fussy-difficult factor) is an extremely stable one compared to the characteristics measured by NYLS questionnaires. Explanations for this could include the relatively greater emphasis on the mother's perceptions rather than actual ratings of infant behavioral frequencies or the more general nature of the difficult construct that Bates employs. Either of these explanations would be consistent with the finding of low concurrent validity of the ICQ with observations of mother-infant behavior (Bates, Freeland, & Lounsbury, 1979), with more stability, but less specificity of the construct at each developmental period.

Laboratory assessment of temperamental stability from 6 to 12 months has been conducted by Wilson (1982). Preliminary results showed interrelationships between temperament questionnaires and lab scores at both 6 and 12 months but not stability over this time period. Technical problems with the 6-month lab assessments were cited as the most likely source of difficulty. However, this period of instability is the one absent link in temperament consistency from birth to 2-years-of-age in this program of research and, it would appear noteworthy if the measurement problems cannot be resolved. The absence of a link in the stability of individual differences from 6–12 months, particularly when convergence between lab and questionnaire results is found, would indicate a specific period of developmental transformation or discontinuity in temperament. The factors affecting such a transformation would most likely be contextually determined, since questionnaire stability across the 6–12 month age period is fairly well established.

ONE-YEAR PREDICTION

The NYLS data (Thomas & Chess, 1977) remain the most complete set of longitudinal stability estimates through the years 1–5. The methodological and statistical limitations of these data have been thoroughly reviewed by McNeil (1976) but they are included as the standard of comparison for more recent studies and because follow-up of the sample in adulthood has now been accomplished (Thomas & Chess, 1982; Chess & Thomas, 1984). At 1–2 years-of-age median stability of .38 was found, with six of nine characteristics showing individual stability. In spite of the availability of an NYLS based questionnaire (Fullard, McDevitt, & Carey, 1984) for this age period no 12–24 or 24–36 month stability data have yet been reported.

Matheny, Wilson, and Nuss (1984) have reported 6 month stabilities of lab and questionnaire assessments of temperament during the second year of life. With about 66% of the total variance being reliable, substantially higher proportions of stability variance were found in comparison with prediction just 6 months earlier. Consistent with increasing stability at this period, Plomin and DeFries (1985) found a median stability of .54 using midparental CCTI data with about half of the reliable variance accounting for stability and half being associated with change. IBR and videotape ratings of temperament showed much lower levels of stability over the same interval, again suggesting that the contextual features of observational data may reduce predictive power over time.

Both Matheny, et al. and the Plomin and DeFries studies employed aggregates of variables to increase predictive power of their measures (see Epstein, 1980). In the Matheny data the predictive power appears to have been enhanced but Plomin and DeFries reported aggregate r's to be at the level of the average for their separate stabilities. Thus there was no beneficial effect associated with this method. This raises the question of why aggregation works in some instances but not in others. It may be that when the intercorrelations of the variables aggregated are significant but not high the effect is to reduce sampling error around a true mean score, thereby making aggregate reliability higher than the reliabilities of the component measures. Low intercorrelations would suggest sampling of different means with no increased reliability of the aggregate measure. Data on this point are not available for the studies mentioned, however.

Another study using prediction from the second year of life has been reported by Kagan, Reznick, Clarke, Snidman, and Coll (1984). Using a dimension of behavioral inhibition with extreme groups (inhibited vs. uninhibited) they found moderate stability of individual difference from 21–48 months. The study is noteworthy in showing fairly long-term prediction of a temperament-related dimension from an early age with a level of observed stability similar to 6-month stabilities in the 12–24 month period. In addition, the behavioral data are supported by consistent differences in heart rate patterns, connecting the behavioral stability with a biological correlate. Although the inflationary effect of using extreme groups to increase stability cannot be overlooked, these findings suggest the potential power of temperamental characteristics to influence early behavior and development.

TWO-YEAR PREDICTION

Data showing temperamental consistency from 24–36 months onward are sparse. In fact, the NYLS data remain the only report found in the literature. Six of nine characteristics showed significant stability with a median r or .28. Neither short- nor long-term predictive power, using questionnaires or laboratory assessments are known. This is not an unimportant gap in our knowledge of temperamental stability, since data prior to 2-years-of-age show increased stability compared with early infancy and the early childhood data show very high interyear correlations. Data from 24–36 months onward would complete the overview of the basic developmental function of stability between infancy and early childhood.

EARLY CHILDHOOD PREDICTION

Stability data from the 3–7 year age range pertains almost exclusively to the NYLS characteristics. One year stability data from ages 3 to 7 has been reported by Fox (1979) and similar data for 3–6 years are available from Matheny (1984). Both utilized the Behavioral Style Questionnaire at 1-year intervals on separate samples of children. Results indicated much higher levels of stability (.5–.7 range) than seen in the NYLS, suggesting that improvements in the psychometric characteristics of temperament measures has allowed greater stability to be found.

The trend in both studies was for increasing levels of stability as age increased. By age 5 almost two thirds of the reliable variance was stable. For the

6–7 year interval the Fox data show nearly three fourths of the reliable variance is associated with stability. This almost completely reverses the proportions of stability to change seen for prediction from 6 months of age in the McDevitt and Carey (1981) data using similar measures and time intervals (e.g., 12 months). Although this is clearly a developmental function there are not presently sufficient data to chart its outline throughout the first 7 years of life.

Longer term prediction of individual temperamental characteristics from early childhood (Hegvik, McDevitt, & Carey, 1981) indicates that there continue to be significant increments of change throughout middle childhood. With an average interval of $4\frac{1}{2}$ years between assessments, all 8 NYLS characteristics remained significantly stable, though the median stability coefficient was .42. Thus, it is clear that even with the increased stability in early childhood, temperament does not become fixed at any point in early or middle childhood.

Follow-up data on the NYLS subjects into adolescence and adulthood has been reported by Thomas and Chess (1982) and Korn (1984). No stability was found for the individual temperamental characteristics. However, an average of scores in the categories making up difficult temperament showed significant prediction for years 3 and 4 to teenage and young adult summary scores (Korn, 1984). An interesting feature of Korn's analysis was that using this aggregate measure the interyear correlations *within* the 1–5 year period were increased from a median stability of .30 to a median composite of .39, again suggesting the increased predictive power of more global indices of temperament. A quartile analysis also suggested that difficult boys and easy girls were likely to remain so into later years.

Thomas and Chess (1982), using sophisticated set correlation analyses and with the addition of nontemperament predictor and criterion variables, showed significant prediction of adult adjustment of 34% of the total variance. Temperament scores in the years 3–4 and 4–5 predicted a composite adjustment score and presence or absence of a clinical diagnosis in adulthood with low but significant correlations.

Thus within early childhood, temperament shows moderate to high stability. Individual characteristics remain stable at least into early childhood and global measures of difficultness show significant links to teen and young adult periods.

SUMMARY AND IMPLICATIONS

The patchwork of studies reviewed above does not permit firm conclusions to be made about the continuity of temperament. Several issues and trends do appear to have some implications to future research: (1) There is fairly good evidence that temperamental characteristics show some significant (nonzero) stability from birth to adulthood. The magnitude and duration of stability appears to increase dramatically after the age of three but the trajectory of this developmental function is not precisely defined; (2) In the first 3 months of life there is insufficient reliable variance in temperament measures to detect many of the possible links. A questionnaire utilizing parental observation over a period of weeks might increase the amount of reliable variation. Alternately measuring the factors suppressing stability (e.g., maturational differences) and partialling them out of the stability correlation would seem necessary before higher levels of consistency could be attained. Finally there is some question about the equivalence of neonatal behavior and behavioral style as variables and greater stability might be expected if the variables assessed were matched more closely (see Carey, 1983); (3) More global concepts and measures of temperaments appear more stable than more narrowly defined ones. While questionnaire measures have demonstrated significant stability from 6 months to 1 year, laboratory assessments have not. Related to this, individual temperament characteristics do not show stability into the teen and adult years though composite scores do. What seems to emerge from these observations is the general notion that continuities in temperament are more enduring and more easily detected as the level of analysis becomes less specific, situational, or contextual and more global or general. On the other hand, as the generality of a concept or measure increases, its sensitivity and ability to provide useful information clinically or theoretically decreases. It is one thing to know that a child is temperamentally difficult but without knowing which dimensions are problematic it would be impossible to offer meaningful assistance. Specific or contextually defined dimensions of temperament may show age-related developmental transformations that would be lost if combined with other dimensions into a more global construct. To the extent that these transformations have theoretical significance, compensating for the instability they create may not be advantageous. In these cases aggregation of occasions rather than variables might capture the nuances of development with adequate levels of reliability.

As sophistication of research in the temperament area increases and is guided by additional empirical work perhaps the focus of inquiry will shift from the current emphasis on demonstrating only that stability exists to developing an understanding of the processes by which both stability and change are created. Current research suggests that they coexist in systematically changing proportions during the first years of life, and this developmental process will require supporting theory and concept to adequately explain once the psychometric issues have been resolved.

REFERENCES

Bates, J. E. (1982, March). *The role of temperamental difficultness in social relationships.* Paper presented at the International Conference on Infant Studies, Austin, Texas.
Bates, J. E., Freeland, C. A. B., & Lounsbury, M. L. (1979). Measurement of infant difficultness. *Child Development, 50,* 794–803.

Buss, A. H., & Plomin, R. (1975). *A temperament theory of personality development.* New York: Wiley-Interscience.

Buss, A. H., & Plomin, R. (1984). *Temperament: Early developing personality traits.* Hillsdale, NJ: Lawrence Erlbaum Associates.

Carey, W. B. (1981). The importance of temperament-environment interaction for child health and development. In M. Lewis & L. Rosenblum (Eds.), *The uncommon child.* New York: Plenum.

Carey, W. B. (1983). Some pitfalls in infant temperament research. *Infant Behavior and Development, 6,* 247–254.

Chess, S., & Thomas, A. (1984). *Origins and evolution of behavior disorders: Infancy to early adult life.* New York: Brunner/Mazel.

Epstein, S. (1980). The stability of behavior, II. Implications for psychological research. *American Psychologist, 35,* 790–806.

Fox, M. M. (1979). *A longitudinal study of temperament in early childhood.* Unpublished doctoral dissertation. Temple University.

Fullard, W., McDevitt, S. C., & Carey, W. B. (1984). Assessing temperament in 1 to 3 year old children. *Journal of Pediatric Psychology, 9* (2), 205–217.

Hagekull, B., & Bohlin, G. (1981). Individual stability in dimensions of infant behavior. *Infant Behavior and Development, 4,* 97–108.

Hegvik, R., McDevitt, S. C., & Carey, W. B. (1981). *Longitudinal stability of temperament characteristics in the elementary school period.* Paper presented at the International Society for the Study of Behavioral Development, Toronto.

Hubert, N. C., Wachs, T. D., Peters-Martin, P., & Gandour, M. J. (1982). The study of early temperament: Measurement and conceptual issues. *Child Development, 53,* 571–600.

Huttunen, M., & Nyman, G. (1982). On the continuity, change and clinical value of infant temperament in a prospective epidemiological study. In R. Porter & G. Collins (Eds.), *Temperamental differences in infants and young children.* London: Pitman Books, Ltd. (Ciba Foundation symposium series 89)

Kagan, J., Reznick, S. J., Clarke, C., Sidman, N., & Garcia-Coll, C. G. (1984). Behavioral inhibition in children. *Child Development, 55,* 2212–2225.

Kaye, K. (1978). Discriminating among normal infants by multivariate analysis of Brazelton scores: lumping and smoothing. In A. J. Sameroff (Ed.), Organization and stability of newborn behavior: A commentary on the Brazelton Neonatal Behavior Assessment Scale. *Monographs of the Society for Research in Child Development, 43,* 60–80.

Korn, S. J. (1984). Continuities and discontinuities in difficult/easy temperament: Infancy to young adulthood. *Merrill-Palmer Quarterly.*

Matheny, A. P. (1984). Personal communication.

Matheny, A. P., Wilson, R. S., & Nuss, S. M. (1984). Toddler temperament: Stability across settings and over ages. *Child Development.*

McDevitt, S. C. (1976). *A longitudinal assessment of continuity and stability in temperamental characteristics from infancy to early childhood.* Unpublished doctoral dissertation, Temple University.

McDevitt, S. C., & Carey, W. B. (1981). Stability of ratings vs. perceptions of temperament from early infancy to 1–3 years. *American Journal of Orthopsychiatry, 51,* 341–345.

McNeil, T. F. (1976). *Temperament revisited: A research oriented critique of the New York Longitudinal Study.* Unpublished manuscript, University of Lund, Malmo, Sweden.

Persson-Blennow, I., & McNeil, T. F. (1980). Questionnaires for measurement of temperament in one- and two-year-old children: Development and standardization. *Journal of Child Psychology, Psychiatry, and Allied Disciplines, 21,* 37–46.

Peters-Martin, P., & Wachs, T. D. (in press). A longitudinal study of temperament and its correlates in the first 12 months. *Infant Behavior and Development.*

Plomin, R. (1983). Childhood temperament. In B. B. Lahey & A. E. Kazdin, (Eds.), *Advances in clinical child psychology, 6*. New York: Plenum.

Plomin, R., & DeFries, J. C. (1985). *Origins of individual differences in infancy: The Colorado Adoption Project*. New York: Academic Press.

Rutter, M. (1982). Temperament, concepts, issues and problems. In R. Porter & G. M. Collins (Eds.), *Temperamental differences in infants and young children*. London: Pitman Books, Ltd. (Ciba Foundation symposium 89).

Stevenson-Hinde, J., & Simpson, A. E. (1982). Temperament and relationships. In R. Porter & G. Collins (Eds.), *Temperamental differences in infants and young children*. London: Pitman Books, Ltd. (Ciba Foundation symposium 89).

Sullivan, J. W., Horowitz, F. D., & Pannabecker, B. J. (1982). *Continuity of temperament from birth to six months of age*. Paper presented at the Temperament Conference, Salem, Massachusetts.

Thomas, A., & Chess, S. (1977). *Temperament and development*. New York: Brunner/Mazel.

Thomas, A., & Chess, S. (1982). Temperament and follow-up to adulthood. In R. Porter and G. M. Collins (Eds.), *Temperamental differences in infants and young children*. London: Pitman.

Wilson, R. S. (1982). Intrinsic determanents of temperament. In R. Porter & G. Collins, *Temperamental differences in infants and young children*. London: Pitman Books, Ltd. (Ciba Foundation symposium 89).

4

The New York Longitudinal Study: From Infancy to Early Adult Life

Alexander Thomas
Stella Chess
New York University Medical Center

The New York Longitudinal Study (NYLS) has now followed the behavioral development of 133 subjects from middle- and upper-middle class families from early infancy to early adult life. A major focus of this project has been the identification of categories of temperamental individuality and their functional significance for both normal and deviant psychological development (Chess & Thomas, 1984; Thomas & Chess, 1977).

With this focus of the study, our concern has been to gather and analyze data not only on temperamental characteristics at different age groups, but also on levels of psychological functioning, including the presence or absence of a behavior disorder, and the course of such a disorder over time. Our commitment to the interactionist/transactional view from the beginning, in which the influence of temperament on development could be conceptualized only in terms of its continuous interaction over time with the subject's other characteristics and with the influence of the environment, also led us to collect data on IQ, special attributes of the subject, parental practices and attitudes, and special environmental events.

Our data-gathering and analytic procedures and findings for the childhood period are detailed in our earlier volumes (Thomas, Chess, Birch, Hertzig, & Korn, 1963; Thomas, Chess, & Birch, 1968), and for the early adult period in our latest one (Chess & Thomas, 1984). This report concentrates on our findings with regard to our data on change and continuity in temperament, and their implications for developmental theory. For details concerning methods and measures, the reader is referred to Chess and Thomas (1984).

MEASURES UTILIZED

The measures we have utilized for this presentation can be tabulated as follows:

1. *Temperament*—nine categories (activity level, rhythmicity, approach/withdrawal, adaptability, sensory threshold, quality of mood, intensity of mood expression, distractibility, and persistence/attention span). Three constellations were also identified by qualitative judgment and factor analysis: (a) easy temperament-rhythmic, high approach, predominantly positive mood of mild to moderate intensity, and quick adaptability; (b) difficult temperament—arhythmic, many withdrawal responses to the new, relatively frequent negative mood of high intensity, and slow adaptability; and (c) slow-to-warm-up temperament—many withdrawal responses to the new of mild to moderate intensity, and slow adaptability. (Children with this last constellation are frequently labeled as "shy" or "inhibited" by family, friends, or themselves.)

Temperament was rated in the childhood years by item scoring of the parental interview protocols. Interrater reliability was at the 0.9 level. In the early adult years, temperament was rated by the interviewer, one of us (A.T.), who also sat in on most of the interviews, and by a naive rater from the interview audiotapes. Interrater reliabilities were moderate, ranging from .59 to .80, except for .48 for quality of mood, .46 for persistence, .23 for threshold, and .01 for intensity. It was clear that the rating of intensity especially presented special problems. The reliability levels were improved by pooling the ratings of the three raters, and these were used in the various analyses.

2. *Global adjustment scores at 3 and 5 years*—The information obtained from parents and teachers made possible the rating of levels of the child's adjustment in 12 areas—sleeping, eating, elimination, sex, motor activity, speech and communication, fears, discipline, relationship with parents, relationship with sibs, non-family relationships, and task mastery. A further category, relationship to school, was added for the 5-year parent interview. A similar rating scale, with appropriate modification, was developed for the 5-year teacher interview. Interrater reliabilities for the 3-year scale were above .80 for 8 categories, .64 to .75 for three others, and .32 for coping. For the 5-year parent and teacher interviews, the interrater reliabilities were all above .88. For each protocol, a global adjustment score was calculated by adding up the average score for each category and dividing by the number of categories.

3. *Parental attitudes and practices*—These ratings were made from special structured interviews with both parents, simultaneously but separately, done when the subjects were 3-years-old, and by two interviewers who had no other contact with the NYLS. Immediately following the interview, the interviewers rated the parent on a total of 99 items derived from the interview. It was not possible to obtain interrater reliabilities for these ratings. The ratings of the

mothers were then subjected to a cluster analysis by means of the Tryon system (Cameron, 1977). Eight clusters were extracted: (1) parental disapproval, intolerance and rejection; (2) parental conflict with each other, especially over childcare practices; (3) parental strictness vs. permissiveness; (4) maternal concern and protectiveness; (5) relatively depressed living standards; (6) limitations on the child's material supports; (7) inconsistent parental discipline; and (8) large family orientation.

4. *Early adult adjustment scores*—From the early adult subject interviews, the raters scored each subject on a 7-point scale for 13 items—self-evaluation, relationship with family, school functioning, social functioning, sexual adjustment, patterns of coping, goals, implementation of goals, person orientation, task orientation, routines of daily life, communication, and emotional expressiveness. In addition, each subject received an overall global adjustment rating on a 9-point scale. Interrater reliabilities for the individual items were moderate; for the overall global rating they varied from 0.82 to 0.87. For the determination of the final behavioral adjustment score in early adult life, the bootstrapping technique was used (Goldberg, 1970). With this technique a set of elements (the specific areas of adjustment) is first subjected to an overall clinical judgment (the global adjustment score). Then, using that judgment as a criterion in a multiple regression analysis with the element scores as independent variables, the regression equation is generated that estimates the overall judgment. The data finally used are not the actual judgments, but their regression estimates. The rationale for this procedure is that the regression equation distills the implicit rating policies that are implicit when the overall judgment is made, but unlike the latter, are not subject to day-to-day variation in rater judgment, or the intrusion of irrelevant factors into the judgment.

5. *Clinical diagnosis*—Whenever a parent or teacher reported apparently deviant behavior in a child, the staff interviewer consulted one of us (S.C.). If the reporter suggested the possibility of a clinical behavior disorder, a full-scale clinical evaluation was done, consisting of a full clinical history from the parents, followed by a play session with the younger children, and a focused interview with the older ones. Special sensory, neurological or psychological studies were undertaken as indicated. In each case where a clinical diagnosis was made, a schedule of follow-up evaluations was arranged.

In the early adult interviews, which ranged from 18 to 24 years, with 4 subjects being only 17-years-of-age, the clinical evaluations were made from the subject interviews. Interrater reliability among the three raters was high, at the 0.90 level. In the few cases of disagreements, the judgment of one of us (A.T.) was chosen.

6. *Special life events*—The only special events with a sufficient N for quantitative analysis were separation/divorce of the parents, or death of a parent. Idiosyncratic life events did play a significant role in certain individual subjects, as indicated in the qualitative analyses.

The NYLS records also include other data, such as temperament ratings from teachers, IQ data and temperament and adjustment ratings in adolescence, whose analyses are as yet not completed, and therefore are not included in this report.

CONTINUITY AND CHANGE IN TEMPERAMENT

As we originally began to observe clinically and impressionistically the temperamental characteristics of individuals we knew, in the years before we began the NYLS, we were struck by the many dramatic instances of continuity in one or another aspect of their behavioral styles, sometimes even from early childhood to adulthood. It was tempting to generalize from these observations to the concept that temperament might be a behavioral attribute characterized by continuity over time, and that an adult's temperamental pattern might be predicted from a knowledge of his behavioral style in early childhood. However, such a formulation would be completely at variance with our fundamental commitment to an interactionist viewpoint, in which the behavioral development of any individual is conceptualized as a constantly evolving process of organism-environment interaction. Such a process involves both change and continuity, and change at one age-period can turn into continuity at another period, or continuity turn into change.

Beyond this overall implication of the interactionist view, there are a number of conceptual and methodological problems in the study of temperamental continuity. Dunn (1980) has pointed out that "individual differences at any one age may reflect differences in rate of maturation rather than differences in temperament" (p. 103). Individual differences in the timing of genetic influences may also affect the patterning of behavior, including temperament (Wilson, 1978). Rutter (1970) has emphasized a number of methodological problems: reliance on adjectives used by parents or observers in describing children's behavior; the possibility of selective bias in deciding which episodes of behavior the parent or other observer reports; and the effect that the changing context of the child's behavior might have on the temperament ratings.

NYLS QUANTITATIVE ANALYSES OF CONTINUITY IN TEMPERAMENT

With these conceptual and methodological issues in mind, it has been no surprise to find limited continuity in our nine individual temperamental categories.

The quantitative temperament scores for the first 5-years-of-life were utilized to calculate interyear product-moment correlations for each of the nine categories. The scores for each child were pooled arithmetically for each year, and the calculations were based on these pooled weighted scores. These correlations have been previously reported (Thomas & Chess, 1977, p. 161), but with a smaller N than in the present tabulation. The variable N from year to year and category to category is the result of missing data in some cases, especially in the youngest subjects for the fifth year.

As can be seen from Table 4.1, there are significant correlations from one year to the next for all categories except approach/withdrawal, distractibility, and persistence. These three categories are also the ones with skewed distribution curves for each of the first 5 years. The other six categories, with higher interyear correlations, all approximate normal distribution curves. This suggests that a lack of sufficient differentiation of the subjects by the quantitative scores for approach/withdrawal, distractibility, and persistence may be at least partially responsible for the low level of interyear correlations.

Table 4.1 also shows that as the time span for the comparison is increased, from 1 year to 2, 3, or 4 years the number of significant correlations decreases sharply. Only activity level shows significant correlations for all the interyear comparisons. Several analyses were done to examine this finding of dwindling in significant correlations over longer time-periods. First, the means were tabulated.

For the six categories with consistent significant correlations for contiguous years, the means for activity level and threshold showed overall consistency for the 5 years. (Activity level was the one category with significant correlations for all ten interyear comparisons; threshold and adaptability were next, with 7 out of

TABLE 4.1
Interyear Correlations for First Five Years

Interyear	1-2	2-3	3-4	4-5	1-3	2-4	3-5	1-4	2-5	1-5
Activity	.30*	.38*	.33*	.37*	.37*	.29*	.25*	.24*	.20*	.18*
(N)	131	125	121	116	125	126	114	126	117	117
Rhyth.	.41*	.38*	.18	.35*	.36*	.02	.15	.23*	.10	.22*
(N)	131	125	120	113	125	125	112	125	115	115
Adapt.	.33*	.41*	.45*	.52*	.14	.34*	.31*	.13	.29*	.14
(N)	130	124	121	116	125	125	114	126	116	117
A./With.	.09	.02	.20*	.40*	.17	.20*	.03	.01	.06	-.03
(N)	131	125	121	116	125	126	114	126	117	117
Thresh.	.43*	.22*	.30*	.28*	.25*	.16	.24*	.15	.03	.22*
(N)	131	125	121	116	125	126	114	126	117	117
Intens.	.45*	.39*	.33*	.33*	.19*	.11	.11	.16	.09	.02
(N)	131	125	121	116	125	126	114	126	117	117
Mood	.52*	.19*	.28*	.29*	.18*	.13	.13	.17	.12	.08
(N)	131	125	121	116	125	126	114	126	117	117
Distract.	-.07	.17	.19*	.11	.10	.05	.34*	-.06	-.05	.15
(N)	129	123	114	97	125	117	99	118	100	103
Persist.	.09	.35*	.22*	.14	-.02	.21*	.24*	-.03	.14	.02
(N)	131	125	121	116	125	126	114	126	117	117

*Significant at the .05 level of confidence (two-tailed).

10). The mean for rhythmicity showed a gradual consistent shift toward greater regularity and for mood a similar shift to more positive mood. This may account, in part at least, for the drop in significant correlations as the interyear periods lengthen. Adaptability showed a shift to lower adaptability at 2 years and then a gradual return to greater adaptability. A similar trend was evident for intensity, with a shift to greater intensity in the second year and then a gradual return to milder intensity. This shift to lower adaptability and greater intensity in the second year may correspond to the oft-described "2-year negativism."

Variability score—It is possible that some children are characterized by greater variability and others by lesser variability in temperament over time. In other words, the overall group trends may conceal the existence of two subgroups. This possibility was explored by developing a variability score for each category for each child. For each of the nine categories, the S.D of the scores of that category of that child for years 1–5 was determined. The mean of these nine S.D.s was then calculated, giving one score of mean variability of all the nine categories for each child.

The mean variability scores were then compared by regression analysis to our various ratings: the adult temperament scores, the adult bootstrap score, global adjustment scores at ages 3 and 5, clinical versus nonclinical, and the temperamentally difficult child and difficult adult scores. No significant relationships were found. There is, therefore, no evidence from these limited analyses that variability in temperament over the first 5 years is clinically a functionally significant characteristic. The analysis of variability in temperament has as yet not been carried beyond this point.

Correlation of childhood with early adult temperament—This analysis is tabulated in Table 4.2.

As can be seen from Table 4.2, there is only one significant correlation between years 1 and 2 and the young adult. For year 3, the significant correlations increase to two, with a third (Quality of Mood) almost reaching the .05 level

TABLE 4.2
Correlations Between Temperament in Years 1-5
and Early Adult Temperament (Two-Tailed) in 131 Subjects

Category	Year 1 -Adult	Year 2 -Adult	Year 3 -Adult	Year 4 -Adult	Year 5 -Adult
Activity	.06	.08	.02	.15	.07
Rhythmicity	-.10	.00	.11	-.05	.02
Adaptability	.14	.15	.21*	.22**	.18
App./Withdraw.	-.02	-.01	.29**	.20*	.16
Threshold	.15	.06	.14	.04	.04
Intensity	.20*	.01	.09	.26**	.03
Quality Mood	-.07	-.03	.17	.18*	.10
Distract.	.03	-.08	-.15	-.01	.01
Persist.	-.13	-.18*	-.03	-.12	.02

* .05 level
** .001 level

(.058). For year 4 the significant correlations increase sharply, to drop away in year 5. The significant correlations in years 3 and 4 comprise categories of the easy-difficult child constellation, namely approach/withdrawal, adaptability, intensity, and quality of mood.

EASY-DIFFICULT TEMPERAMENT: CONTINUITY AND PREDICTABILITY

In view of this finding of significant correlations between elements of easy-difficult temperament in childhood and young adulthood, the issue of continuity of this temperamental constellation was explored further. For this purpose, an overall easy-difficult temperament score was constructed by taking the means of the scores of the five categories making up this constellation. The interyear correlations for the first 5 years, and the correlations between each of the first 5 years and the adult easy-different temperament score were calculated, and are presented in Table 4.3.

The findings in Table 4.3 correspond overall with the findings of Tables 4.1 and 4.2.

The correlations between the easy–difficult temperament score in each of the first 5 years and the global adjustment scores at home at 3 years, and in school at 5 years, and in early adulthood, as well as the presence of a clinical psychiatric disorder in early adulthood, were then calculated, and are presented in Table 4.4.

In Table 4.4, all correlations are in the expected direction, i.e., positive correlation of the difficult temperament end of the continuum with lower adjustment at 3 and 5 years, and in early adult life, and negative correlation with better

TABLE 4.3
Easy-Difficult Temperament Interyear Correlations

Years	Years	Years	Years
1-2 .42*	1-3 .26*	1-4 .7	1-5 .05
2-3 .37*	2-4 .24*	2-5 .20*	
3-4 .29*	3-5 .14		
4-5 .44*			

Easy-Difficult Child to Easy-Difficult Adult
Correlations

Age	Adult Score
1 yr.	.17
2 yr.	.09
3 yr.	.31*
4 yr.	.37*
5 yr.	.15

* Statistically significant beyond the .05 level

TABLE 4.4
Easy- Difficult Temperament and Adjustment Correlations

Easy - Difficult Score Age	Adjustment Score			Early Adult Ratings	
	Home- Year 3	Home- Year 5	School- Year 5	Adjustment Score	Clinical Diagnosis
0-1 yr.	.03	-.03	-.02	.08	.03
1-2	.14	.02	-.06	-.09	-.03
2-3	.38*	.21*	-.02	-.21*	.05
3-4	.55*	.36*	.30*	-.32*	.24*
4-5	.24*	.58*	.11	-.23*	.19*
N Range	111- 127	113- 117	82- 84	115- 131	116- 132

* Statistically significant beyond the .05 level

Note: The adjustment scores for the childhood and early adult periods are in opposite directions. The lower the childhood score, whether at age 3 or 5 years, the better the adjustment, whereas the higher the early adult score the better the adjustment.

adjustment in early adulthood, as well as a positive correlation with an early adult clinical psychiatric diagnosis.

As can be seen from Table 4.4, there are no significant correlations with easy–difficult temperament for the first 2-years-of-life. Then, in years 2 to 3 a number of significant correlations appear, with a further increase in years 3 to 4. In the fifth year, the significant correlations remain high, though slightly decreased from the fourth year. These findings suggest a stabilization of at least those temperamental characteristics comprising easy-difficult temperament by the third year of life. This may reflect a leveling-off of individual differences in maturation and genetic influences, as compared to the infancy period. Also, there may be the beginning of a stabilization of parent-child interactional patterns by the third year. Finally, the definitional criteria for the five temperamental categories characterizing the easy versus difficult child constellation may begin to stabilize by the third year, so that there begins to be a closer correspondence with the rating criteria for the later years. As to which of the above possibilities are pertinent to our findings, further research is necessary to decide this issue. Our own hypothesis is that this stabilization of easy–difficult temperament in the third and fourth years basically reflects a functional developmental phenomenon, rather than a methodological issue.

Finally, the relationships between childhood temperament at 3 years as the independent variable, and early adult easy-difficult temperament and adjustment as the dependent variables, was studied through a series of multiple regression analyses.

To summarize these analyses, which are reported in detail elsewhere (Chess & Thomas, 1984), easy-difficult temperament at age 3 years is significantly related to early adult easy-difficult temperament, even when adjustment and maternal attitudes at year 3 are controlled for. Overall temperament at year 3, including all nine categories, is also significantly related to easy-difficult adult score, but this relationship becomes nonsignificant when adjustment at year 3 is controlled for. Of the various attributes of maternal attitudes rated when the child was 3-years-of-age, parental conflict was significantly related to young adult adjustment, even when controlling for age 3 adjustment, adjustment and temperament, and adjustment and easy-difficult temperament.

We have also utilized the recently developed set correlation method (Cohen, 1982), which is a multivariate generalization of multiple regression/correlation. Unlike the latter, set correlation makes it possible to create sets of dependent variables and relate them in one analysis to sets of independent variables. With this procedure, sets of dependent variables can be partialled out from each other, as well as partialling out independent variables. In our set correlation analysis, in addition to the age 3 independent variables of the multiple regression analysis, adjustment and easy-difficult temperament at 5 years, and parental death or separation/divorce at any age were added. The dependent variables included clinical diagnosis in early adult life, as well as adjustment and easy-difficult temperament at the same age-period.

This set correlation analysis confirmed the findings from the multiple regression analysis of the predictive significance of both parental conflict and easy-difficult temperament at 3 years for adult adjustment. The analysis also showed a correlation between difficult temperament at age 5, but not at age 3, and early adult clinical psychiatric status. Death of a parent or separation/divorce did not correlate significantly with early adult adjustment. Parental conflict at age 3 was significantly correlated with later parental separation or divorce.

Sex differences—Sex differences in any of these analyses were not striking in any of their findings. However, Korn (1984), using a quartile analysis approach to the NYLS data, found a significant correlation between boys in the extreme quartile for difficult temperament at 3 years and in early adulthood. In girls, a similar analysis showed a significant correlation between the two age-periods for easy temperament.

QUALITATIVE STUDY OF INDIVIDUAL SUBJECTS

Quantitative methods are crucial for the study of continuity and change in temperament, as for a host of other behavioral issue. But, at least as of now, quantitative analyses gave us only partial answers. A correlation of 0.7 in a behavioral study is impressive, but it still accounts for only 50% of the variance. Not all children with difficult temperament develop behavior disorders, and some children with easy temperament do develop a behavior disorder. And some youngsters are able to cope successfully with a home atmosphere rife with parental conflict. As the developmental psychiatrist Rutter (1980, p. 5) has suggested, the complexities and variabilities of person-situation interactions may make it necessary not only to pursue nomothetic principles of general applicability, but also "to take an ideographic approach which explicitly focuses on the *individuality* of human beings—not just in the degree to which they show particular traits or even in terms of the traits which are relevant to them, but more generally in terms of the idiosyncracies which make each person uniquely different from all others." The developmental psychologist McCall (1983) has pointed up this same issue: "To expect the human organism not to be susceptible to or benefit from momentary or unique opportunities oversimplifies the nature of mental development and the plasticity and adaptability of the human species. . . . We need to abandon our arm's-length approach and get closer to our subjects and their families and friends" (p. 414).

As we have reviewed the individual developmental courses of our NYLS subjects with regard to continuity and change in temperament, we have been struck with the differences among them. Overall, no subject has shown striking consistency over the years in *all* nine categories. Some have shown continuity in some categories; others have evidenced consistency in some categories over one period and in other categories subsequently. In other cases, change in conspicuous temperamental trait over time has been present. Any individual subject may show a combination of several of these possibilities, i.e., continuity in one or more categories and variability in others.

What has been striking, has been the evidence that one or more temperamental categories in any subject may show a combination of consistency and yet variability in its expression at different time periods, depending on the influence of other variables, such as environmental factors or psychodynamic patterns. This finding is consistent with an interactionist model of the developmental process. This finding can be illustrated with a case vignette.

Carl was one of our most extreme cases of difficult temperament from the first few months of life through 5-years-of-age. However, he did not develop a behavior disorder, primarily due to optimal handling by his parents and stability of his environment. His father, who himself had an easy temperament, took delight in his son's "lusty" characteristics, recognized on his own Carl's tendency to have intense negative reactions to the new, and had the patience to wait for eventual adaptability to occur. He was clear, without any orientation by us, that these characteristics were in no way due to his or his wife's influences. His wife tended to be anxious and self-accusatory over Carl's tempestuous course. However, her husband was supportive and reassuring and this enabled her to take an appropriately objective and patient approach to her son's development. By the middle childhood and early adolescent years few new situations arose which evoked the difficult temperament responses. The family, school, and social environment was stable and Carl flourished and appeared to be temperamentally easy rather than difficult. An occasional new demand, however, such as the start of piano lessons, again evoked his previous typical response of initial intense negative response, followed by slow adaptability and eventual positive zestful involvement. When Carl went off to college, however, he was faced simultaneously with a host of new situations and demands—an unfamiliar locale, a different living arrangement, new academic subjects and expectations, and a totally new peer group. Within a few weeks his temperamentally difficult traits reappeared in full force. He felt negative about the school, his courses, the other students, couldn't motivate himself to study and was constantly irritable. Carl knew something was wrong, discussed the situation with his family and us and developed an appropriate strategy to cope with his problem. He limited the new demands by dropping several extracurricular activities, limited his social contacts and policed his studying. Gradually he adapted, his distress disappeared and was able to expand his activities and social contacts. When seen by us for the early adult follow-up at age 23 his temperamental rating was not in the difficult group.

In Carl's case, environmental stability in his childhood and adolescent years influenced a change in his temperamental pattern. A sudden and extensive environmental change was then responsible for a reappearance of his early childhood temperament. In other subjects, however, environmental influence on temperamental continuity was quite different. In some instances environmental stability reinforced the childhood pattern; in other subjects environmental change was reinforcing. In other words, all kinds of permutations and combinations have been evident, depending on the specific dynamics of the person-environment interaction in the individual subjects.

GOODNESS OF FIT

It is these qualitative studies of the developmental courses of the individual subjects that led us to the "goodness of fit" theoretical model. We could find no one single pattern of person-environment interaction that could be applied as a general rule for predicting the developmental course of all our subjects (Thomas, Chess, & Birch, 1968). Rather, for each subject healthy or deviant functioning and development was determined by whether there was a goodness (consonance) or poorness (dissonance) of fit between the properties of the environment and its expectations and demands and the subject's temperament and other characteristics. In some cases goodness of fit made for continuity of temperament, as when parents approved of their child's easy temperament, or persistence, or high activity level, and reinforced these temperamental characteristics by their responses to the child. In other cases, as in Carl above, goodness of fit in his childhood and adolescent years resulted in temperamental discontinuity. The same is true of poorness of fit. A parent who responded to her child's tantrums by intense negative outbursts of her own, only reinforced these negative intense mood expressions of her child. And a parent or teacher who discouraged a child's persistent absorption in an activity because it was inconvenient sometimes motivated the child to be less persistent. This same conceptual model of goodness of fit we have found useful not only for the question of continuity and change in temperament, but also for analyzing social functioning, academic performance, and in tracing the origins and evolution of behavior disorders in individual subjects.

Goodness of fit does not imply an absence of stress and conflict. Quite the contrary. Stress and conflicts are inevitable attributes of the developmental process. When they are consonant with the child's capacities, the consequences are constructive; when they are dissonant, the stress becomes excessive for *that* child, with unfavorable developmental consequences.

This concept of goodness of fit is similar to that employed by Kagan (1971) in studying perceptual schemata in infants and their interaction with new environmental stimuli. He emphasized that excessive stress and distress depended on the degree of discrepancy from an established scheme and not from the novelty of the stimulation as such. It is also of interest that a number of developmental psychologists and psychiatrists have begun to use the goodness of fit model in recent years in their analysis of the dynamic interplay between child and environment, though not all use the actual term "goodness of fit" itself (Greenspan, 1981; Murphy, 1981; Stern, 1977).

THE CONCEPT OF DIFFICULT TEMPERAMENT

We devised the term "difficult temperament" after listening to certain parents in the routinely scheduled NYLS interviews. These parents kept telling us, in interview after interview, how difficult it was to manage their infants in the routines of daily care, and how different these babies were from their other children or the children of their relatives or friends. Almost everything new—the bath, new foods, new people, new surroundings—became the occasion for noisy outbursts of crying. Sleeping and feeding schedules were irregular, and positive changes came slowly. It became clear that these parents were describing children who were irregular, withdrew from most new situations, adapted slowly, and had many expressions of intense negative mood. The term "difficult" indeed seemed appropriate. This temperamental constellation then appeared as a strong factor in our factor analyses (Thomas et al., 1968). Finally, Rutter (Rutter, Birch, Thomas, & Chess, 1966) discovered a significant predictive correlation between the difficult temperament NYLS subjects and the later development of behavior disorders, a finding confirmed in other research centers (Thomas, Chess, & Korn, 1982). The analyses reported earlier in this paper add further evidence to the high risk potential these children have for maladaptive functioning, which may carry into early adult life.

The identification of difficult temperament, therefore, has importance for prevention and treatment in clinical practice. However, several objections can, and have been raised to the use of the term "difficult." It does have a pejorative connotation, even if most parents can accept the reassurance that this style is one normal form of behavioral individuality in children. Then, some parents find other temperamental characteristics difficult to manage, such as high activity level or marked distractibility. Finally, other cultures or subcultures with different expectations of their children and different routines of daily life may not find the child with difficult temperament as difficult to manage as did our NYLS parents (Korn & Gannon, 1983; Super & Harkness, 1981).

These considerations certainly do have merit, and we ourselves have pondered the possibility of finding a more neutral label than "difficult," and have discussed this question with various colleagues. Thus far, no alternative term has been suggested that did not have as many, if different, objections than the label "difficult." So, for the present we can only recommend the continued use of the term "difficult temperament," with the cautions that it not be reified and that its specific imperfections be kept in mind at all times.

DIRECTIONS FOR FUTURE RESEARCH

The study of the dialectic interplay between continuity and changes in temperament is of interest in itself. Much more important, however, is the indication that such studies may help to illuminate a number of basic issues in developmental psychology and psychiatry—genetic-environment interaction, developmental transitions and transformations, dynamics of family relationships, and the origins and evolution of behavior disorders. These issues and their research implications are highlighted in a number of the chapters in this volume.

There is a further most intriguing question linked with continuity and change, which we and others have barely begun to consider. When and how do individuals develop insight into their own temperamental patterns, and the influence these characteristics have on their functioning? What relationship does this insight have to other attributes of the person? What mechanisms does an individual use to reinforce certain temperamental traits and to try to modify or change others? What determines the degree of success in achieving such temperamental change, and what effects do these efforts have on the subsequent life-course?

These questions pose a formidable challenge to temperament research, both conceptually and methodologically. Yet, their exploration holds the promise of developing a new and fruitful dimension to our work.

REFERENCES

Cameron, J. R. (1977). Parental treatment, children's temperament, and the risk of childhood behavior problems. *American Journal of Orthopsychiatry, 47,* 568–576.

Chess, S., & Thomas, A. (1984). *Origins and evolution of behavior disorders: Infancy to early adult life.* New York: Brunner/Mazel.

Cohen, J. (1982). Set correlation as a general multivariate data-analytic method. *Multivariate Behavioral Research, 17,* 301–341.

Dunn, J. (1980). Individual differences in temperament. In M. Rutter (Ed.), *Scientific foundations of developmental psychiatry.* London: Heinemann.

Goldberg, L. R. (1970). Man versus model of man: A rationale plus evidence for a method of improving on clinical inferences. *Psychological Bulletin, 73,* 422–432.

Greenspan, S. I. (1981). *Psychopathology and adaptation in infancy and early childhood.* New York: International Universities Press.

Kagan, J. (1971). *Change and continuity in infancy.* New York: Wiley.

Korn, S. (1984). Continuities and discontinuities in difficult/easy temperament: Infancy to young adulthood. *Merrill-Palmer Quarterly, 30,* 189–199.

Korn, S., & Gannon, S. (1983). Temperament, culture variation and behavior disorders in preschool children. *Child Psychiatry and Human Development, 13,* 203–212.

McCall, R. B. (1983). Environmental effects on intelligence: The forgotten realm of discontinuous nonshared within family factors. *Child Development, 54,* 408–415.

Murphy, L. B. (1981). Explorations in child personality. In A. I. Rabin, J. Aronoff, A. M. Barclay, & P. A. Zucker (Eds.), Further explorations in personality. New York: Wiley.

Rutter, M. (1970). Psychological development: Predictions from infancy. *Journal of Child Psychology and Psychiatry, 11,* 49–62.

Rutter, M. (1980). Introduction. In M. Rutter (Ed.), *Scientific foundations of developmental psychiatry.* London: Heinemann.

Rutter, M., Birch, H., Thomas, A., & Chess, S. (1964). Temperamental characteristics in infancy and later development of behavioral disorders. *British Journal of Psychiatry, 110,* 651–661.

Stern, D. (1977). *The first relationship.* Cambridge, MA: Harvard University Press.

Super, C. M., & Harkness, S. (1981). Figure, ground and gestalt: The cultural context of the active individual. In R. M. Lerner & N. A. Busch-Rossnagel (Eds.), *Individuals as producers of their development.* New York: Academic Press.

Thomas, A., & Chess, S. (1977). *Temperament and development.* New York: Brunner/Mazel.

Thomas, A., Chess, S., & Birch, H. (1968). *Temperament and behavior disorders in children.* New York: New York University Press.

Thomas, A., Chess, S., Birch, H., Hertzig, M., & Korn, S. (1963). *Behavioral individuality in early childhood.* New York: New York University Press.

Thomas, A., Chess, S., & Korn, S. (1982). The reality of difficult temperament. *Merrill-Palmer Quarterly, 28,* 1–20.

Wilson, R. S. (1978). Synchronies in mental development: An epigenetic perspective. *Science, 202,* 939–948.

5 Temperamental Inhibition in Early Childhood

Jerome Kagan
J. Steven Reznick
Nancy Snidman
Harvard University

During most of this century explanations of stable patterns of social behavior among young children have emphasized variation in environmental experiences and ignored, sometimes to exclusion, the influence of those infant qualities that psychologists call temperamental. A seminal axiom of the disciplines that study life processes is that the inherent properties of the form under study make some contribution to the growth of that form as it exploits successive encounters with the surroundings. Whenever a generation of theorists overemphasizes the influence of the surroundings and ignores the endogenous characteristics of the form, or awards too much power to the form and not enough to the environment, future generations make the necessary correction. The sciences of human behavior are in a transition during which the relevance of the child's inherent characteristics, which are only partially revealed in temperamental predispositions, is being recognized. Thomas and Chess (1977), Plomin and Rowe (1979), Rothbart and Derryberry (1981), Carey and McDevitt (1978), and many others have helped to effect this change in attitude. This body of work implies that the obvious variation among infants in behavioral characteristics invites different treatments by family members and peers, influences the child's selection of actions, and constrains the sequence of choices the child makes across the eras of growth.

It is too early to list a minimal set of fundamental temperamental dispositions. However, two related candidates refer to the child's initial behavioral reactions to unfamiliar people, objects, and contexts or challenging situations. The tendency to withdraw or to approach such incentives, which is moderately stable, is seen most clearly during the transition from infancy to early childhood. The child's behavior with an unfamiliar peer provides a very sensitive index of these two qualities in the third year of life. One small group of children becomes extremely quiet and stares at the unfamiliar peer while remaining close to the caregiver for a period of 5 to 15 min. But even after the initial period of obvious inhibition has passed, these children rarely approach the unfamiliar peer. A second, somewhat larger, group of children shows no signs of timidity, begins to play immediately, and usually makes the first social overture to the other child. The former group seems to be a young version of the prototypic introvert; the latter appears to be an early representative of the extravert (Garcia-Coll, Kagan & Reznick, 1984; Kagan, Reznick, Clarke, Snidman, & Garcia-Coll, 1984).

These two behavioral styles displayed with unfamiliar children are only the most obvious signs of a more general quality; namely, the tendency to display or not to display an initial period of inhibition of speech and play, associated with a retreat to a target of attachment, when the child encounters an unfamiliar or challenging event. In searching for concise adjectives to capture the differences between the two kinds of children, recognizing that any word distorts what is observed, the words restrained, watchful, and gentle capture the essence of the inhibited child; free, energetic, and spontaneous capture the style of the uninhibited youngster. When the inhibited child throws a ball, knocks down a tower of blocks, or hits a large toy clown, the act is monitored, restrained, almost soft. The same act performed by the uninhibited child seems relaxed, vigorous, and free. Each style is a reliable characteristic of about 10% of American children.

Why should these behavioral categories of inhibition and lack of inhibition to the unfamiliar assume this particular form during the transition between infancy and childhood? It is possible that maturation of the brain is accompanied by cognitive abilities that permit the child to make inferences about the possible consequences of an unfamiliar event. If a 2-year-old attempts to predict what might happen after meeting an unfamiliar person and cannot solve that problem, the child becomes vulnerable to uncertainty. Ten-month-old infants are not mature enough to attempt such an inference. Additionally, during the second year, children become better able to remember the past and to compare representations of the past and present over longer periods of time. Hence, if assimilation is not possible, a state of uncertainty emerges. Finally, during the second year, children display their first appreciation of correct and incorrect performance, dysphoric emotion to broken or flawed objects, and empathy with those who are hurt (Kagan, 1981). The realization that one can make a mistake or violate a prohibition is an important origin of uncertainty and, therefore, of behavioral inhibition.

There are, therefore, good reasons for expecting the emergence of individual differences in behavioral inhibition and lack of inhibition with unfamiliar children during the second and third years. Although these particular behavioral clusters are salient during the transition to childhood, the underlying predisposition may be observed both earlier and later, albeit in different form. If the biological bases for the differences in inhibition among 3-year-old children are present during the first months of life, they might be reflected in extreme distress to frustration, extreme irritability, quality of sleep, chronic constipation, allergies, and other symptoms reflecting high levels of arousal in the central nervous system circuits that involve the hypothalamus, pituitary, adrenal, reticular activating system, and the sympathetic arm of the autonomic nervous system. Chen and Miyake (1983) have reported that newborn infants who react with extreme distress to repeated removals of a nipple and are difficult to soothe are more likely to become fearful and inhibited children. Newborns who do not become extremely upset and who soothe easily after an initial cry are less likely to show the later signs of fear and inhibition. Lester (in press) and Garcia-Coll (1979), as well as others, have found that behaviors observed during the newborn period predict psychological characteristics that are similar to behavioral inhibition during later infancy.

Other investigators have also noted the stability of these qualities. Bronson (1970) has commented on the preservation of individual differences in fearfulness, and Emmerich (1964) has found that behaviors resembling inhibition and lack of inhibition were preserved among nursery school children who were observed from 3 to 5 years of age. (See also Halverson & Waldrop, 1976, as well as Simpson & Stevenson-Hinde, in press).

These qualities can persist into adulthood, for extremely shy and withdrawn preschool children who had been seen in a child guidance clinic were likely, as adults, to choose relatively secure bureaucratic jobs with minimal risk rather than enterpreneurial vocations with their attendant increase in unpredictability (Morris, Soroker, & Burruss, 1954; see also Coolidge, Brodie, & Feeney, 1964). Further, psychiatrists make a useful distinction between adult patients who are chronic worriers and a much smaller group—less than 1%—who are vulnerable to sudden panic reactions. The latter patients were more likely to have been extremely fearful and timid during childhood (Gittelman & Klein, 1984), implying that a very small proportion of extremely fearful, inhibited children may be predisposed to be adult panic patients.

The 71 members of the Fels Research Institute's longitudinal sample—Caucasian and primarily middle-class—were observed and tested from infancy through adolescence and evaluated again as young adults. Of the many individual qualities quantified during the first 3 years of life, only inhibition and lack of inhibition were preserved across adolescence and young adulthood (Kagan & Moss, 1962). The children who were extremely shy, timid, and fearful during the opening 3 years displayed a coherent cluster of behaviors during the early school years. They avoided dangerous activities, were minimally aggressive, conformed to parental requests, and avoided unfamiliar social encounters. As adolescents, they avoided contact sports and other traditional masculine activities, and the four boys who were most inhibited during the first 6 years chose intellectual careers as adults (music, physics, biology, and psychology). The four boys who were least inhibited during the first 6 years chose more traditional masculine vocations (football coach, salesman, and two chose engineering). Further, the extremely inhibited children became adults who showed more dependency on their love objects and more conscious feelings of anxiety in social situations than did those who were extremely uninhibited as young children.

In a second longitudinal study, Kagan, Kearsley, and Zelazo (1978) compared 53 Chinese-American children with 63 Caucasian children across the period from 4 to 29 months. Forty-nine of these children were either in full- or part-time day care, while 67 were raised at home without surrogate care. The most significant result was that the Chinese children, whether raised at home or in the day care center, were consistently more inhibited than the Caucasians during infancy and the transition to childhood. For example, each child was observed in a laboratory setting during which unfamiliar visual and auditory events were presented. On most of the procedures, the Chinese children vocalized and smiled less often than did the Caucasians. The Chinese were more likely than the Caucasians to cry intensely following temporary separation from the mother and when the 20-month-old children were brought to an unfamiliar room with their mother, a familiar adult, and a stranger, the Chinese children stayed close to their mother for a longer period of time than did the Caucasians. These ethnic differences were most dramatic across the period from 7- to 20-months of-age. Additionally, each mother ranked sixteen different personality qualities in their 2-year-old, from most to least characteristic. The Chinese parents regarded fearfulness and timidity as more characteristic of their child than did the Caucasian mothers. For example, the Chinese mothers rated the statement ''stays close to mother'' as a salient quality of the child, while the Caucasian mothers regarded talkativeness, a sense of humor, and emotional spontaneity as more characteristic of their children.

An important difference between the two groups of children provides a clue to the deeper bases for the inhibition and lack of inhibition. The Chinese children had more stable heart rates while processing unfamiliar visual and auditory information than did the Caucasians, and the differences in heart rate variability represented the best preserved dimension across the 26 months of the investigation. This physiological index was much more stable than behavioral qualities like attentiveness, irritability, vocalization, or smiling.

Heart rate variability, as well as absolute heart rate, are regulated by both the sympathetic and parasympathetic branches of the autonomic nervous system. Heart rate and blood pressure typically increase during inspiration as vagal tone is inhibited, but decrease with expiration as the vagus is disinhibited. As a result, the heart rate of children and adults at rest usually displays a regular cycle that is yoked to breathing and is moderately variable over epochs of 5 to 10 sec. However, when the vagal influence is restrained, the cardiac deceleration that normally accompanies expiration is muted, and heart rate rises slightly and becomes much less variable (Bunnell, 1982). The mental effort associated with working at cognitive problems is one of the conditions typically associated with the loss of respiratory sinus arrhythmia and an accompanying rise and stabilization of heart rate (Light, 1984). It is a well-established fact that under cognitive stress adults show an increase in epinephrine secretion and heart rate, but a decrease in heart rate variability. This phenomenon is often part of a general bodily response to unfamiliarity or challenge originating in the hypothalamus and involving the pituitary, adrenal gland, reticular activating system, and sympathetic nervous system—what physiologists might call the HPARS system (Axelrod & Reisine, 1984; Smith & DeVito, 1984). It is generally assumed that following encounter with the unfamiliar or challenge discharge of the hypothalamus leads simultaneously to (a) secretion of ACTH by the pituitary resulting in the release of glucocorticoids from the adrenal cortex, (b) discharge of the reticular activating system and subsequent increases in muscle tension, and (c) discharge of the sympathetic nervous system resulting in a rise and stabilization of heart rate, pupil dilation, and other appropriate reactions of target organs in the sympathetic nervous system. The involvement of the sympathetic nervous system in the reaction to challenge is supported by the fact that if the sympathetic nervous system is blocked, for example by the drug propanolol, the rise in heart rate to a cognitive problem is reduced or absent. Thus, the fact that inhibited children are more likely than uninhibited ones to show a rise and stabilization of heart rate to cognitive tasks implies a lower threshold in parts of the HPARS system (Frankenhaeuser, 1979). This difference in threshold of reactivity of the HPARS circuit among humans may be a homologue of similar variation noted in rats (Blizard, 1981) and monkeys (Suomi, Kraemer, Baysinger, & DeLizio, 1981).

There are stable individual differences among adults in the tendency to react to cognitive problems with a rise and stabilization of heart rate. Manuck and Garland (1980) tested 19 college men on two occasions about a year apart. Ten very reactive men showed heart rate increases to the tasks, while nine men were much less reactive. The tendency to display a rise in heart rate was stable over the 13 months of the study—correlations were about 0.8. Light and Obrist (1983) administered to college males a reaction time task in which winning was made easy, difficult, or impossible. The men who showed a larger increase in heart rate at task onset maintained higher heart rate levels than those who did not show the initial rise in cardiac rate, leading the authors to posit an individual difference dimension in the ease of sympathetic activation to a cognitive task. If inhibited and uninhibited children differed in the ease of discharge of the HPARS circuits following encounter with unfamiliarity or challenge, those with a low threshold for such discharge would display the rise and stabilization of heart rate we have noted.

SUMMARY OF CURRENT WORK

We are currently studying two cohorts of children longitudinally. One cohort of 46 children has been seen at 21, 48, and 67 months-of-age and consists of equal numbers of inhibited and uninhibited children. The second cohort of 54 children, half inhibited and half uninhibited, has been seen at 31 and 43 months-of-age and are being seen at 5 years of age (Garcia-Coll et al., 1984; Kagan et al., 1984; Snidman, 1984). The index of behavioral inhibition and lack of inhibition in the first cohort at 21 months was based on behavioral reactions to unfamiliar adults and objects. The primary index in the second cohort seen at 31 months was based on the child's profile of reactions to an unfamiliar peer of the same age and sex. As indicated earlier, inhibited children wait a long time before they play with toys, talk, or approach an unfamiliar person. Initially, they spend long periods of time proximal to their mother while staring at the other person, and are unlikely to approach or talk to an unfamiliar adult or peer. Differences in both behavior, as well as heart rate variability, are preserved to a significant degree. The stability correlations for Cohort One for both behavior and heart rate variability across the period from 21 months to $5\frac{1}{2}$ years ranged between 0.4 and 0.6 (See Table 5.1). For Cohort Two, the stability coefficient for behavior was .59; for heart rate variability it was .50.

Because respiration rate exerts an influence on heart rate it is important to note that even though there is considerable variation in respiration rate—from 18 to 33 cycles per min.—there is no relation between respiration rate and either heart rate or heart rate variability during baseline or cognitive testing, and the two groups do not differ in respiration rate.

Persuasive evidence for the hypothesis that the more stable heart rates of inhibited children are due to higher sympathetic tone was revealed in a spectral analysis of the cardiac data from Cohort Two. The value of a spectral analysis is that it permits the investigator to infer the contribution of sympathetic activity to a decrease in heart rate variability. The data from the children in Cohort Two revealed a significant positive relation between inhibited behavior at 43 months

TABLE 5.1
Preservation of Differences in Behavior and Heart Rate Variability in Cohort One

Dependent Variables	Inhibited Behavior at 21 Months	Inhibited Behavior at Age 4	Heart Rate Var. at 21 Months	Heart Rate Var. at Age 4
Inhibited behavior: Age 4 years	.51**	----	.15	-.39*
Inhibited behavior: Age 5½ years	.43**	.66***	-.03	-.11
Heart rate variability: Age 4 years	-.32*	-.33*	.49**	----
Heart rate variability: Age 5½ years	-.38*	-.43*	.39**	.64***

* = $p < .05$
** = $p < .01$
*** = $p < .001$

of age and relatively more power in that portion of the heart rate spectrum that is presumed to be influenced by sympathetic activity.

Very few uninhibited children became inhibited over the period of study. About one half of the inhibited children remained extremely inhibited, while the remaining half have changed toward a less inhibited style, but one that was still less spontaneous than that of the typical uninhibited youngster. However, the inhibited children who displayed very high and stable heart rates at the early ages (21 months in Cohort One and 31 months in Cohort Two) were much more likely to remain inhibited than were the inhibited children who had lower and more variable heart rates at the initial assessment.

The older inhibited children also showed more obvious psychological signs of anxiety and tension while being tested than did the uninhibited children. At 4- and $5\frac{1}{2}$-years-of-age the inhibited children in Cohort One were quiet, looked at the examiner frequently, more often refused to offer an answer to a difficult problem, and sat with a tense posture of the trunk, often accompanied by small motor movements of the fingers, lips, or tongue. The uninhibited children, by contrast, sat with a relaxed posture or, as the session wore on, displayed gross motor restless movements of trunk and limbs.

The inhibited 5-year-olds in Cohort One seemed to become more uncertain following mild cognitive stress than the uninhibited youngsters. The basis for this claim comes from a change in errors on a test of recognition memory for pictures of familiar objects. Early in the session each child was shown a set of 24 unrelated pictures and was then tested on a set of 24 pictures, half of which the child had just seen, half of which were new. The child was asked to indicate which pictures were new and which old. After an intervening set of three cognitive procedures intended to be difficult, the child was given a parallel test of recognition memory. Over two-thirds of the uninhibited children showed fewer errors on the second than on the first test, while over two-thirds of the inhibited children showed an increase in errors on the second test. Less stressful cognitive tasks revealed no performance difference between the inhibited and uninhibited children. Because performance on recognition and retrieval memory tests is affected by anxiety, these data imply that the inhibited children became increasingly uncertain over the course of testing.

This suggestion is affirmed by the fact that more inhibited than uninhibited children displayed a rise in heart rate over the trials of most of the cognitive tests. For example, three-quarters of the inhibited children but only one-third of the uninhibited children showed a rise in heart rate while listening to a series of three to six words they had to recall. The two groups also differed in the tendency to show a rise in heart rate over the 24 test items of the recognition memory procedure. On the first administration of recognition memory about one-third of each group showed a small but steady rise in heart rate over the 24 test trials. However, on the second test, 76% of the inhibited, but only 23% of the uninhibited, children showed a steady rise in heart rate over the 24 trials. This cardiac acceleration over the course of the second testing, together with the increase in errors, implies a higher level of task-related uncertainty for the inhibited children. This hypothesis is also affirmed by the tonically larger pupillary dilations and the maintenance of a large pupil over the 15 min test episode by the inhibited children. Further, more inhibited than uninhibited children showed lower variabilities of the pitch periods of words spoken under stressful conditions than when the same words were spoken under nonstressful conditions. This latter finding implies higher levels of arousal in the nucleus ambiguus which sends efferents to the muscles of the larynx and vocal cords. This difference in variability of the pitch periods of vocal utterances, which was independent of fundamental frequency, implied greater levels of discharge of the reticular activating system to cognitive stress. Finally, the inhibited children in Cohort 1 had higher levels of cortisol (based on salivary analyses) both during a laboratory session as well as during the early morning hours.

The hypothesis of higher levels of arousal of the HPARS circuit among the inhibited children is supported by interview data gathered from the mothers of both cohorts. The incidence of symptoms suggestive of higher arousal, like chronic constipation, allergies, fears, and sleeplessness during the first 2 years of life were significantly more frequent among inhibited than among uninhibited children, and especially among the inhibited children with high and stable heart rates.

It also appears that inhibited 4-year-old children may have some conception of their characteristics, for they are more likely to attend to drawings of passive agents than to drawings of active agents. The 4-year-old children were shown ten pictures, each illustrating the interaction of an active and a passive figure. The figures were animals, people, or an animal and a person (for example, a woman feeding a child, a man pointing a finger at a woman). The right and left positions of the active and passive agents were counterbalanced. The coder noted whether the child was looking to the right or to the left during successive fixations of each picture. Inhibited children looked less often at the active than at the passive figures and, when asked to describe the picture, first named the passive rather than the active agent more often in their verbal descriptions. The uninhibited children showed the opposite profile.

When these children were seen at $5\frac{1}{2}$-years-of-age, they heard a story supported by twenty pictures about two children—one bold and one fearful. For eighteen of the scenes the two illustrated figures were separated physically so that an observer could code the duration of fixation of each figure. The inhibited children looked significantly less often at the bold figure than did the uninhibited youngsters. Further, the children who had looked more at the active than at the passive figures at 4-years-of-age were the ones who looked more often at the bold than the fearful figure. Over 40% of the uninhibited, but only 15% of the inhibited children looked at the active figure at age 4 and the bold figure at $5\frac{1}{2}$-years-of-age.

The mothers' descriptions of their children revealed that most were aware of their child's typical style, even though a few mothers of our uninhibited children described them as shy and a few parents of inhibited children described them as bold. But the correlations between the maternal descriptions and our behavioral observations averaged about 0.5. We believe that the mothers' rankings were moderately valid in this study because of unusual conditions rarely met in most investigations. First, we were evaluating children who are at the extremes for these behavioral qualities. Second, we had established rapport with the mothers over the several years of the investigation, and perhaps had raised each parent's consciousness about the qualities of inhibition and lack of inhibition.

CONCLUSIONS

The corpus of evidence gathered to date implies that the behavioral qualities of inhibition and lack of inhibition to the unfamiliar are robust and moderately stable traits, even though the underlying predisposition can be expressed in various ways. In infants under 2 years of age, these qualities are displayed in reactions to unfamiliar toys, unfamiliar situations, and unfamiliar adults. In older children, especially those between 2 and 4 years of age, the disposition is seen best in reactions to an unfamiliar child, and in children between 4 and 6 years of age, the dispositions are revealed in frequent glances at an examiner, staring at others in social situations, and a cautious approach to new or dangerous tasks. No single setting or procedure captures this predisposition across the first five years of life. Thus, as the child ages, it is necessary to look for more subtle expressions of this predisposition.

Second, it is likely that a combination of inhibited behavior, together with a high and stable heart rate to cognitive stress, indexes the children who are most extreme on this dimension. About one half of the inhibited children have shown a high and stable heart rate on all assessments, in contrast to about one-fifth of the uninhibited children. We have shown in other investigations (Kagan & Reznick, 1984) that among a sample of 3-year-olds that was not selected to be extremely inhibited or uninhibited, those who were highly motivated to master cognitive tasks showed a rise and stabilization of heart rate and some of our uninhibited children show such a heart rate profile to cognitive procedures. Thus, a rise and stabilization of heart rate to cognitive tasks can reflect motivational involvement as well as the temperamental quality of inhibition. It is also possible for a child to display an inhibited behavioral surface that is the result of socialization experiences rather than a lower threshold in the HPARS circuits. About one third of our behaviorally inhibited group has not shown a high and stable heart rate on any of the assessments and it is likely that their behavioral surface is primarily a result of socialization. Environmental conditions determine the degree to which this biological tendency will be actualized. It is likely that an unusually benevolent environment that gently promotes an uninhibited coping style might create a socially outgoing demeanor in a child born with a potential for an inhibited temperament. Analogously, an overly stressful environment can create inhibited behavior in a child who is born with a temperamental disposition that favored an uninhibited coping style.

The complete corpus of data suggests that inhibition and lack of inhibition to the unfamiliar might be influenced by biological processes that predispose some children to one or the other style. We do not suggest that all shy, timid children—or adults—are born with this temperamental disposition, only that possession of this disposition makes it a little more likely that a child will develop one of these sets of characteristics. Of course, the environment has an important influence on these psychological attributes. A small group of extremely inhibited children in Cohort One is becoming less inhibited as their parents impose pressure on them to adopt a bolder and more fearless approach to environmental challenge.

The strongest support for the claim that these two profiles involve inherent biological influences comes from the data on heart rate, pupillary dilation, cortisol, and perturbation of the voice to mild cognitive stress. The fact that significantly more of the inhibited children showed a higher and more stable heart rate, tonically larger pupillary dilations, higher cortisol and less variability in their vocal utterances implies a lower threshold in the HPARS circuits. A recent review of the factors controlling autonomic responses suggests that the paraventricular nucleus of the hypothalamus may be one place where psychological incentives are transduced to become important influences on the autonomic nervous system (Smith & DeVito, 1984). When the paraventricular nucleus is stimulated there is a rise in blood pressure and heart rate and an inhibition of reflex bradycardia. These facts suggest that this area of the lateral hypothalamus is one site of control over emotional responsibity to stressful events. This region has a monosynaptic connection to the intermediolateral cells of the spinal cord and, thence, to the sympathetic nervous system. Perhaps this is one of the important places where mind meets body, with individuals varying in the ease with which the hypothalamus responds to psychological uncertainty. One possible, albeit speculative, basis for this difference in threshold would be higher levels of central norepinephrine. Recent analyses of the urines of the 5-year-old children in Cohort One following a 90-min test battery revealed that the inhibited children had higher total norepinephrine turnover than did the uninhibited children. This finding represents indirect support for the above hypothesis.[1]

There is some evidence that ethnic groups may differ in thresholds within the HPARS system. It will be recalled that the Chinese children studied in the day care investigation were more inhibited and had a more stable heart rate than the

---

[1]These analyses were performed as part of a collaborative study with Richard J. Wyatt and Farouk Karoum of St. Elizabeth's Hospital, Washington, D.C.

Caucasians during the first $2\frac{1}{2}$ years of life. Kleinman (1982) has reported that symptoms of anxiety, panic, and neurasthenia are more frequent among Chinese psychiatric patients than among European and American patient populations. This seemingly odd asymmetry in modal diagnostic category implies, in addition to the influence of culture, a possible genetic vulnerability to specific symptoms. This admittedly speculative idea deserves further study.

Inhibition and lack of inhibition to the unfamiliar are only two of the fundamental temperamental dispositions. It is likely that future research will reveal that other candidates, like activity level, lability of emotional mood, and even predominant affective states, may prove to be as stable and theoretically significant as inhibition and lack of inhibition, with each of these characteristics expressed in different forms during the successive stages of development and each associated with a specific cluster of biological processes. Perhaps the empirical strategy used in our research will prove useful in investigations of these other characteristics. Rather than study variation in a volunteer sample, we deliberately selected children who belong to extreme groups because we believe that such a strategy facilitates understanding. Psychiatrists and behavioral geneticists interested in the etiology of schizophrenia do not evaluate mood and thought processes in a random sample of children but select youngsters who are the offspring of schizophrenic parents because of the reasonable assumption that the cluster of qualities that define this category do not fall on a continuum. It may be equally advantageous to supplement studies of volunteer groups by selecting children who are at the extremes of qualities like activity, regularity of sleep, irritability to frustration, lability of emotional states, and intensity of expression of anger, sadness, fear, and joy.

ACKNOWLEDGMENT

This research was supported in part by the John D. and Catherine T. MacArthur Foundation.

REFERENCES

Axelrod, J., & Reisine, T. D. (1984). Stress hormones: Their interaction and regulation. *Science*, *224*, 452–459.

Blizard, D. A. (1981). The Maudsley reactive and non-reactive strains: A North-American perspective. *Behavioral Genetics*, *11*, 469–489.

Bronson, G. W. (1970). Fear of visual novelty. *Developmental Psychology*, *2*, 33–40.

Bunnell, D. E. (1982). Autonomic myocardial influences as a factor determining intertask consistency of heart rate reactivity. *Psychophysiology*, *19*, 442–448.

Carey, W. B., & McDevitt, S. C. (1978). Stability and change in individual temperament diagnoses from infancy to early childhood. *Journal of the American Academy of Child Psychiatry, 17,* 331–337.

Chen, S., & Miyake, K. (1982/1983). Japanese versus United States comparison of mother-infant interaction and infant development. In Miyake, K. (Ed.), *Annual Report of the Research and Clinical Center for Child Development.* Faculty of Education, Hokkaido University, pp. 13–26.

Coolidge, J. C., Brodie, R. D., & Feeney, B. (1964). A ten-year follow-up study of sixty-six school phobic children. *American Journal of Orthopsychiatry, 34,* 675–684.

Emmerich, W. (1964). Continuity and stability in early social development. *Child Development, 35,* 311–332.

Frankenhaeuser, M. (1979). Psychobiological aspects of life stress. In P. H. Venables & M. J. Christie (Eds.), *Research in psychophysiology* (pp. 203–223). New York: Wiley.

Garcia-Coll, C. (1979, July). *Temperament in early development.* Presented at annual meeting of the Interamerican Congress of Psychology, Peru.

Garcia-Coll, C., Kagan, J., & Reznick, J. S. (1984). Behavioral inhibition in young children. *Child Development, 55,* 1005–1019.

Gittelman, R., & Klein, D. F. (1984). Relationship between separation anxiety and panic and agoraphobic disorders. *Psychopathology,* Suppl. 1, *17,* 56–65.

Halverson, C. F., & Waldrop, M. F. (1976). Relations between preschool activity and aspects of intellectual and social behavior at age seven-and-a-half. *Developmental Psychology, 12,* 107–112.

Kagan, J. (1981). *The second year.* Cambridge: Harvard University Press.

Kagan, J., Kearsley, R. B., & Zelazo, P. R. (1978). *Infancy: Its place in human development.* Cambridge: Harvard University Press.

Kagan, J., & Moss. H. A. (1962). *Birth to maturity.* New York: Wiley. (Reprinted, New Haven: Yale University Press, 1983).

Kagan, J., & Reznick, J. S. (1984). Cardiac reaction as an index of task involvement. *Australian Journal of Psychology, 36,* 135–147.

Kagan, J., Reznick, J. S., Clarke, C., Snidman, N., & Garcia-Coll, C. (1984). Behavioral inhibition to the unfamiliar. *Child Development, 55,* 2212–2225.

Kleinman, A. (1982). Neurasthenia and depression. *Culture, Medicine, and Psychiatry, 6,* 117–190.

Lester, B. M. (in press). A method for the study of change in neonatal behavior. In T. B. Brazelton & B. M. Lester (Eds.), *Infants at risk: Towards plasticity and intervention.* New York: Elsevier.

Light, K. C. (1984). Cardiovascular and renal responses to competitive mental challenges. In J. F. Orlebeke, G. Mulder, & L. J. P. van Doornen (Eds.), *Cardiovascular psychophysiology: Theory and methods.* New York: Plenum.

Light, K. C., & Obrist, P. A. (1983). Task difficulty, heart rate reactivity, and cardiovascular responses to an appetitive reaction time task. *Psychophysiology, 20,* 301–312.

Manuck, S. B., & Garland, N. F. (1980). Stability of individual differences in cardiovascular reactivity: A 13-month follow-up. *Physiology and Behavior, 24,* 621–624.

Morris, D. P., Soroker, E., & Burruss, G. (1954). Follow-up studies of shy, withdrawn children, I: Evaluation of later adjustment. *American Journal of Orthopsychiatry, 24,* 743–754.

Plomin, R. A., & Rowe, D. C. (1979). Genetic and environmental etiology of scoial behavior in infancy. *Developmental Psychology, 15,* 62–72.

Rothbart, M. K., & Derryberry, D. (1981). Development of individual differences in temperament. In M. E. Lamb & A. L. Brown (Eds.), *Advances in developmental psychology,* Volume 1.

Simpson, A. E., & Stevenson-Hinde, J. (in press). Temperamental characteristics in three- to four-year-old boys and girls in child-family interactions. *Journal of Comparative and Physiological Psychology.*

Smith, O. A., & DeVito, J. L. (1984). Central neural integration for the control of autonomic responses associated with emotion. In W. M. Cowan (Ed.), *Annual review of neuroscience*. Palo Alto: CA: *Annual Reviews, 7,* 43–65.

Snidman, N. (1984). *Behavioral restraint and the central nervous system: Predicting performance on cognitive tasks from autonomic nervous system activity.* Unpublished doctoral dissertation, University of California, Los Angeles.

Suomi, S. J., Kraemer, G. W., Baysinger, C. M., & DeLizio, R. D. (1981). Inherited and experiential factors associated with individual differences in anxious behavior displayed by rhesus monkeys. In D. F. Kline & J. Rabkin (Eds.), *Anxiety: New research and changing concepts* (pp. 179–199). New York: Raven Press.

Thomas, A., & Chess, S. (1977). *Temperament and development.* New York: Brunner/Mazel.

6

The EAS Approach to Temperament

Arnold H. Buss
University of Texas, Austin

Robert Plomin
University of Colorado, Boulder

Temperament has been approached from three major directions. The main pediatric approach is that of Thomas, Chess, Birch, Hertzig, and Korn (1963) and Thomas, Chess, and Birch (1968), who launched the modern era of temperament research in the 1950s by rebelling against the psychoanalytic tradition and the environmentalism that dominated child development. They delineated nine temperaments and this approach has generated an outpouring of research (see chapter 4, this volume) including the construction of questionnaires to assess the nine temperaments (Carey, chapter 11; Lerner & Lerner, chapter 8).

Another approach could be called the personality tradition. In 1957, Diamond published a book, *Personality and Temperament,* that emphasized the constitutional origins of personality:

> A crucial problem in the study of personality is to determine what are the most fundamental respects in which individuals differ from each other. All attempts to do this on the basis of observation of adult human behavior, no matter how sophisticated in either a statistical or a clinical sense, have the common failing that they are unable to distinguish between the essential foundations of individuality and its cultural elaboration. (pp. 3–4)

Diamond described four temperaments shared by all primates and social mammals: fearfulness, aggressiveness, affiliativeness, and impulsiveness. He conducted no research on human behavior, however, nor did he provide any instruments to assess his temperaments. Following the lead of Diamond, we published a theory of temperament in 1975 (Buss & Plomin, 1975) that identified emotionality, activity, sociability, and impulsivity (EASI) as the essential foundations of individuality for our species in the sense that they appeared early in

67

development, showed some stability, and were among the most heritable traits in personality as indicated by behavioral genetic research.

A third perspective on temperament emanates from research on individual differences among infants. One of the most striking ways in which infants differ is in arousal. Three approaches to temperament that emphasize arousal in infancy are the *behavioral inhibition* approach of Kagan, Reznick and Snidman (see chapter 5), the *temperament as affect* approach of Goldsmith and Campos (1982a, 1982b) which focuses on anger, fearfulness, pleasure/joy, interest/persistence, and motoric activity (Goldsmith, 1982), and the *reactivity and self-regulation* approach described by Rothbart and Derryberry (1981), which is similar to the theory proposed by Strelau (1965, 1983) for adults. These approaches justify their use of the term *temperament* by referring to Allport's definition:

> Temperament refers to the characteristic phenomena of an individual's emotional nature, including his susceptibility to emotional stimulation, his customary strength and speed of response, the quality of his prevailing mood, and all the peculiarities of fluctuation and intensity of mood, these phenomena being regarded as dependent upon constitutional make-up and therefore largely hereditary in origin. (1961, p. 34)

In this chapter, we provide an overview of our revised theory of temperament which focuses on three broad dimensions of personality: emotionality, activity, and sociability (Buss & Plomin, 1984). Though we have retained much of the theory stated in our 1975 book, there are changes. Previously, there were five criteria of temperament, the crucial one being inheritance. We have retained inheritance as crucial and added presence early in life as part of the definition. These two criteria serve to define temperaments as inherited personality traits present in early childhood.

The second change is that we have dropped impulsivity from our list of temperaments, the original acronym of which was EASI. Ten years ago, the heritability of impulsivity was not established, for there was both positive and negative evidence. Nothing has happened since to alter this picture, but in an attempt to be scientifically conservative, we have dropped impulsivity as a temperament and the abbreviation is EAS.

The third change is in the conceptualization of the three temperaments. Concerning activity, its components of vigor and tempo were found to correlate so highly that they have been combined into a single index, and that is the only change. The additions to emotionality and sociability require further elaboration.

CONCEPTUAL CHANGES

Emotionality

Traditionally, emotion has been divided into the components of feelings, expression, and arousal. In terms of temperament, arousal is the crucial component that yields inherited individual differences. We also distinguish between high-arousal and low-arousal emotions. Three high-arousal emotions are crucial for survival of the individual (fear and anger) or survival of the species (sexual arousal), and they are present in all mammals. Low-arousal emotions include love, elation, depression, and a variety of cognitively toned emotions such as pride and contempt. Any individual differences in these emotions are assumed not to be inherited. Also, the evolutionary significance of high arousal seen in fear and anger leads us to focus on these two aspects of emotionality. The other high-arousal emotion, sexual arousal, is not relevant to childhood.

We consider distress, the tendency to become upset easily and intensely, to be primordial emotionality. We mean not only being upset but also being in a state of high autonomic arousal. In everyday usage, distress is a broad term that includes not only such high-arousal states as pain and acute frustration but also low-arousal states such as bereavement. We exclude grief because it involves only low arousal. We follow Bridges (1932; see also Sroufe, 1979) in assuming that distress, the most primitive negative emotion, differentiates during infancy into fear and anger.

Sociability

Sociability is the tendency to prefer the presence of others to being alone. Why do we want to be with others? We consider five categories of intrinsically social rewards: their presence, attention, sharing of activities, responsivity, and stimulation. Sociability consists of seeking and being especially gratified by these rewards. Correlated with this need to be with people is a tendency to respond warmly to others.

Attachment.   Like other temperament researchers (Chess & Thomas, 1982; Goldsmith & Campos, 1982a; Kagan, 1982), we relate temperament to attachment. Secure infants are likely to be at least moderately sociable and not especially emotional. Avoidant infants are likely to be unsociable and so play less with the stranger and are less interested in the mother when she returns. Resistant infants are likely to be emotional: They are fearful when the mother leaves and angry with her when she returns. Some evidence supports these hypotheses. Ambivalently attached infants cry nearly twice as much as securely attached infants as early as the first few months of life (Ainsworth, Blehar, Waters, & Wall, 1978). Securely attached infants are more sociable with peers (Easterbrooks & Lamb, 1979; Lieberman, 1977; Pastor, 1981, Waters, Wippman, & Sroufe, 1979), and they are more sociable and less shy with strange adults (Main, 1974; Thompson & Lamb, 1983). Some attachment researchers explain the relationship between security of attachment and infant sociability as being caused environmentally (Thompson & Lamb, 1983). Our approach leads to a different interpretation: Children differ initially in sociability and emotionality and these temperaments affect social interaction with both mother and stranger.

Sociability and shyness.   Sociability is the tendency to affiliate with others and to prefer being with others rather than being alone. Shyness refers to one's behavior when with people who are casual acquaintances or strangers. The relationship between sociability and shyness is only moderate in adults ($-.30$), and shyness is more related to emotionality than to sociability (Cheek & Buss, 1981). Similar results have been found in infancy: Infants rated by their parents as emotional display more fear of strangers in the laboratory (Berberian & Snyder, 1982). In infancy, shyness appears mainly in the form of stranger anxiety whereas sociability appears in the form of preferring to play with other children and not wanting to be left alone by adults. Although both shyness and sociability are heritable, we consider sociability primary and suggest that shyness may be attributed to a combination of fearfulness and low sociability.

Neuroticism and Extraversion

Neuroticism and extraversion, promulgated by Eysenck (1983), appear as higher-order factors in nearly all systems of personality. For example, Cattell's approach to personality emphasizes 16 primary factors (Cattell, Eber, & Tatsuoka, 1970). However, second-order factors derived from the 16 primaries are nearly identical to Eysenck's extraversion and neuroticism (e.g., Royce, 1973). We suggest that in childhood, emotionality is the core of neuroticism without conditioned anxiety, and sociability is the core of extraversion stripped of its liveliness component (such as "liking parties").

NATURE

Differential Heritability

Since our 1975 book, a new development in behavioral genetic research is an awareness of the lack of solid evidence for differential heritability among traits. Although it seems reasonable to expect that some personality traits show less genetic influence than others, Loehlin and Nichols (1976) reported that in their large adolescent twin sample all the scales of the California Psychological Inventory (CPI) manifested differences between identical and fraternal twin correlations of about .20, suggesting a heritability—the proportion of phenotypic variance that can be accounted for by genetic variance—of about 40%:

> Thus, in the CPI data, we fail to find evidence of any consistent tendency for some scales to show greater differences in identical-fraternal resemblance than other scales do; the identicals are consistently more alike than the fraternals but about equally so on the various scales. (p. 28)

They also examined clusters of items from the CPI, as well as from an objective behavior inventory, adjective checklists, self-concept measures, and interests and attitudes. Similar results were found for these measures as well as in a survey of other twin studies:

> In short, for personality . . . the existing literature appears to agree with our own finding that, while identical-twin pairs tend to be more similar than fraternal-twin pairs, it is difficult to demonstrate that they are consistently more similar on some traits than on others. (p. 46)

However, some research suggested that emotionality and sociability were more heritable than other personality traits (Carey, Goldsmith, Tellegen, & Gottesman, 1978; Horn, Plomin, & Rosenman, 1976; Zonderman, 1982). Of the 480 CPI items, 38% overlap at least two of the 18 scales. When overlapping items are eliminated, some scales—Responsibility and Femininity—showed heritabilities near zero (Horn et al., 1976). Moreover, when 41 of the most heritable CPI items were isolated using cross-validation criteria, one large factor emerged from these heritable items: shyness, which we suggest is a combination of sociability and emotionality.

Perhaps identical twins merely *perceive* themselves as more similar than fraternal twins, a thought that led us to conduct several twin studies using parental ratings of children's personality. However, several twin studies using parental ratings revealed that most traits appeared to be influenced by heredity, although one exception to this rule consistently appeared: Reaction to foods, a dimension that emerges from items derived from the protocols of the New York Longitudinal Study (Rowe & Plomin, 1977), yields no evidence of genetic influence. We also explored twin correlations based on cross-ratings of parents—mothers' ratings of one twin and fathers' ratings of the other twin—and found similar results.

Perhaps the finding is real: Self-reports and ratings of personality are nearly all moderately heritable. Correlations for identical twins reared apart are most difficult to explain in any other way. In two older studies, identical twins reared apart were as similar as identical twins reared together for extraversion and neuroticism (Newman, Freeman, & Holzinger, 1937; Shields, 1962). The on-going Minnesota Study of Twins Reared Apart (Bouchard, 1984) uses the Tellegen Differential Personality Questionnaire; the median correlation for 28 pairs of twins reared apart is .65, compared to a correlation of .53 for identical twins reared together. A second-order factor called negative affect is similar to neuroticism, and it yields a correlation of .64 for the separated identical twins in the Minnesota study.

Loehlin (1982) has suggested a possible explanation for the lack of evidence for differential heritability of self-report personality questionnaires. His argument begins by noting that extraversion and neuroticism are found in many personality questionnaires and both traits appear to be substantially heritable. For example, in a recent Swedish study using nearly 13,000 twin pairs, the twin correlations for extraversion are .51 for identical twins and .21 for fraternal twins; for neuroticism the correlations are .50 and .23, respectively, for identical and fraternal twins. These twin correlations suggest heritabilities of about 50% for both traits. In addition, Loehlin (1982) reanalyzed his twin data mentioned earlier to form seven orthogonal factor scales, two of which were extraversion and neuroticism. These two scales yielded the expected high heritabilities; other scales such as stereotyped masculinity, intolerance of ambiguity, and persistence yielded much lower heritability estimates.

Loehlin suggested that extraversion and neuroticism are such pervasive super-traits that they mask the differential heritability of other traits. In our approach to temperament, sociability is the main component of extraversion, and emotionality is the core of neuroticism. Moreover, the most heritable component of extraversion appears to be sociability (Canter, 1973; Eaves & Eysenck, 1975). Although seldom assessed, activity shows substantial genetic influence.

Genetic Influence on the EAS Temperaments

We have reviewed recent studies, primarily on twins, relevant to the heritability of the EAS temperaments (Buss & Plomin, 1984). The usual measures are parental ratings and interviews, although studies are beginning to use ratings of behavior observed in structured situations, which yield greater evidence for differential heritability than self-report or rating measures (Plomin, 1981; Plomin & Foch, 1980).

Our twin studies using parental ratings on EAS questionnaires include 228 pairs of identical twins and 172 pairs of fraternal twins whose average age is 5 years. Identical twin correlations exceed .50, and fraternal twin correlations are near zero. The fraternal twin correlations are lower than one would expect for a heritable trait unless nonadditive genetic variance and contrast effects are important. It is not just our studies employing parental rating questionnaires that suggest substantial genetic influence for the EAS traits. Parental reports have been used in seven other twin studies of children, five of them since the publication of our 1975 book. In one study, mothers rated their twin children on 23 bipolar rating scales, comprising six factors (Matheny & Dolan, 1980). Three of these factors were emotionality, activity, and sociability and they showed substantial genetic influence:

> According to method, behaviors, and the age of the twins, previous efforts by Buss and Plomin (1975) were most comparable to the present study. Buss and Plomin isolated emotionality, activity, sociability, and, to a lesser extent impulsivity, as the primary factors of a temperament theory of personality development, and presented evidence from highly homogeneous scales that there was a pronounced genetic influence on these four temperaments. The first three of their factors were

identified in the present study, and both lines of investigation indicate that emotionality, sociability, and activity are isolable, and genetically influenced, aspects of children's behavior. (Matheny & Dolan, 1980, pp. 232–233)

Because parental ratings have dominated research in this area, studies using observational ratings in structured settings are particularly noteworthy. The most widely used instrument is Bayley's Infant Behavior Record (IBR; Bayley, 1969) which is used by testers to rate an infant's behavior during administration of the Bayley test. It offers the important advantages of assessing infants' reactions to a standard, mildly stressful, situation and of providing comparable data across studies. The IBR consists of 30 items representing broad dimensions of behavior and such as social responsiveness, activity, and attention. Matheny (1980) found three factors at several ages: Test Affect-Extraversion, Activity, and Task Orientation. Test Affect-Extraversion appears to be related to emotionality and sociability. The activity factor includes IBR items of activity, body motion, and energy and would thus appear to be an adequate representative of EAS activity. Twin correlations averaged during the first 2 years for the Test Affect-Extraversion factor are .50 for identical twins and .14 for fraternal twins, with no discernible developmental change in the correlations. For the Activity factor, the average twin correlations are .40 and .17, respectively, with an apparent trend toward increasing heritability in the second year of life. These results are particularly important because each member of the twin pairs was rated by a different examiner. The IBR has also been modified for use in rating videotapes of laboratory assessments of infant temperament (Matheny & Wilson, 1981) which is the focus of the ongoing temperament research in the longitudinal Louisville Twin Study (see chapter 7).

A laboratory-based twin study by Goldsmith and Campos (1982b) focused on emotionality and provides results important to EAS emotionality and to the issue of differential heritability. Genetic influence on the high-arousal emotion of fear was found in such situations as approach of strangers and the visual cliff. Less aroused emotional expressiveness of a positive nature such as smiling and laughing showed no genetic influence (Goldsmith, 1983). A similar lack of genetic influence for individual differences in smiling and laughing was found when parental reports were employed in twin analyses (Goldsmith & Campos, 1982a). An early report from the Louisville Twin Study also found no evidence for genetic influence on smiling during infancy and early childhood (Wilson, Brown, & Matheny, 1971).

In summary, behavioral genetic research during the last decade has added to knowledge about the heritability of the EAS temperaments. Diverse measures have been used in both twin and family studies, the results pointing to the conclusion that activity, emotionality, and sociability are heritable.

NURTURE

Environmental Main Effects

Genetic influence on temperament does not imply that temperament is un-
modifiable; moreover, the same behavioral genetic research reviewed above
provides the best available evidence for the importance of environment. We
expect the EAS temperaments to interact with the environment in terms of
selecting environments, affecting social environments, and modifying the impact
of the environment (Buss & Plomin, 1984).

Genetic propensities in temperament need to be studied as they interact with
the environment in development. Wachs and Gruen (1982) conclude that the
highest priority for environmental research involves:

> . . . the question of the interface between individual differences and reactivity to
> environmental stimulation. Both from basic and applied data it has become in-
> creasingly clear that the relationship of early experience to development will be
> mediated by the nature of the organism on which the experience impinges. Unfortu-
> nately, virtually nothing is known about the specific organismic characteristics
> which mediate differential reactivity to the early environment. One hopes that
> future research and theory will begin to delineate the specific organismic charac-
> teristics which are relevant to this process. (p. 247)

In our view, emotionality, activity, and sociability are among the "organismic
characteristics" being sought.

Almost nothing has been reported concerning environmental correlates of
temperament, although one justification given for the study of temperament is
that it provides the child's input to parent-child interaction. The only information
about environmental correlates comes from nonspecific distal factors such as
socioeconomic class and race (Thomas & Chess, 1977, pp. 146–151). These
data involve parental ratings, however, and parental expectations for children's
behavior might differ across cultural groups.

Part of the problem is that there are no standard measures of the environment
relevant to the development of temperament. For cognitive development, the
Home Observation for Measurement of the Environment inventory (HOME;
Caldwell & Bradley, 1978) has become standard. No significant correlations
were found when the HOME was related to parental ratings of EAS temperaments in infants in the Colorado Adoption Project (Plomin & DeFries, 1985).
Another widely used measure of the family environment, the Family Environment Scale (FES; Moos & Moos, 1981) also yielded few significant correlations
with the EAS temperaments.

Genetic Mediation of Environmental Relationships

In nonadoptive families, in which parents share heredity as well as family environment with their children, relationships between parental childrearing and

children's temperament could be mediated indirectly via heredity. However, in adoptive families, parents share only family environment with their adopted children. Thus, the adoption design is able to assess the influence of heredity in ostensibly environmental relationships (Plomin, Loehlin, & DeFries, 1985). For example, one of the few relationships that have been found between environment and temperament involves children's emotionality and sociability as related to parental permissiveness. For over 150 adoptive families and over 150 nonadoptive families in the Colorado Adoption Project, the correlation between an FES second-order permissiveness-like factor called Personal Growth and infant emotionality is $-.39$ in nonadoptive families and $-.10$ in adoptive families (Plomin & DeFries, 1985). Similar results emerged for sociability: The correlation with FES Personal Growth in nonadoptive homes is .34 and in adoptive homes, .16. Thus, the few obtained environmental relationships with temperament may be mediated genetically, not environmentally.

Temperament-Environment Interaction

Interactions represent conditional relationships: The relationship between X and Y depends upon another variable, Z. Temperament interactions can treat temperament as an independent variable, as a dependent variable, or as both an independent and a dependent variable (Plomin & Daniels, 1984). Most research on temperament interactions has been of the first type: The interaction between temperament and environment has been used to predict outcome measures such as school performance and adjustment (see the Lerners' chapter in the present volume). In an analysis of infancy data from the Colorado Adoption Project, 23 interactions were studied treating temperament as an independent variable (Plomin & Daniels, 1984). Only a chance number of significant interactions emerged from hierarchical multiple regression analyses of temperament interactions.

Over 50 interactions of the second category, temperament as a dependent variable, were examined in the same study. Genotype-environment interaction is an example of the second category, in which temperament is treated as a dependent variable predicted by genetic factors, environmental factors, and their interaction. Using data from the Colorado Adoption Project, temperament characteristics of biological mothers who relinquished their children for adoption at birth were used to estimate genotype of the adopted-away infants. Among the environmental measures were characteristics of the adoptees' adoptive mothers and HOME and FES scores of the adoptive home. The power of these analyses permitted detection of interactions that accounted for as little as 5% of the variance, but no significant interactions emerged. So far, then, the environment has been shown to have little significant impact either as a main effect or as an interaction.

Nonshared Environmental Influence

Although behavioral genetic research indicates that environmental variance accounts for about half of the variance for temperament, the same research suggests that environmental factors relevant to personality development seem to consist almost exclusively of individual experiences that make members of the same family as different from one another as are members of different families (Rowe & Plomin, 1981). This finding jeopardizes the assumption, made in nearly all previous research on environmental influences on development, that children in the same family share roughly the same experiences. These studies have yielded few significant and no substantial relationships (Maccoby & Martin, 1983). We need to examine more than one child per family in order to explore the possible environmental sources of differences between children in the same family.

The interest in nonshared environmental influences is so new that there is little research on the topic, nearly all of it on adolescents. Results of this research suggest that parental treatment is not a likely source of nonshared family environment: Parents usually report that they treat their children similarly and pairs of siblings also perceive similar treatment by their parents (e.g., Daniels, Dunn, Furstenberg, & Plomin, in press; Daniels & Plomin, in press). Siblings' interactions with each other (Dunn & Kendrick, 1982) and extrafamilial influences such as differential peer experiences are more likely candidates.

CONCLUSION

Our theory differs from other approaches to temperament in its insistence on a genetic origin for this subclass of the personality traits that emerge early in life. This assumption requires behavioral genetic data, and these support the heritability of emotionality, activity, and sociability.

We also differ in our personality orientation, which has two consequences. First, in temperament, as in any group of personality traits, the major psychometric criteria of internal consistency and reliability must be met. Factor analyses have yielded clusters entirely consistent with our three temperaments, and they have been shown to demonstrate reasonable stability over time. The second consequence is that the temperamental traits that emerge in infancy should be linked with personality traits that appear in older children and adults. All three temperaments have been observed in older children and adults, and it seems likely that emotionality is the core of what has been labeled neuroticism and sociability is the core of extraversion.

No single perspective on temperament can suffice, for each approach yields insights not perceived by others. Our claim is that the insistence on linking temperaments to behavioral genetics and to traditional personality traits offers its

own distinctive insights and places the study of temperament in the context of
lifespan development.

REFERENCES

Ainsworth, M., Blehar, M., Waters, E., & Wall, S. (1978). *Patterns of attachment*. Hillsdale, NJ:
Lawrence Erlbaum Associates.

Allport, G. W. (1961). *Pattern and growth in personality*. New York: Holt, Rinehart & Winston.

Bayley, N. (1969). *Manual for the Bayley Scales of Infant Development*. New York: Psychological
Corporation.

Berberian, K. E., & Snyder, S. S. (1982). The relationship of temperament and stranger reaction for
younger and older infants. *Merrill-Palmer Quarterly, 28,* 79–94.

Bouchard, T. J. (1984). Twins reared together and apart: What they tell us about human diversity. In
S. W. Fox (Ed.), *Individuality and determinism* (pp. 147–178). New York: Plenum.

Bridges, K. (1932). Emotional development in early infancy. *Child Development, 2,* 324–341.

Buss, A. H., & Plomin, R. (1975). *A temperament theory of personality development*. New York:
Wiley-Interscience.

Buss, A. H., & Plomin, R. (1984). *Temperament: Early developing personality traits*. Hillsdale,
NJ: Lawrence Erlbaum Associates.

Caldwell, B. M., & Bradley, R. H. (1978). *Home observation for measurement of the environment*.
Little Rock: University of Arkansas.

Canter, S. (1973). Personality traits in twins. In G. Claridge, S. Canter, & W. I. Hume (Eds.),
Personality differences and biological variations. New York: Pergamon Press.

Carey, G., Goldsmith, H. H., Tellegen, A., & Gottesman, I. I. (1978). Genetics and personality
inventories: The limits of replication with twin data. *Behavior Genetics, 8,* 299–314.

Cattell, R. B., Eber, H., & Tatsuoka, M. M. (1970). *Handbook for the Sixteen Personality Factor
questionnaire*. Champaign, IL: IPAT.

Cheek, J. M., & Buss, A. H. (1981). Shyness and sociability. *Journal of Personality and Social
Psychology, 41,* 330–339.

Chess, S., & Thomas, A. (1982) Infant bonding: Mystique and reality. *American Journal of Orthopsychiatry, 52,* 211–222.

Daniels, D., Dunn, J., Furstenberg, F. F., Jr., & Plomin, R. (in press). Environmental differences
within the family and adjustment differences within pairs of adolescent siblings. *Child
Development*.

Daniels, D., & Plomin, R. (in press). Differential experience of siblings in the same family.
Developmental Psychology.

Diamond, S. (1957). *Personality and temperament*. New York: Harper.

Dunn, J. F., & Kendrick, C. (1982). *Siblings: Love, envy, and understanding*. London: Grant
McIntyre.

Easterbrooks, M. A., & Lamb, M. E. (1979). The relationship between quality of mother-infant
attachment and infant competence in initial encounters with peers. *Child Development, 50,* 380–
387.

Eaves, L. J., & Eysenck, H. J. (1975). The nature of extraversion: A genetical analysis. *Journal of
Personality and Social Psychology, 32,* 102–112.

Eysenck, H. J. (1983). A biometrical-genetical analysis of impulsive and sensation seeking behavior. In M. Zuckerman (Ed.), *Biological bases of sensation seeking, impulsivity, and anxiety*.
Hillsdale, NJ: Lawrence Erlbaum Associates.

Goldsmith, H. H. (1982). *The objective measurement of infants*. Unpublished manuscript, University of Texas.

78   BUSS AND PLOMIN

Goldsmith, H. H. (1983). Emotionality in infant twins: Longitudinal results. *Abstracts of the Fourth International Congress on Twin Studies, London.*

Goldsmith, H. H., & Campos, J. J. (1982a). Toward a theory of infant temperament. In R. N. Emde & R. Harmon (Eds.), *The development of attachment and affiliative systems.* New York: Plenum.

Goldsmith, H. H., & Campos, J. J. (1982b). Genetic influence on individual differences in emotionality. *Infant Behavior and Development, 5,* 99.

Horn, J., Plomin, R., & Rosenman, R. (1976). Heritability of personality traits in adult male twins. *Behavior Genetics, 6,* 17–30.

Kagan, J. (1982). Comments on the construct of difficult temperament. *Merrill-Palmer Quarterly, 28,* 21–24.

Lieberman, A. F. (1977). Preschoolers' competence with a peer: Relations with attachment and peer experience. *Child Development, 48,* 1277–1287.

Loehlin, J. C. (1982). Are personality traits differentially heritable? *Behavior Genetics, 12,* 417–428.

Loehlin, J. C., & Nichols, R. C. (1976). *Heredity, environment and personality.* Austin: University of Texas Press.

Maccoby, E. E., & Martin, J. A. (1983). Socialization in the context of the family: Parent-child interaction. In P. H. Mussen (Ed.), *Handbook of child psychology (4th ed.): Vol. IV. Socialization, personality, and social development.* New York: Wiley.

Main, M. (1974). Exploration, play, and cognitive functioning as related to child-mother attachment. *Dissertation Abstracts International, 34,* 5718B.

Matheny, A. P., Jr. (1980). Bayley's Infant Behavior Record: Behavioral components and twin analyses. *Child Development, 51,* 1157–1167.

Matheny, A. P., & Dolan, A. B. (1980). A twin study of personality and temperament during middle childhood. *Journal of Research in Personality, 14,* 224–234.

Matheny, A. P., Jr., & Wilson, R. S. (1981). Developmental tasks and rating scales for the laboratory assessment of infant temperament. *JSAS Catalog of Selected Documents in Psychology, 11,* 81–82.

Moos, R. H., & Moos, B. S. (1981). *Family Environment Scale manual.* Palo Alto, CA: Consulting Psychologists Press.

Newman, J., Freeman, F., & Holzinger, K. (1937). *Twins: A study of heredity and environment.* Chicago: University of Chicago Press.

Pastor, D. L. (1981). The quality of mother-infant attachment and its relationship to toddler's initial sociability with peers. *Developmental Psychology, 17,* 326–335.

Plomin, R. (1981). Heredity and temperament: A comparison of twin data for self-report questionnaires, parental ratings, and objectively assessed behavior. In L. Gedda, P. Parisi, & W. E. Nance (Eds.), Progress in clinical and biological research, Vol. 69B: *Twin research 3, Part B. Intelligence, personality, and development.* New York: Alan R. Liss.

Plomin, R., & Daniels, D. (1984). The interaction between temperament and environment: Methodological considerations. *Merrill-Palmer Quarterly, 30,* 149–162.

Plomin, R., & DeFries, J. C. (1985). *Origins of individual differences in infancy: The Colorado Adoption Project.* New York: Academic Press.

Plomin, R., & Foch, T. T. (1980). A twin study of objectively assessed personality in childhood. *Journal of Personality and Social Psychology, 39,* 680–688.

Plomin, R., Loehlin, J. C., & DeFries, J. C. (1985). Genetic and environmental components of "environmental" influences. *Developmental Psychology, 21,* 391–402.

Rothbart, M. K., & Derryberry, D. (1981). Development of individual differences in temperament. In M. E. Lamb & A. L. Brown (Eds.), *Advances in developmental psychology.* Hillsdale, NJ: Lawrence Erlbaum Associates.

Rowe, D. C., & Plomin, R. (1977). Temperament in early childhood. *Journal of Personality Assessment, 41,* 150–156.

Rowe, D. C., & Plomin, R. (1981). The importance of nonshared environmental influences in behavioral development. *Developmental Psychology, 17,* 517–531.

Royce, J. R. (1973). The conceptual framework for a multi-factor theory of individuality. In J. R. Royce (Ed.), *Multivariate analysis and psychological theory.* New York: Academic.

Shields, J. (1962). *Monozygotic twins brought up apart and brought up together.* London: Oxford University Press.

Sroufe, L. A. (1979). Socioemotional development. In J. D. Osofsky (Ed.), *Handbook of infant development* (pp. 462–516). New York: Wiley.

Strelau, J. (1965). *Problems and methods of investigation into types of nervous system in man.* Warsaw, Poland: Ossolineum.

Strelau, J. (1983). *Temperament-personality-activity.* New York: Academic.

Thomas, A., & Chess, S. (1977). *Temperament and development.* New York: Brunner/Mazel.

Thomas, A., Chess, S., Birch, H., Hertzig, M., & Korn, S. (1963). *Behavioral individuality in early childhood.* New York: New York University Press.

Thomas, A., Chess, S., & Birch, H. G. (1968). *Temperament and behavior disorders in children.* New York: New York University Press.

Thompson, R. A., & Lamb, M. E. (1983). Security of attachment and stranger sociability in infancy. *Developmental Psychology, 19,* 184–191.

Wachs, T., & Gruen, G. (1982). *Early experience and human development.* New York: Plenum.

Waters, E., Wippman, J., & Sroufe, L. A. (1979). Attachment, positive affect, and competence in the peer group: Two studies in construct validation. *Child Development, 50,* 821–829.

Wilson, R. S., Brown, A., & Matheny, A. P., Jr. (1971). Emergence and persistence of behavioral differences in twins. *Child Development, 42,* 1381–1398.

Zonderman, A. B. (1982). Differential heritability and consistency: A reanalysis of the National Merit Scholarship Qualifying Test (NMSQT) California Psychological Inventory (CPI) data. *Behavior Genetics, 12,* 193–208.

7
Behavior-Genetics Research In Infant Temperament: The Louisville Twin Study

Ronald S. Wilson
Adam P. Matheny, Jr.
University of Louisville School of Medicine

Formal behavior-genetics research in infant temperament is of recent origin, but the premise of some biological influences on temperament certainly has a long history. At bottom, such a premise seems inescapable when faced with the marked individual differences in temperament among young infants (Bell, 1968; Escalona, 1968).

Much of the current research in temperament has been inspired by the pioneering work at the New York Longitudinal Study (Thomas & Chess, 1977; Thomas, Chess, Birch, Hertzig, & Korn, 1963). These authors focused on nine categories of temperament as inductively derived from interviews with the parents; and indeed, two of their examples nicely illustrated the potential for behavior-genetics research. One was a pair of DZ twins with markedly dissimilar patterns of reactivity from birth onward, which ultimately led the mother to develop different emotional bonds and responses to each twin.

The other was a pair of MZ twins adopted into separate families and raised apart, but who showed strikingly similar temperamental traits in the preschool years. The authors remarked, "They were highly irregular in sleep patterns, had marked intensity of negative mood expression, and were moderately active and adaptable, distractible and persistent" (Thomas & Chess, 1977, p. 135).

More formal studies of temperament using the twin method have increased in number and sophistication, and for recent excellent reviews, see Buss & Plomin (1984), Goldsmith (1983), and Plomin (1983). While the studies are diverse in terms of methodology and concept, nevertheless there is general agreement about the properties that the reference behaviors should show. The behaviors should be detectable in early childhood, they should be relatively stable over some period of time, and they should show some influence of genetic factors. Representative findings from several data sources may be briefly mentioned.

PARENTAL REPORTS

For practical reasons, the largest collection of data on young twins' temperament has been obtained from cross-sectional studies based on maternal reports. Goldsmith's thorough review (1983) lists the assortment of affective and social behaviors from neonates, infants, and preschoolers incorporated into these studies. The results suggested that the genetic influence might be somewhat invariant across ages. Yet a different picture emerged when longitudinal studies were considered.

Torgersen (1982; also see Torgersen & Kringlen, 1978) scored maternal interviews for the NYLS categories of temperament in order to obtain evidence of MZ and DZ twin differences. At 2-months-of-age, only three characteristics of temperament provided significant differences, whereas at 9 months and 6 years all of the temperament characteristics provided significant differences. It was interesting to note that within-pair variances for the DZ twins increased with age, while that of the MZ twins remained somewhat constant.

Questionnaires have largely replaced interviews as a data source, and one popular questionnaire has been the EASI (Buss & Plomin, 1975). Aspects of emotionality, activity, and sociability have been repeatedly isolated at several ages, and there has been evidence for genetic influence (see Buss & Plomin, 1984, for updated references). However, the magnitude of the genetic influence, as expressed by twin correlations, varied considerably according to the age of the twins. Although it would appear that genotypic influences may wax and wane with development (Gottesman, 1974), the fluctuations could also be attributed to transformations in the behavior being sampled from one age to the next.

DIRECT OBSERVATIONS

In a pioneering study, Freedman (1965) filmed the behavior of 20 pairs of infant twins in their homes during 8 consecutive months. The infants were rated once on Bayley's Infant Behavior Profile so that a single score represented the pooled judgment of each behavior displayed for the entire 8-month interval. From those ratings, behaviors denoting sociability, fearfulness, and object orientation were most prominent for demonstrating genetic influences.

Observations of temperament as displayed in a test setting were reported by Goldsmith and Gottesman (1981), who made use of twins from the Collaborative Study that had been tested at 8 months, 4 years and 7 years. The results suggested that there were age-dependent variations in the structure of temperament and the genotypic influences on temperament. Somewhat similar conclusions can be drawn from other direct observations of twin temperament as displayed in home or laboratory settings (Goldsmith & Campos, 1982; Lytton, 1980; Plomin & Rowe, 1977).

Overview. Taken as a whole, the results have demonstrated that the behavioral phenomena of temperament are detectable early and are influenced genetically. The results are far less conclusive, however, about the factors that influence the developmental course of temperament. There are few behavior-genetic studies that have examined the structure of temperament at various ages, the continuity and stability of temperament measures over age, and the appearance of synchronized developmental trends in temperament for twins (e.g., Goldsmith & Campos, 1982).

The Louisville Twin Study has recently focused on these issues, and has employed a multimethod design with repeated assessments throughout infancy to obtain the target data. The design and conceptual framework have evolved progressively during a 10-year period in which temperament data were collected as an auxiliary to the mental testing program. The data were powerfully persuasive, however, about the central role of temperament in infant development. Perhaps the salient results can be reviewed as keystones for the current research.

Early Studies of Temperament

Temperament research at Louisville began over 15 years ago with interviews in which the mother was queried about the twins' behavior at home. The twins were brought to the research center on a regular basis for mental testing, and at each visit the mother reported whether the twins had been alike or different for various aspects of behavior. A wide variety of behaviors was covered, touching on everything from feeding/sleeping problems to temper tantrums to accepting strangers or new routines, etc.

The twins were classified as being concordant or discordant for each item of behavior, and the analysis then proceeded to identify behaviors that clustered together—if Twin A was reported to show temper more frequently, did he/she also demand more attention and cry more often? The analysis was repeated at later ages to see if Twin A continued to show these behaviors more often than Twin B, and if the same behaviors were clustered together.

The results showed a nuclear temperament cluster at 12 months made up of temper frequency, temper intensity, irritability, crying, and demanding attention (Wilson, Brown, & Matheny, 1971). If the twins were discordant, one twin typically displayed all these behaviors more than the co-twin, but was shorter on attention span. This nuclear cluster appeared as early as 6 months and continued as a tightly organized cluster to 36 months, so there was a recurrence of the same patterning among temperament variables during early childhood. Similarly, the twins tended to preserve the same relationship on the major variables over time—if Twin A cried more at 12 months than B, he would likely do so at 24 months also.

In addition to temperament and attention span, a third cluster termed sociability was identified from the data. Initially it was made up of two modestly related components—(a) smiling and accepting people, and (b) seeking affection and demanding attention—but by 4 years these variables had coalesced into a well-defined cluster. In fact, the major differences reported within twin pairs at 4 years involved differences in sociability, whereas in earlier years it had involved differences in temperament. Some progressive transformation seemed to quiet the more hectic aspects of temperament, and enhanced the social outgoing aspects.

The comparison of monozygotic (MZ) with dizygotic (DZ) twins showed evidence of a genetic influence on the temperament cluster, and on vegetative processes such as feeding problems and sleep disorders. The distinction was not clear-cut in the first year, in the sense that MZ twins and DZ twins showed the same levels of concordance; but by 2 years the zygosity groups had clearly separated, with MZ twins significantly more concordant for temperament and vegetative functions (Matheny, Wilson, Dolan, & Krantz, 1981). Zygosity differences were less evident for sociability. Nevertheless, this first body of data on temperament pointed to a significant genetic influence for some aspects of temperament, especially the negative mood expressed via irritability, crying, and temper displays.

Bayley's Infant Behavior Record

While the interview data were very informative, some direct method for obtaining temperament data by trained observers seemed highly desirable. Therefore, as an adjunct to the mental testing program, each examiner completed an Infant Behavior Record (Bayley, 1969) for each infant after testing. The Infant Behavior Record (IBR) basically covered the infant's adaptation to the test setting via some 25 ratings of emotional tone, fear, goal-directedness, and social response to the examiner. Since the infants had been tested repeatedly at 3, 6, 9, 12, 18, and 24 months, a large body of data was built up on the stability of these behaviors over age.

After a preliminary report of MZ concordance for two clusters of ratings termed primary cognition and extraversion (Matheny, Dolan, & Wilson, 1976), a full-scale factor analysis was carried out for the IBR ratings at every age, with the sample size ranging between 300–400 infants. Five factors were extracted with factor weights that remained moderately consistent over ages, and of these, the first three factors accounted for the largest proportion of the variance. They were termed task orientation, test affect-extraversion, and activity (Matheny, 1980).

Task orientation was composed chiefly of ratings for goal-directedness, attention span, and orientation to test materials, as a general measure of cognitive set during testing. The second factor was composed chiefly of ratings for fear, cooperation, emotional tone, and social response to the examiner, as a measure of temperament in the test setting. The final factor was composed of ratings for activity, energy, and body motion.

The twin analysis revealed greater MZ concordance for the three factor scores, especially from 12 months to 24 months. At the latter age, the MZ correlations averaged $R_{MZ} = 0.53$, while the DZ correlations averaged $R_{DZ} = 0.13$. The MZ/DZ differences were more sharply drawn with increasing age, making it evident that MZ twins progressively matched each other more closely for behavior in the test setting, even though being tested by separate examiners.

The analysis also revealed a genetic influence on the patterning of scores in the temperament profile. MZ twins matched each other more closely for the profile of factor scores at every age, making it apparent that their relative high and low points were more closely duplicated than for DZ twins. Whatever the patterning of IBR factor scores might be, it coincided more closely for MZ twins.

The profile analysis was further employed for a test of age-to-age stability in the factor scores (Matheny, 1983). The factor structure had remained reasonably consistent over ages, demonstrating some continuity in the organization of these temperament variables. The further question was whether individual differences remained reasonably stable over ages as well.

Factor scores were generated at each age on the three primary factors listed above. The factor scores were then intercorrelated over ages (6 to 24 months), as a measure of whether each infant retained the same relative position. The correlations were highest for 18- to 24-months, with rs of 0.46 and 0.35 for task orientation and test affect-extraversion, respectively. The correlations confirmed some degree of stability, but they also indicated that a substantial reordering of individual differences was taking place between ages.

If the changes were due in part to maturational processes, then MZ twins might be more closely synchronized for the pattern of changes over age. The profile analysis was thus applied to each set of factor scores obtained at 12, 18, and 24 months, and the MZ profile correlations were 0.49 for task orientation, 0.37 for test affect-extraversion, and 0.52 for activity. By contrast, the DZ correlations were significantly lower, being 0.21, 0.12, and 0.18, respectively.

It was apparent that the pattern of change was more coherently organized for MZ twins, so the age-to-age instabilities in the factor scores were not due solely to error variance, but rather represented changes that were partially determined by genetic factors. In the broader perspective of transitions in temperament, these results opened up the prospect of a genetic basis for developmental change.

Laboratory Assessment of Temperament

With this as background, the research program in 1976 was redirected entirely to the assessment of temperament, with a special emphasis on laboratory observations. In large part, this was to capitalize on our long-term experience in dealing with infant twins, and to create a protocol in which trained observers could rate the infant's temperament as displayed in a standardized setting. It also furnished an opportunity to compare the mother's reports of temperament at home with directly observed behaviors in the laboratory.

For the lab protocol, the infant was confronted with a succession of typical age-related challenges, and the staff employed a graded series of soothing techniques and diversionary play activities, as required. The predominant behavioral style was then reflected in how the infant responded to these challenges; and if upset, how responsive or resistant the infant was to being soothed or diverted in play. The sessions were videotaped, and the staff subsequently rated the infant's behavior from videotapes.[1]

The primary rating scales employed in the Lab assessment were emotional tone, activity, attentiveness, and orientation to staff. All ratings were made on 9-point bipolar scales, with emotional tone, for example, ranging from (1) extremely upset, crying vigorously . . . to (9) excited, animated, laughing. Ratings were made for each 2-min period of the protocol, then the periods were combined to yield a single composite rating on each scale. The infant's temperament profile as revealed in the laboratory was thus defined by the vector of composite ratings.

The initial analysis was performed at 12 months, and it showed a strong association between positive emotional tone and sustained attention, or conversely, between very distressed emotional tone and fleeting attention (Wilson & Matheny, 1983). This clustering of behaviors in the laboratory recalled the primary cluster from the 12-month interview data, wherein the more irritable, temperamental twin also displayed a shorter attention span.

Emotional tone was also significantly related to activity (the distressed child tended to be less active in play), and to staff orientation (the distressed child was avoidant and withdrawn). By contrast, the child with positive emotional tone was more active, eager, and responsive with the staff—in a word, more sociable.

Subsequently, a factor analysis was performed on the laboratory ratings, and the first factor was loaded heavily with the ratings of emotional tone (.82), attention (.84), and orientation to/cooperation with staff (.65). This factor became the composite representation of the main temperament cluster described above, as revealed under the successive challenges of the playroom assessment.

The initial study was followed by an analysis of the temperament ratings for the same infants at 18 and 24 months (Matheny, Wilson, & Nuss, 1984). In terms of individual differences and whether they remained stable over ages, first-factor scores were generated for all infants at each age, and then correlated over ages. The correlation for Factor I scores between 12 and 18 months was $r =$

---

[1]A fuller discussion of the laboratory assessment may be found in Wilson & Matheny (1983), and the complete protocol of vignettes and rating scales is documented in Matheny & Wilson (1981).

0.38, and between 18 and 24 months was $r = .66$. Thus, there appeared to be an increasing degree of stability in the temperament ratings for each infant as captured in the lab, and it suggested that individual differences in temperament became more sharply drawn and predictable during the second year.

Temperament Questionnaire

As an adjunct to the laboratory assessment, the mothers completed the Toddler Temperament Questionnaire (Fullard, McDevitt, & Carey, 1984) for the twins at each visit. This enabled us to draw on the rich reservoir of the mother's experiences with the twins, and to make use of a well-developed questionnaire as a replacement for the earlier interviews. Among other advantages, the questionnaires yielded numerical scores for each twin on nine categories of temperament, rather than a simple designation of more than/less than for specific behavioral items. The nine categories are listed below, with brief descriptors for each category.

1. Activity level—motor activity during daily routines as well as motility during sleep-wake cycles.
2. Rhythmicity—regularity of vegetative functions.
3. Approach/withdrawal—initial positive or negative response to a new stimulus.
4. Adaptability—ease of transition to new or altered situations.
5. Intensity of reaction—degree of response.
6. Quality of mood—amount of positive or negative affect.
7. Attention span and persistence—degree to which an interest is maintained or an activity is pursued in the face of obstacles.
8. Distractibility—effectiveness of extraneous stimuli to shift ongoing behavior.
9. Threshold of responsiveness—level of sensory stimulation required to evoke a response.

The category scores defined the infant's temperament profile, and after the scores were intercorrelated, a principal-components factor analysis was performed. For the first factor, there emerged a clear network of relations pertaining to approach, adaptability, mood, attention span, and resistance to distraction (factor loadings of .84 to .63, respectively). With minor variations, all correlated moderately well with one another, and seemed to sketch (at one extreme) the profile of an infant who was positive in mood, adapted easily, approached others readily, and maintained attention in the face of superfluous distractions. The opposite extreme was of an infant predominantly negative in mood, avoidant of others, slow to adapt, short in attention span, and easily distracted. Clearly, the questionnaires filled out by the mothers at 12 months seemed to be capturing the same cluster of attributes that had previously appeared in the interview data and the lab ratings.

The questionnaire data at 18 and 24 months yielded similar first factors, and as a measure of age-to-age stability, the first-factor scores for all infants were intercorrelated at adjacent ages. Between 12 and 18 months, the correlation for first-factor scores was $r = .44$, while for 18–24 months the correlation was $r = .65$. As in the case of the laboratory ratings, individual differences in temperament became more sharply drawn and predictable over age.

Further, the cluster of temperament variables defining Factor I for both the questionnaire data and the lab ratings seemed to be very much alike, suggesting that what the infant displayed in the lab was similar to its behavior at home. This high-lighted the issue of convergent validity, and as a measure of such validity, the Factor I scores for lab and questionnaire were correlated. The resultant correlation yielded $r = 0.52$ ($p < .001$) at 12 months, and comparable correlations at 18 and 24 months (0.38 and 0.52).

Thus, when each infant's temperament profile was condensed into a single factor score, there was a highly significant relation between the factor scores based on direct observations and those based on maternal ratings. Obviously there was a strong core element of temperament that was systematically detected in both data sets.

RESULTS FOR EXPANDED SAMPLE

The sample size has increased substantially since these results were published, and the analysis has been extended back to 9 months. In addition, most of the twins have now been bloodtyped, so a zygosity analysis was possible. With this expanded data set available, the analysis was refocused to bear upon the queries raised by the prior results. Specifically, does the organization of temperament variables maintain continuity over ages? Do individual differences remain stable? Do measures of temperament from different sources display convergent validity? And if there are transformations in temperament over ages, do these transformations occur in parallel for MZ twins?

Laboratory Ratings

Initially, the stability of individual differences was appraised by computing the age-to-age correlations for the laboratory ratings, and the results are shown in Table 7.1.

The correlations were moderate and generally comparable for 9–12 and 12–18 months, with the longer time span offsetting any trend towards improved stability. For 18–24 months, however, the correlations increased substantially, especially for the core variables of emotional tone and attentiveness. The array of

TABLE 7.1
Age-to-Age Correlations For Laboratory Ratings of Temperament

	Ages		
Rating	9-12 Months	12-18 Months	18-24 Months
Emotional tone	.38	.36	.62
Attentiveness	.39	.37	.56
Activity	.28	.33	.39
Orientation to staff	.47	.28	.33
Multivariate R	.41	.40	.56
Shared Variance	17.1%	16.0%	31.3%

*N*s per age: 102-122

individual differences became more firmly established and predictable, and the total predictive variance exceeded 31%. In correlational terms, the relationship between the two sets of temperament ratings[2] could be expressed as a multivariate $R_{18-24} = 0.56$. In the structured laboratory setting, infants began to display consistent patterns of temperament in the second year, with emotional tone being notable.

Organization of Temperament.   To identify the structure of temperament at each age, the laboratory ratings were factor analyzed for the augmented sample, and the resultant 1st-factor loadings are presented in Table 7.2.

Emotional tone was the most consistently high-loading variable at every age, and it served as the anchor for the first-factor. It was followed by attentiveness with slightly lower loadings, then social orientation moved into the cluster as the activity loadings gradually declined.

TABLE 7.2
Continuity of Factor Structure for Lab Ratings Over Ages
(Factor I Loadings > .60)

Ratings	9 Mos	12 Mos	18 Mos	24 Mos
Emotional tone	.86	.92	.92	.93
Attentiveness	.74	.86	.82	.89
Activity	.73	.73	---	---
Orientation to staff	---	.68	.58	.82
Variance accounted for:	40.3%	46.7%	46.2%	45.2%

---

[2]The shared relationship between data sets is derived from a canonical analysis, which captures all common variance via a succession of canonical variates (CV). When the variance accounted for is summed over all CVs, it yields an aggregate measure of shared variance. The aggregate measure may be expressed as a porportion of total variance, or in square root form, as a multivariate R. The latter is analogous to the more typical multiple R except that there are several related outcome variables rather than a single one. See Cooley & Lohnes (1971) and Sympson (1981).

The two core variables retained high values at every age, and thus demonstrated a continuity in the basic organization of temperament variables from 9 to 24 months. Again, the consistency of the factor structure for emotional tone and attentiveness recalled the original link between distressed temperament and short attention span in the interview data, which had persisted as a tightly organized cluster to age 3 years. The replication of factor structure, plus the heavy loading of emotional tone at each age, suggested a basic pattern of temperament variables organized around emotional activity. The changing weights of the auxiliary variables, however, made it apparent that some transformations were taking place with age.

Questionnaire Ratings

How consistently were the infants rated on the nine categories of temperament from age to age? The correlations are presented in Table 7.3.

The results showed generally improving correlations over age, with high values for most categories between 18 and 24 months. In six of the categories, the 18–24 months correlations exceeded $r = .60$, which was higher than for any laboratory variable except emotional tone. The total predictable variance for this period was 47%, which signified a surprising degree of consistency in temperament over this half-year period.

On an individual basis, several categories showed remarkable changes in stability from 9–12 to 18–24 months. Approach, adaptability, mood, and distractibility all moved from low values initially to much higher correlations in the final period (18–24 mo. rs of 0.61 to 0.76). Individual differences became much more consistent and sharply drawn for these variables by 18 months, although

TABLE 7.3
Age-to-Age Correlations for Questionnaire
Categories of Temperament

| | Ages | | |
| | 9–12 Months | 12–18 Months | 18–24 Months |
Categories			
Activity	.46	.56	.74
Rhythmicity	.54	.58	.38
Approach	.21	.54	.70
Adaptability	.13	.43	.61
Intensity	.54	.31	.50
Mood	.29	.57	.64
Persistence	.44	.30	.48
Distractability	-.07	.27	.76
Threshold of Response	.34	.36	.62
Multivariate R	.51	.57	.69
Shared variance	25.8%	32.7%	47.3%

*N*s per age: 86-102

they had been notably unstable in the first period (rs of 0.07 to 0.29). By contrast, intensity and persistence started at a higher level initially and maintained it into the final period, while the age-to-age correlations for rhythmicity actually dropped. The temperament profile for each infant appeared to coalesce in the second year, and maintained a notable degree of consistency during a period of rapid growth.

Continuity of Temperament Structure

From the standpoint of the nine temperament categories, how were they organized over successive ages? The category correlations were factor analyzed at each age, and the first-factor loadings greater than .50 are shown in Table 7.4.

The core nucleus of variables was built around adaptability, approach and mood, all of which appeared with substantial loadings at every age. Recalling the earlier prototype description, this factor was anchored at one end by infants who were good-humored, adaptable, and positive when faced with new situations, while the opposite end was anchored by irritable, slow-to-adapt, withdrawing infants. This core cluster was replicated at every age, although other variables joined the cluster at separate ages.

The pattern of loadings for this larger sample basically confirmed what had been found previously at 18 and 24 months (Matheny, Wilson, & Nuss, 1984), and it extended the appearance of the basic cluster back to 9 months. Interestingly, the core variables were among those that made the largest gains in age-to-age stability in Table 7.3. At 9 and 12 months particularly, the factor weights were very similar for adaptability, approach, and mood, although the distribution of individual differences was considerably rearranged between ages. While the cluster remained consistent, it was not the same infants who got high factor scores at each age. By 18–24 months, however, individual differences had stabilized considerably, and the core cluster was characterized by a consistent pattern of factor weights plus a predictable array of individual differences.

TABLE 7.4
Continuity of Factor Structure For Questionnaire Categories
Over Ages (Factor I Loadings > .50)

Category	Ages			
	9 Mos	12 Mos	18 Mos	24 Mos
Adaptability	.83	.79	.72	.82
Approach	.80	.70	.65	.50
Mood	.64	.70	.84	.77
Persistence	---	.75	---	.53
Intensity	---	---	.62	.55
Activity	---	---	---	.62
Variance accounted for:	30.8%	27.4%	28.3%	29.2%

Convergent Validity: Laboratory and Questionnaire

With the expanded sample, factor scores were not used to measure convergent validity, since each factor accounted for only a limited portion of the data, and the factor composition did change somewhat over age. Rather, a multivariate canonical analysis was employed which would take into account the full set of relationships between the lab ratings and the questionnaire scores. These relationships can be illustrated by showing selected correlations between the lab variables and questionnaire variables at 24 months (see Table 7.5). For example, infants who were upset and distressed in the lab (low emotional-tone scores) were reported by the mothers to be less adaptable and withdrawn.

The canonical analysis (Cooley & Lohnes, 1971) decomposed each data set into a series of independent linear composites, then calculated the shared variance between the two data sets. In effect, it took all intercorrelations between the laboratory ratings and questionnaire scores, and after partialling out the overlapping relationships, it expressed the remaining covariance between data sets as a multivariate R, with an associated percentage of shared variance (see also footnote 2). The results are presented in Table 7.6.

From 12 months onward, the collective relationship between the two data sets yielded Rs near .50, with 22–25% of the variance being shared in common. There was a strong convergent view of temperament as displayed in the laboratory, and temperament as reported by the mother. Despite all differences in settings, instruments, and observers, the core characteristics of each infant reached through the surface variations and produced a common consensus.

In examining the individual variables that carried the relationship, it was apparent that emotional tone and orientation to staff were the principal laboratory variables from 12 months onward, while approach, adaptability, and mood were the principal questionnaire variables. All had high canonical loadings, with emotional tone and approach respectively being the most heavily loaded in each data set. Thus, the core variables that furnished the strongest link between laboratory and questionnaire were also the ones that had anchored the first factors in each data set (cf. Tables 7.2 and 7.4). Evidently some basic rudiment of temperament was being picked up by these core variables.

TABLE 7.5
Intercorrelations Between Selected Lab Variables
And Questionnaire Variables at 24 Months

	Laboratory Variables			
Questionnaire	Emotional Tone	Attention	Activity	Orientation to Staff
Approach	.43	.31	.31	.36
Adaptability	.22	.21	.25	.37
Mood	.13	.08	.28	.17
Attention/Persistence	.14	.20	.25	.24

Note: N = 88. Signs inverted to preserve directional scoring between scales.

TABLE 7.6
Convergent Validity: Correlations Between
Lab Ratings and Questionnaire Measures

	Ages			
	9 Mos	12 Mos	18 Mos	24 Mos
Multivariate R	.36	.47*	.50*	.48*
Shared Variance	12.8%	21.9%	24.9%	22.6%

* $p < .001$

Zygosity and Temperament

Bloodtyping has recently been completed for many of these twins, with all concordant pairs being designated as MZ (Wilson, 1980). The remaining untyped pairs have been classified as MZ or DZ by consensus of the staff. When compared with bloodtyping results, staff consensus has turned out to be very reliable for twins that have been observed repeatedly from birth to 24 months (98%).

Twin correlations have been computed for the four laboratory rating scales, and the results are presented in Table 7.7.

For emotional tone, MZ twins and DZ twins were equally similar through 12 months, but in the ensuing year, MZ twins became increasingly concordant while DZ twins drifted apart. In fact, the MZ correlations at 18 and 24 months exceeded the age-to-age correlations in Table 7.1, so each MZ twin was a better predictor of the co-twin's score at the same age than of his own score at a later age. For emotional tone particularly, and for activity and attentiveness to a somewhat lesser degree, the pattern of MZ/DZ correlations argued for a significant genetic influence on the expression of temperament during the second year. As each infant's temperament profile gradually coalesced and became more stable, MZ twins became more concordant while DZ twins diverged.

TABLE 7.7
Twin Correlations For Laboratory Measures of Temperament

		Ages			
Variable	Zygosity	9 Mos	12 Mos	18 Mos	24 Mos
Emotional Tone	MZ	.57	.51	.74*	.81**
	DZ	.37	.55	.42	.40
Attentiveness	MZ	.52	.24	.64	.73
	DZ	.34	.60	.43	.50
Activity	MZ	.46	.53	.49*	.37
	DZ	.48	.45	.08	.20
Orientation to Staff	MZ	.63	.32	.76	.58
	DZ	.68	.47	.54	.59

No. Pairs: 27-33 MZ, 25-31 DZ
$*p < .05$; $**p < .01$ for $R_{MZ} > R_{DZ}$

Synchronized Changes for MZ Twins

If MZ concordance exceeded age-to-age consistency for the temperament scores, it suggested that MZ twins might be making synchronized changes over ages. If so, some of the age-to-age changes might be attributed to systematic maturational effects shared by both twins, rather than simply error variance.

For illustration, the emotional-tone scores were plotted for several MZ and DZ pairs, and the resultant curves are presented in Fig. 7.1.

Each data point represented the infant's mean emotional-tone score for the visit, with lower scores signifying irritability and distress. Some pairs became very irritable over ages (the bottom MZ pair); some remained positive and cooperative throughout (the middle MZ pair); and in some pairs, there was a sharp divergence within the pair during the second year, as in the top and middle DZ pairs.

To express these trends on a sample-wide basis, within-pair correlations were computed for concordance in the emotional-tone curves. The concordance in

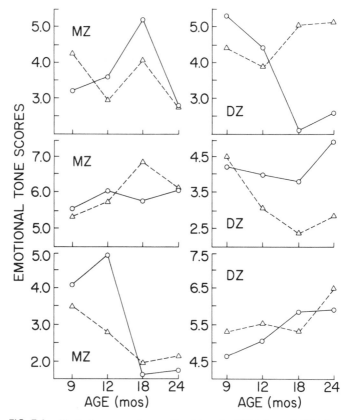

FIG. 7.1.   Illustrative curves for emotional tone for MZ twins and DZ twins.

trend takes into account both the elevation of the scores and the profile of age-to-age changes, so the trend correlation represents how closely the curves were matched overall (Wilson, 1979).

Initially, the trend correlations were computed over each adjacent time span, to identify where MZ/DZ differences first became manifest; then the final analysis compared the emotional tone curves over 12, 18, and 24 months. The trend correlations are presented in Table 7.8.

The trends in the emotional-tone curves were the same for MZ pairs and DZ pairs over 9–12 months, but thereafter the trend correlations steadily increased for MZ twins, while the DZ correlations regressed slightly. Although the 18–24 months period showed the sharpest MZ/DZ differentiation for matching trends, even the full three-age span showed significantly greater MZ concordance. Therefore, the age-to-age changes were more closely synchronized for MZ twins, and appeared to represent a coherent pattern of developmental change arising from genetic sources.

Summary of Zygosity Analyses

These results may be incorporated into a synthesis of results from the earlier studies. In the original interviews, MZ twins were significantly more concordant than DZ twins for aspects of temperament and for vegetative processes. In the test situation, the IBR ratings of behavior showed MZ twins to be more concordant on the factors of goal orientation and test affect-extraversion, especially during the second year. Further, MZ twins were more concordant for the profile of factor scores—an illustration of matching patterns of temperament—and more concordant for the profile of age-to-age change in the factor scores. The latter suggested a genetic influence on developmental change itself, such that MZ twins would display synchronized pathways of change.

It is this result which was further clarified by the trends in emotional tone discussed above. MZ twins displayed parallel trends in emotional tone from 12 months onward, so even if there were a marked change in emotional tone, it

TABLE 7.8
Twin Correlations For Trends in
Emotional Tone Over Ages

	Correlations	
Age Periods	MZ	DZ
9-12 Mos	.50	.48
12-18 Mos	.63	.51
18-24 Mos	.80**	.41
12-18-24 Mos	.73**	.47

$**p < .01$ for $R_{MZ} > R_{DZ}$

tended to occur in synchrony for MZ twins. The genotype appeared to be guiding the direction of change between ages, perhaps in analogous fashion to the spurts and lags in mental development (Wilson, 1978).

In broad view, a prospective genetic influence on temperament may be inferred not just from stabilities over age, but also from synchronized patterns of change. For each infant, some transformations in the temperament profile may be plausibly related to programmed maturational schedules that originate in the genotype. As Rothbart and Derryberry (1981) have emphasized, temperament is a psychobiological concept, and constitutional factors will play a prominent role in guiding the course of development. Perhaps an appreciation of this fact will lead to a more comprehensive framework for understanding the development of temperament.

ACKNOWLEDGMENT

The research reviewed in this paper has been supported in part by USPHS research grants OCD 90-C-922, HD 03217 and HD 14352, and by a research grant from the John D. and Catherine T. MacArthur Foundation. We are indebted to the many co-workers who have contributed so much to the program, including R. Arbegust, P. Gefert, M. Hinkle, J. Lechleiter, B. Moss, S. Nuss, D. Sanders, and A. Thoben.

REFERENCES

Bayley, N. (1969). *Bayley scales of infant development*. New York: Psychological Coporation.
Bell, R. Q. (1968). A reinterpretation of the direction of effects in studies of socialization. *Psychological Review, 75*, 81–95.
Buss, A. H., & Plomin, R. (1975). *A temperament theory of personality development*. New York: Wiley.
Buss, A. H., & Plomin, R. (1984). *Temperament: Early developing personality traits*. Hillsdale, NJ: Lawrence Erlbaum Associates.
Cooley, W. W., & Lohnes, P. R. (1971). *Multivariate data analysis* (2nd ed.). New York: Wiley.
Escalona, S. K. (1968). *Roots of individuality*. Chicago: Aldine.
Freedman, D. G. (1965). An ethological approach to the genetic study of human behavior. In S. Vandenberg (Ed.), *Methods and goals in human behavior genetics*. New York: Academic Press.
Fullard, W., McDevitt, S. C., & Carey, W. B. (1984). Assessing temperament in one to three-year-old children. *Journal of Pediatric Psychology, 9*, 205–217.
Goldsmith, H. H. (1983). Genetic influences on personality from infancy to adulthood. *Child Development, 54*, 331–355.
Goldsmith, H. H., & Campos, J. J. (1982). Genetic influences on individual differences in emotionality. *Infant Behavior and Development, 5*, 99. (Abstract)
Goldsmith, H. H., & Gottesman, I. I. (1981). Origins of variation in behavioral style: A longitudinal study of temperament in young twins. *Child Development, 52*, 91–103.
Gottesman, I. I. (1974). Developmental genetics and ontogenetic psychology: Overdue detente and propositions from a matchmaker. In A. D. Pick (Ed.), *Minnesota Symposia on Child Psychology*, Vol. 8. (pp. 55–80). Minneapolis: University of Minnesota Press.

Lytton, H. (1980). *Parent-child interaction: The socialization process observed in twin and singleton families.* New York: Plenum.

Matheny, A. P. (1980). Bayley's Infant Behavior Record: Behavioral components and twin analyses. *Child Development, 51,* 1157–1167.

Matheny, A. P. (1983). A longitudinal twin study of stability of components from Bayley's Infant Behavior Record. *Child Development, 54,* 356–360.

Matheny, A. P., Dolan, A. B., & Wilson, R. S. (1976). Twins: Within-pair similarity on Bayley's Infant Behavior Record. *Journal of Genetic Psychology, 28,* 263–270.

Matheny, A. P., & Wilson, R. S. (1981). Developmental tasks and rating scales for the laboratory assessment of infant temperament. *JSAS Catalog of Selected Documents in Psychology, 11,* 81.

Matheny, A. P., Wilson, R. S., Dolan, A. B., & Krantz, J. Z. (1981). Behavioral contrasts in twinships: Stability and patterns of differences in childhood. *Child Development, 52,* 579–588.

Matheny, A. P., Wilson, R. S., & Nuss, S. N. (1984). Toddler temperament: Stability across settings and over ages. *Child Development, 55,* 1200–1211.

Plomin, R. (1983). Childhood temperament. In B. Lahey & A. Kazdin (Eds.), *Advances in clinical child psychology* (Vol. 6). New York: Plenum Press.

Plomin, R., & Rowe, D. C. (1977). A twin study of temperament in young children. *The Journal of Psychology, 97,* 107–113.

Rothbart, M. K., & Derryberry, D. (1981). Development of individual differences in temperament. In M. E. Lamb & A. L. Brown (Eds.), *Advances in developmental psychology* (Vol. 1). Hillsdale, NJ: Lawrence Erlbaum Associates.

Sympson, J. B. (1981). Redundancy re-evaluated: Further comments on "A General Canonical Correlation Index." *JSAS Catalog of Selected Documents in Psychology, 11,* 72 (Ms. 2344).

Thomas, A., & Chess, S. (1977). *Temperament and development.* New York: Brunner/Mazel.

Thomas, A., Chess, S., Birch, H. G., Hertzig, M. E., & Korn, S. (1963). *Behavioral individuality in early childhood.* New York: New York University Press.

Torgersen, A. M. (1982). Influence of genetic factors on temperament development in early childhood. In CIBA Symposium 89, *Temperamental Differences in Infants and Young Children.* London: Pitman.

Torgersen, A. M., & Kringlen, E. (1978). Genetic aspects of temperament differences in twins. *Journal of the American Academy of Child Psychiatry, 17,* 433–444.

Wilson, R. S. (1978). Synchronies in mental development: An epigenetic perspective. *Science, 202,* 939–948.

Wilson, R. S. (1979). Analysis of longitudinal twin data: Basic model and applications to physical growth measures. *Acta Geneticae Medicae et Gemellologiae, 28,* 93–105.

Wilson, R. S. (1980). Bloodtyping and twin zygosity: Reassessment and extension. *Acta Geneticae Medicae et Gemellologiae, 29,* 103–120.

Wilson, R. S., Brown, A. M., & Matheny, A. P. (1971). Emergence and persistence of behavioral differences in twins. *Child Development, 42,* 1381–1398.

Wilson, R. S., & Matheny, A. P., Jr. (1983). Assessment of temperament in infant twins. *Developmental Psychology, 19,* 172–183.

8 Children and Adolescents in Their Contexts: Tests of a Goodness of Fit Model

Richard M. Lerner
Jacqueline V. Lerner
Michael Windle
Karen Hooker
Kathleen Lenerz
Patricia L. East
The Pennsylvania State University

The noted child psychiatrist, Stella Chess, once observed that "All parents are environmentalists . . . until they have their second child!" A central theme in our research on the contextual significance of temperament is that children possess characteristics that allow them to be agents in their own development. This idea is certainly not news to those who have been involved over the past 15 years in reading and generating the literature on personality and social development. However, it *was* only about 17 years ago that Bell (1968) published his influential paper on a reinterpretation of the direction of effects in socialization research. Nevertheless, 10 years later, Hartup (1978) found it still useful to remind colleagues that socialization is best viewed as a reciprocal process, rather than as one involving a unidirectional social molding of children by parents. Even more recently, Scarr and McCartney (1983) argued that a child's organismic characteristics, represented by his or her genotype, may be the "driving force" of cognitive, personality, and even social developments.

It is important to emphasize, however, that the scholars who have argued for the role of the child as an agent in his or her own development do *not* view those characteristics of children which promote their own development as acting in a predetermined or fixed manner (R. Lerner, 1982; Scarr & McCartney, 1983). Instead, the probabilistic character of such "child effects," and of development in general, is emphasized. This stress occurs because the reciprocal nature of all child effects is given prominence. The context enveloping a child is composed of, for example, a specific physical ecology and other individually different and developing people with whom the child interacts. This context is as unique and changing as is the child lawfully individually distinct. One cannot completely

99

specify in advance what particular features of the context will exist at a specific time in a given child's life. As a consequence, we may only speak probabilistically of the effects a given child may have on his or her context, of the feedback the child is likely to receive from the context, and of the nature of the child's development that will therefore ensue.

Thus, child effects are not as simple as they may seem at first. Indeed, the probabilism of development represents a formidable challenge for theory and research. To understand how children may influence their own development we need to: (1) have a conceptualization of the nature of the *individual* characteristics or processes involved in such effects; (2) conceptualize and operationalize the features of the context, or of the ecology, wherein significant interactions occur for the child (but as Bronfenbrenner, 1979, has noted, psychologists are neither readily prone nor typically adequately trained to do this); (3) devise some means, some model, by which child effects and contextual features may be integrated; and (4) translate Steps 1–3 into methodologically sound research.

In the research in our laboratory we have followed these steps, and devised a conceptual model and an empirical strategy, with which we have *begun* to study ways in which children, as a consequence of their temperamental individuality, may promote their own development through their interactions in a changing and multidimensional world. To explain our research program it is necessary first to present the general features of the model that has guided our research.

THE GOODNESS OF FIT MODEL

Both individuals and the world they inhabit are composed of multiple "levels of being," or multiple dimensions, (e.g., the inner-biological, individual-psychological, and sociocultural levels). These dimensions are thought to be interdependent, and developing and/or changing over time (e.g., see R. Lerner, 1984, 1985; R. Lerner & J. Lerner, 1983). Moreover, both person and context will be individually distinct as a consequence of the unique combination of genotypic and phenotypic features of the person and of the specific attributes of his or her context. The presence of such individuality is central to understanding the model that has guided our research: the goodness of fit model of person-context relations.

The details of this model have been presented elsewhere (e.g., J. Lerner, 1984; J. Lerner & R. Lerner, 1983). To briefly summarize these earlier presentations, we may note that as a consequence of characteristics of physical individuality, for example, in regard to body type or facial attractiveness (Sorell & Nowak, 1981) and/or of psychological individuality, for instance, in regard to conceptual tempo or temperament (Kagan, 1966; Thomas & Chess, 1977), children promote differential reactions in their socializing others; these reactions may feed back to children, increase the individuality of their developmental milieu, and provide a basis for their further development. Schneirla (1957) termed these relations "circular functions." Through the establishment of such functions in ontogeny people may be conceived of as producers of their own development (R. Lerner, 1982; R. Lerner & Busch-Rossnagel, 1981). However, this circular functions idea needs to be extended since it is mute regarding the specific characteristics of the feedback (for example, its positive or negative valence) a child will receive as a consequence of his/her individuality. What may provide a basis for this feedback?

The child's individuality, in differentially meeting the demands of the context, provides a basis for the feedback he or she gets from the socializing environment. That is, just as a child brings his or her characteristics of individuality to a particular social setting, there are demands placed on the child by virtue of the social and physical components of the setting. First, these demands may take the form of attitudes, values, or expectations held by others in the context regarding the child's physical or behavioral characteristics. Second, demands exist as a consequence of the behavioral attributes of others in the context with whom the child must coordinate, or fit, his or her behavioral attributes for adaptive interactions to exist. Third, the physical characteristics of a setting (such as the presence or absence of access ramps for the handicapped) constitute contextual demands. Such physical presses require the child to possess certain behavioral attributes for optimal interaction with the setting to occur.

For example, considering the demand "domain" of attitudes, values, or expectations, teachers and parents may have relatively distinct expectations about behaviors desired of their students and children, respectively. Teachers may want students who show little distractibility, since they would not want attention diverted from the lesson by the activity of other children in the classroom. Parents, however, might desire their children to be moderately distractible, for example, when they require their children to move from watching television to dinner. Children whose behavioral individuality is either generally distractible or generally not distractible would thus differentially meet the demands of these two contexts. Further, the degree of fit in one context may influence the fit in a related context, such as when a child's failure to meet the demands of a teacher is communicated to the parents. Problems of adjustment to school or to home might thus develop as a consequence of a child's lack of match, or "goodness of fit," in either or both settings.

From the perspective of the goodness of fit model, adaptive psychological and social functioning do not derive directly from either the nature of the person's characteristics of individuality per se or the nature of the demands of the contexts within which the person functions (J. Lerner, 1984; J. Lerner & R. Lerner, 1983). Rather, to the extent that a person's characteristics of individuality fit (or exceed) the demands of a particular setting, adaptive outcomes in that setting will accrue. In turn, people whose characteristics do not fit (or fall short of) the context's demands should show evidence of nonadaptive outcomes.

To test these expectations, the "unit" of analysis used in statistical analyses must be a relational one. That is, basically, the goodness of fit model is a contextual one which stresses that psychosocial functioning can be predicted best when one relates person to context. As such, in the research in our laboratory we have devised various means to arrive at such a relational unit. For example, we have used often a difference, or discrepancy, score derived by subtracting a subject's score on a given temperament attribute (e.g., attention span) from the attitudinal demand regarding attention span held by a significant other (e.g., the classroom teacher) in a given context. Discrepancy scores indicative of poor fit are expected to predict poorer psychosocial functioning.

For instance, consider a teacher who indicates that low-attention span in a student makes for difficult interaction. In this case a student whose attention span score was low would show a small discrepancy from the level of functioning difficult for the teacher. A student whose attention span was high would have a larger discrepancy from the level of functioning difficult for the teacher. Thus, with such discrepancy (difference) scores, a large difference from what is seen as difficult is indicative of good fit with the context; in our data analyses we test the model by seeing if such scores covary positively with favorable psychosocial functioning.

Moreover, we standardly compare such tests of our contextual model with what we may term the personological (or temperament-alone) model. That is, as explained by Plomin and Daniels (1984), if the goodness of fit model is to be supported it must be shown to account for more variance than is the case when just temperament alone is interrelated with psychosocial functioning, i.e., when the context and its demands are not used to make predictions and/or to form a unit of analysis. Let us summarize then the general format of our research and some of our major findings which, we believe, suggest the use of the model and encourage its further refinement.

TESTS OF THE GOODNESS OF FIT MODEL

Because temperament has been identified (Thomas & Chess, 1977) as a key dimension of behavioral individuality in infancy and throughout childhood, our tests of the goodness of fit model have focused on this construct. By temperament we mean only behavioral style, that is, how a person does whatever he/she does (Thomas & Chess, 1977). For example, because all people engage in eating, sleeping, and toileting behaviors, the absence or presence of such contents of the behavior repertoire would not differentiate among them. But whether these behaviors occur with regularity (i.e., rhythmically), or with a lot of or a little intensity, might serve to differentiate among people.

In addition, although most current temperament research involves studying infants or young children, our research has focused on the adolescent age range.

Indeed, our major focus has been on the two ends of this age range, that is, on people making the transition from childhood to adolescence (early adolescents) and people making the transition from adolescence to young adulthood (late adolescents). As noted, our focus on temperamental individuality derives from our theoretical interest in person-context relations. The transition periods on which we focus involve, we believe, a much wider and richer array of contexts and contextual transitions than is the case in infancy or early childhood. This is especially the case when one considers that in the transitions involved in early and late adolescence ontogenetically new contexts, such as the work place, become salient; moreover, the person plays a more active role in selecting his or her settings and associates.

Procedures in Testing the Model

Our research, to date, has followed a methodological strategy adhering to the four steps previously described. First, two instruments have been developed to measure temperament. They have been labeled the Dimensions of Temperament Survey, or the DOTS (R. Lerner, Palermo, Spiro, & Nesselroade, 1982), and the Revised Dimensions of Temperament Survey, or the DOTS-R (Windle, 1984). The DOTS is a 34-item instrument with true-false response alternatives. Five factors have been identified in the DOTS (Attention Span-Persistence versus Distractibility; Adaptability-Approach versus Withdrawal; Activity Level; Rhythmicity; and Reactivity, a factor composed of items relating to threshold, intensity, and activity level). The DOTS-R is a 54-item instrument, has a four choice response format, and assesses nine temperament attributes among children and ten attributes among adults. The nine childhood attributes are: Activity Level (General); Activity Level (Sleep); Rhythmicity; Approach-Withdrawal; Flexibility-Rigidity; Mood; Rhythmicity (Sleep); Rhythmicity (Eating); Rhythmicity (Daily Habits); and Task Orientation. Among adults, this last attribute differentiates into the attributes of Distractibility and Persistence. Both the DOTS and the DOTS-R questionnaires can be completed reliably by children in the fourth grade and beyond. In addition parents or other caregivers who know the child well can report about the child's temperament.[1] An example of a child-report item, in this case for Rhythmicity (Sleep), is "I get sleepy at a different

---

[1]The reliability of the DOTS has been noted in previous papers (e.g., J. Lerner et al., 1985; R. Lerner et al., 1982). For the DOTS-R attributes of Activity Level (General), Activity Level (Sleep), Approach-Withdrawal, Flexibility-Rigidity, Mood, Rhythmicity (Sleep), Rhythmicity (Eating), Rhythmicity (Daily Habits), and Task Orientation (or Distractibility and Persistence) the internal consistency (Cronbach alpha) reliabilities are, respectively, .84, .87, .84, .79, .91, .80, .80, .70, and .79 for a sample of 115 preschoolers, .75, .81, .77, .62, .80, .69, .75, .54, and .70 for a sample of 224 early adolescents, and .84, .89, .85, .78, .89, .78, .80, .62, .81, and .74 for a sample of 300 late adolescents (Windle, 1984).

time every night." The corresponding item for parents is "My child gets sleepy at a different time every night."

Our second measurement task is to assess a feature of the child's context relevant to his or her temperament. As explained earlier, we have identified at least three contextual presses, or demands, which may be relevant to a child's temperament. These are: the attitudes, expectations, or values about temperament held by significant others; the temperaments of significant others; and the presses on behavior style imposed by the physical ecology. To date, we have focused mostly on expectational demands, although in one study using the DOTS we assessed the demands imposed by the temperament of a significant other (Windle & R. Lerner, 1984).

To assess the expectations about temperament held by a child's significant others, modified versions of the DOTS or the DOTS-R have been used. When we have used the DOTS to measure expectations we have recast each item to relate to the preferences held by either parents, teachers, or peers. For example, a DOTS item, pertinent to attention span-distractibility, is "I stay with an activity for a long time." To assess teachers' expectational demands for this item it is recast to read, "I want my students to stay with an activity for a long time." For the parent and peer group versions of this item the word "students" is deleted, and the word "child" or "friends" is substituted, respectively.

With the DOTS-R we have taken a somewhat different, more explicitly theory-guided approach to measuring expectational demands. Thomas and Chess (1977), as part of their New York Longitudinal Study (NYLS), conducted extensive interviews with parents. If a child had particular scores on a specific set of five of the nine temperament attributes they assessed in the NYLS (i.e., low rhythmicity, slow or low adaptability, high intensity, negative mood, and withdrawal), it was difficult for the parent to have positive interactions with the child. The point of this finding is that the levels of scores, or the "signs" of the difficult child, present difficulty only because they constitute a basis of poor interaction between the child and a significant other in his or her context. And the reason the attribute provides a basis for poor interaction is because it is not something the significant other wants or expects from the child. Thus, temperamental difficulty resides not in the child per se; rather it is the context which defines what is difficult.

Super and Harkness (1982) have further clarified this point. They stress that people in different contexts may have distinct ideas about how difficult a given temperament attribute may be. They term the belief system of people of a particular context an *ethnotheory*, and believe that in different contexts there exist different ethnotheories of temperament difficulty.

Following the lead of Super and Harkness, we have used the DOTS-R items to formulate a means to assess the ethnotheory of temperamental difficulty held by the parents, by the teachers, and by the peers of the samples we have studied. For instance, the DOTS-R item, "My child gets sleepy at different times every night," is rated by a parent in respect to how difficult it would be for the parent to interact with his or her child *if* the child always showed the behavior described in the item. As with the original DOTS-R questionnaire, each DOTS-R ethnotheory questionnaire uses a four choice response format, with high scores indicating greater difficulty of interaction.[2] Finally, as explained above, goodness of fit exists when a large discrepancy exists between temperament and what is seen as difficult. The derivation of such scores leads to the third step of our general methodology, that of putting temperament scores and demands together, and testing the goodness of fit model.

Our general hypotheses are that scores indicative of good fit (e.g., high discrepancy scores between temperament and difficulty scores) should covary with outcome scores indicative of favorable psychosocial functioning, *and* that the variance accounted for by the fit score-outcome score relations should be greater than that accounted for by temperament score-outcome score relations. Testing both hypotheses allows us to evaluate the differential usefulness of the contextual, goodness of fit model and the personological, "temperament-alone" model. Let us now present and evaluate the evidence we have obtained in respect to our hypotheses.

Results of Tests of the Model Using the DOTS

The initial studies in our laboratory (J. Lerner, 1983; J. Lerner, Lerner, & Zabski, 1985; Palermo, 1982; Windle & R. Lerner, 1984) used the DOTS to measure temperament and contextual expectations. The results of these studies have been reviewed recently by J. Lerner (1984), and thus need only to be summarized briefly here. The first three of the above-noted studies used a similar design: the self-rated temperaments of children (ranging in grade level from fourth through eighth grade), and the demands (expectations) of teachers, classroom peers, and/or parents, were assessed; outcome measures assessed variables such as positive and negative peer relations, teacher ratings of academic competence and adjustment, grades, self-esteem, achievement test scores, and parent identification of problem behaviors in the home. The Windle and Lerner (1984) study focused on late adolescents' dating behavior, and found that temperament-temperament (and demand-demand) similarity was more characteristic of late adolescents involved in exclusive dating relationships than of late adolescents who were not dating exclusively.

Within and across the four studies using the DOTS numerous positive findings were obtained, i.e., fit scores did relate in the expected ways to the outcome measures. However, the variance accounted for by the fit scores was only infre-

---

[2]Internal consistency (Cronbach alphas) reliabilities for the DOTS-R Ethnotheory scores are moderate to high, ranging across parents, teachers and adolescent peers—from a low of .65 to a high of .92, and with an average of .81 (Hooker et al., 1985; Windle et al., 1985).

quently greater than the variance accounted for by the temperament scores alone. In fact, while much of the time the fit scores and the temperament-alone scores accounted for corresponding amounts of variance in the outcome measures, when there were differences they tended most often to be in favor of the temperament scores alone; however, in respect to both models, the absolute amount of total variance accounted for was not great (e.g., typically about 5% across outcome measures). Thus, it is accurate to say that across these four studies we did not show that using scores relating person and context allowed us to account for psychosocial functioning to an extent greater than that possible through relying solely on a personological model.

We believe there are several reasons for this. First, as noted in J. Lerner's (1984) review, relatively little variability existed in teacher (or peer or parent) demands; thus, in deriving a difference score between temperament and demands we were, in effect, subtracting a constant from the temperament scores. Second, difference scores, like change scores, are less reliable than their components (when the components are positively related). Third, to support the goodness of fit model we need to find that, in effect, one correlation (between the difference score and an outcome measure) is greater than another correlation (between the temperament-alone score and an outcome measure). Substantially more power is needed when testing if one correlation is greater than another than when testing if a single correlation is greater than zero (Cohen, 1977; Rosenthal & Rosnow, 1984); thus, the sample sizes in our DOTS studies (which averaged less than 200) were not large enough to give us the needed power (given the effect sizes we expected). Fourth, the model specifies that those children who meet (or exceed) contextual demands should have more favorable psychosocial functioning than should children who fall below contextual demands. However, relatively few children in fact fall below the assessed contextual demands (e.g., of the teacher); it may well be that by early adolescence most children who fall below such demands are not in the typical classrooms we assessed in our studies. In any case, the DOTS studies have tested the model without being able to take advantage of the full potential range of variation above and below contextual demands. Fifth, there were problems with the DOTS itself, such as item under-representation of some attribute domains (e.g., Activity Level was measured by three items, all of which dealt only with activity during sleep), and the dichotomous response format (which restricted the potential variability of responses).

Yet, the fact that the goodness of fit model was supported about as well as the temperament-alone model, despite the several problem areas, left us encouraged about the former model's potential utility. As such, we began to try to address these problem domains by, first, developing another measurement instrument, the DOTS-R (Windle, 1984). Thus, after the completion of the four above-noted DOTS studies the work in our laboratory turned from the use of the DOTS to the use of the DOTS-R and to assessment of ethnotheory.

Results of Tests of the Model Using the DOTS-R

We have completed two studies which test the goodness of fit model through the use of the DOTS-R. In the first study, by Hooker, Windle, East, Lenerz, and R. Lerner (1985), the temperaments of early adolescents (sixth graders) were assessed, along with their teachers' ethnotheories of temperamental difficulty. In the second study, by Windle, Hooker, Lenerz, East, and R. Lerner (1985), the temperaments of late adolescents (college students) were assessed, along with their parents' and their peers' ethnotheories. In both studies we reasoned that those adolescents who are interacting best in a context should get feedback from the context which eventuates in their perceiving themselves as meeting the context's demands—as being competent in that context. Accordingly, as an outcome measure in both studies we used scores derived from the Harter (1982) Perceived Competence Scale, i.e., the score for cognitive competence, for social competence, and for general self-worth;[3] a fourth score derived from this instrument—for physical competence—was not used since we had no hypotheses about it. In the Windle et al. (1985) study we administered also to each subject the Center for Epidemiologic Studies-Depression Scale (the CES-D scale) (Radloff, 1977), with the expectation that, since failure to perceive oneself as interactively competent may be associated with feelings of depression (Seligman, 1975), perceived competence should be inversely related to depression.

Several types of data analyses were conducted in order to compare the usefulness of the goodness of fit model with that of the temperament-alone model, e.g., hierarchical regressions (suggested by Plomin & Daniels, 1984), ANOVAs, log-linear analyses, and correlational analyses were done. Since all analyses led to the same basic conclusions, in the interest of brevity we shall present the results of the most straightforward analyses, the correlational ones. In these analyses each temperament (T) attribute was correlated with each outcome score, and this constituted the temperament-alone (T-alone) analyses. In turn, each ethnotheory (E) score for an attribute was subtracted from a subject's temperament (T) score for that attribute, and this difference score was correlated with each outcome measure in order to conduct the goodness of fit, or difference, score (T-E) analyses. In addition, since we have noted the reliability problems associated with differences scores, each T-E/outcome measure correlation was disattenuated; of course, in the service of a balanced comparison of the two models we disattenuated also each T-alone/outcome measure correlation. Final-

---

[3]To test the veridicality of subjects' perceived competence ratings, Hooker et al. correlated each child's (a) cognitive and (b) social competence ratings with his/her classroom teacher's single Likert item, seven point rating of the child's (1) academic competence; and (2) social competence. Significant correlations were found in the (a)–(1), $r(136) = .57, p < .001$, and the (b)–(2), $r(136) = .27, p < .002$, comparisons. Moreover, if these teacher ratings are substituted for the corresponding child ratings, results very similar to those shown in Table 8.1 are found.

ly, for each outcome measure we determined the multiple correlation between the outcome measure and the T-alone scores as well as, of course, the T-E scores. The results of those analyses are presented in Table 8.1 for the Hooker et al. (1985) study and in Table 8.2 for the Windle et al. (1985) study. For the latter study only the results using the parent ethnotheories are presented since they are essentially the same as those found when using the peer ethnotheories.

Indeed, there is marked consistency between the demands of the parents and of the peers of late adolescents, and this means that, in making transitions from one context to the other, the adolescent is faced with a "united front" in respect to ethnotheories of temperamental difficulty. For example, for the demands regarding the attributes of mood and flexibility-rigidity, average ethnotheory scores for the parents and peers respectively, are: 9.5 (SD = 3.4) and 10.0 (SD = 3.9) for mood; and 13.6 (SD = 3.0) and 13.5 (SD = 3.4) for flexibility-rigidity. Moreover, the ethnotheories of the sixth grade teachers studied by Hooker et al. (1985) also are markedly similar to the ethnotheories of the groups studied by Windle et al. (1985). For instance, for the demands noted above in regard to the Windle et al. data (i.e., for mood and for flexibility-rigidity), the corresponding scores for the teachers studied by Hooker et al. were 12.3 (SD = 4.03) and 13.1 (SD = 2.73), respectively. Thus, it may be that a common ethnotheory exists across the early- to late-adolescent span *and* across the key contexts of this period.

Leaving the substantive implications of such findings aside, however, we may note that such consistency presents us with an important methodological problem. As was the case with the DOTS studies, the Hooker et al. and the Windle et al. DOTS-R studies are faced with having to form discrepancy scores with demands that show so little variation within and across context that in effect a constant is being subtracted from the temperament score. Moreover, it is also again the case that few subjects fall below the desired ethnotheory. Nevertheless, despite these statistical constraints, inspection of Tables 1 and 2 reveals that, as was the case for the DOTS studies, the analyses using the DOTS-R indicate that the goodness of fit model does about as well as the temperament-alone model in accounting for variance in the outcome measures.

In regard to Table 8.1, and the early adolescents studied by Hooker et al. (1985), we may note that 14 of the 27 T-alone correlations (i.e., 52%) are significant. We should emphasize that all these correlations are in the direction expected on the basis of inspection of the distribution of pertinent ethnotheory scores. For example, the teachers studied by Hooker et al. found high activity level (general) difficult (possible range of scores = 0–28, actual mean = 20.2, actual SD = 3.3) and low task orientation difficult (possible range of scores 0–32, actual mean = 13.0, actual SD = 4.0); thus, we would expect that (T-E)/outcome score correlations (as well as T-alone/outcome score correlations) for activity level (general) to be negative and for task orientation to be positive. These findings occurred.

The number of significant T-E (early adolescent temperament minus teacher demands)/outcome score correlations is also 14 (of 27), or 52%. Thus, in comparing the relative number of significant relations found for the two models, there is no difference. Moreover, the multiple correlations associated with the two models are all significant and of comparable magnitudes. Finally, when both the T-alone/outcome score correlations and the T-E/outcome score correlations

TABLE 8.1
Correlations (With and Without Disattenuation) Between Temperament Scores, Or Difference Scores (DOTS-R Scores Minus Teacher Ethnotheory Scores), and Perceived Competence (Harter) Scale Scores. For Early Adolescents (N = 136) (Data from Hooker et al., 1985)

| | Perceived Competence Scale Scores For: | | |
DOTS-R Attribute:	Cognitive	Social	General Self-Worth
1. Activity Level (General)	-.28***	-.19*	-.15
Disattenuated	-.37***	-.25**	-.20*
Difference Score	-.23**	-.18*	-.12
Disattenuated	-.31***	-.23**	-.16
2. Activity Level (Sleep)	-.04	-.10	-.10
Disattenuated	-.05	-.13	-.13
Difference Score	-.05	-.09	-.11
Disattenuated	-.06	-.11	-.14
3. Approach-Withdrawal	.33***	.17	.25**
Disattenuated	.43***	.22**	.33***
Difference Score	.22*	.14	.20*
Disattenuated	.29***	.18*	.27**
4. Flexibility-Rigidity	.36***	.23**	.29***
Disattenuated	.52***	.33***	.43***
Difference Score	.27**	.19*	.22**
Disattenuated	.39***	.27**	.33***
5. Mood	.34***	.27**	.21*
Disattenuated	.44***	.34***	.27**
Difference Score	.26**	.26**	.19*
Disattenuated	.33***	.33***	.27**
6. Rhythmicity (Sleep)	.22**	-.03	.11
Disattenuated	.30***	-.04	.16
Difference Score	.20*	.04	.12
Disattenuated	.28***	.06	.17
7. Rhythmicity (Eating)	.12	-.02	.08
Disattenuated	.16	-.03	.11
Difference Score	.09	.04	.07
Disattenuated	.12	.05	.09
8. Rhythmicity (Daily Habits)	.09	.13	.04
Disattenuated	.14	.20*	.06
Difference Score	.09	.15	.06
Disattenuated	.11	.20*	.10
9. Task Orientation	.44***	.18*	.26**
Disattenuated	.60***	.24**	.36***
Difference Score	.37***	.20*	.20*
Disattenuated	.51***	.27**	.28***
Multiple R:	.61***	.40**	.38**
Difference Score Multiple R:	.50***	.39**	.33*

*$p < .05$
**$p < .01$
***$p < .001$

TABLE 8.2
Correlations (With and Without Disattenuation) Between Temperament Scores, Or
Difference Scores (DOTS-R Scores Minus Parent Ethnotheory Scores), And
Perceived Competence (Harter) Scale Scores And CES-D (Depression) Scores
For Late Adolescents[1] (Data from Windle et al., 1985)

DOTS-R Attribute:	Perceived Competence Scale Scores for:			CES-D
	Cognitive	Social	General Self-Worth	Score
1. Activity Level (General)	-.01	.21**	.07	.08
Disattenuated	-.01	.26***	.09	.09
Difference Score	.00	.28***	.20*	.00
Disattenuated	.00	.35***	.26***	.00
2. Activity Level (Sleep)	.00	-.07	-.08	-.03
Disattenuated	.00	-.08	-.10	-.03
Difference Score	-.04	-.05	-.06	-.06
Disattenuated	-.05	-.06	-.07	-.07
3. Approach-Withdrawal	.28***	.46***	.31***	-.26***
Disattenuated	.35***	.57***	.39***	-.30***
Difference Score	.23**	.35***	.16	-.20**
Disattenuated	.29***	.43***	.20*	-.23**
4. Flexibility-Rigidity	.26***	.30***	.24***	-.25***
Disattenuated	.34***	.38***	.32***	-.30***
Difference Score	.18*	.12	-.05	-.08
Disattenuated	.23*	.15	-.07	-.09
5. Mood	.16*	.39***	.24**	-.27***
Disattenuated	.20*	.47***	.30***	-.30***
Difference Score	.17*	.33***	.11	-.21**
Disattenuated	.21**	.40***	.14	-.23**
6. Rhythmicity (Sleep)	.01	-.01	.01	-.07
Disattenuated	.01	-.01	.01	-.08
Difference Score	-.02	-.02	-.02	-.04
Disattenuated	-.03	-.04	-.03	-.05
7. Rhythmicity (Eating)	.09	-.01	.04	-.08
Disattenuated	.12	-.01	.05	-.09
Difference Score	.10	-.03	-.02	-.08
Disattenuated	.13	-.04	-.04	-.09
8. Rhythmicity (Daily Habits)	.12	.02	.05	-.14*
Disattenuated	.18*	.03	.07	-.19*
Difference Score	.15	.02	.01	-.11
Disattenuated	.22**	.03	.02	-.15*
9. Distractability	.37***	.04	.21**	.24***
Disattenuated	.47***	.06	.27***	-.28***
Difference Score	.33***	-.01	.12	-.17*
Disattenuated	.42***	-.03	.16	-.20*
10. Persistence	.37***	.06	.26***	-.17**
Disattenuated	.49***	.08	.35***	-.21**
Difference Score	.35***	.05	.22**	-.13
Disattenuated	.47***	.07	.30***	-.16*
Multiple R:	.49***	.54***	.41***	.40***
Difference Score Multiple R:	.46***	.54***	.35***	.29**

[1] N = 181 for all DOTS-R attribute--Harter Scale score comparisons, and N = 240 for all
DOTS-R attribute--CES-D Scale score comparisons. For the difference score analyses, N =
118 for comparisons involving Harter Scale Scores, and N = 144 for all comparisons involving CES-D Scale scores.

$*p < .05$; $**p < .01$; $***p < .001$

are disattenuated, the percentage of significant correlations associated with the T-alone model is 63%, and the corresponding percentage associated with the T-E model is 59% (or 16 of 27); these two proportions do not differ significantly.

In regard to Table 8.2, and the late adolescents studied by Windle et al. (1985), all significant correlations between, on the one hand, the three relevant Harter (1982) scale scores and the CES-D (Radloff, 1977) score, and on the other hand, the various temperament scores, are again in the expected direction—on the basis of inspection of the pertinent ethnotheory score distributions. However, while the percentage of significant T-alone/outcome score correlations (i.e., 50%) is significantly greater ($z = 2.30$, $p < .05$) than the corresponding percentage for the T-E/outcome score comparisons (33%), when the two sets of correlations are disattenuated the percentage for the T-alone model (i.e., 50%) and for the goodness of fit model (i.e., 43%) are comparable, and not significantly different ($z = 0.63$, $p > .05$). Moreover, the multiple correlations associated with the T-alone model and the T-E model are quite comparable.

Thus, across both the Hooker et al. and the Windle et al. studies it is reasonable to conclude that, in spite of the statistical constraints on the goodness of fit model, it generally does about as well as does the temperament-alone model in accounting for the variance in our outcome measures. Moreover, the amount of variance accounted for by both models is quite respectable, given both other amounts reported in the temperament literature in general (J. Lerner & R. Lerner, 1983), and the amounts found with the DOTS measure in particular (e.g., J. Lerner et al., 1985). These observations lead us to our concluding statements.

CONCLUSIONS

We believe that the DOTS-R—given its reliability and the number and magnitude of the (expected) T-alone correlations it has with the outcome measures—is a quite useful instrument to employ in tests of the goodness of fit model (cf. Windle, 1984). However, as was the case with tests of this model using the DOTS, we find no greater support for the contextual, goodness of fit model than for the personological, temperament-alone model. On the other hand, however, we have found that, by-and-large, the two models do about equally well in accounting for variance in outcome measures. As we noted earlier, this is the case, despite the several constraints that exist in finding support for the goodness of fit model. Thus, such comparability leads us to believe that if we could improve and extend our testing of the model its usefulness could be more unequivocally evaluated.

For instance, if we were able to introduce variation into contextual demands the problems involved with subtracting a constant from temperament scores might be obviated. For example, one solution might be to sample atypical families—wherein only one particular child is abused, neglected, or otherwise "scapegoated," and therefore may not be meeting a significant other's demands while his/her siblings are; such a sample, if large enough, might solve also the problem of not having enough children on both sides of the contextual demand. Of course, another way to introduce contextual variation would be to conduct cross-cultural studies, and here the work of Super and Harkness (1981) already has proven useful.

Finally, we should note that our tests of the model should be extended in several ways. We must begin to triangulate our measures of temperament by including direct assessments of the behavioral exchanges that occur when fit is, or is not, achieved; in this way a richer understanding may be gained of the processes that lead to positive or negative psychosocial outcomes. In addition, domains of individuality other than the temperamental one should be assessed simultaneously with temperament. Contextual demands exist for attributes of the person other than temperament, especially in the period within the life span within which we have focused our work—the adolescent transitionary one. Indeed, several physical, physiological, cognitive, emotional, *and* social transitions mark both ends of the adolescent period. The number and simultaneity of these individual and contextual changes suggest that this time of life may be the exemplary one within which to study the import of developing individuals attaining or not attaining fit with their changing world, and in so doing providing a basis of their own further successful or unsuccessful developments.

ACKNOWLEDGMENT

The preparation of this manuscript was supported in part by grants to the first two authors from the John D. and Catherine T. MacArthur Foundation and the William T. Grant Foundation. The work of Windle and of Hooker was supported in part by National Institute on Aging Grant T32AG00048. The authors thank Karen Cipriani, Athena Droogas, David F. Hultsch, Nancy Owens, M. Bernadette Reidy, and Fred W. Vondracek for their comments about previous drafts of this paper. Reprint requests should be sent to Richard M. Lerner, College of Human Development, The Pennsylvania State University, University Park, PA. 16802.

REFERENCES

Bell, R. Q. (1968). A reinterpretation of the direction of effects in studies of socialization. *Psychological Review, 75,* 81–95.

Bronfenbrenner, U. (1979). *The ecology of human development.* Cambridge, MA: Harvard University Press.

Cohen, J. (1977). *Statistical power analysis for the behavioral sciences.* New York: Academic Press.

Harter, S. (1982). The perceived competence scale for children. *Child Development, 53,* 87–97.

Hartup, W. W. (1978). Perspectives on child and family interaction: Past, present, and future. In R. M. Lerner & G. B. Spanier (Eds), *Child influences on marital and family interaction: A life-span perspective.* New York: Academic Press.

Hooker, K., Windle, M., East, P. L., Lenerz, K., & Lerner, R. M. (1985). *Temperament and competence in early adolescents: A test of a goodness of fit model.* Unpublished manuscript, The Pennsylvania State University.

Kagan, J. (1966). Reflection-impulsivity: The generality and dynamics of conceptual tempo. *Journal of Abnormal Psychology, 71,* 17–24.

Lerner, J. V. (1983). The role of temperament in psychosocial adaptation in early adolescence: A test of a ''goodness of fit'' model. *Journal of Genetic Psychology, 143,* 149–157.

Lerner, J. V. (1984). The import of temperament for psychosocial functioning: Tests of a ''goodness of fit'' model. *Merrill-Palmer Quarterly, 30,* 177–188.

Lerner, J. V., & Lerner, R. M. (1983). Temperament and adaptation across life: Theoretical and empirical issues. In P. B. Baltes & O. G. Brim, Jr. (Eds.), *Life-span development and behavior* (Vol. 5) (pp. 197–231). New York: Academic Press.

Lerner, J. V., Lerner, R. M., & Zabski, S. (1985). Temperament and elementary school children's actual and rated academic performance: A test of a ''goodness of fit'' model. *Journal of Child Psychology and Psychiatry, 26,* 125–136.

Lerner, R. M. (1982). Children and adolescents as producers of their own development. *Developmental Review, 2,* 342–370.

Lerner, R. M. (1984). *On the nature of human plasticity.* New York: Cambridge University Press.

Lerner, R. M. (1985). Individual and context in developmental psychology: Conceptual and theoretical issues. In J. R. Nesselroade & A. von Eye (Eds.), *Individual development and social change: Explanatory analysis* (pp. 155–187). New York: Academic Press.

Lerner, R. M., & Busch-Rossnagel, N. (1981). Individuals as producers of their development: Conceptual and empirical bases. In R. M. Lerner & N. A. Busch-Rossnagel (Eds.), *Individuals as producers of their development: A life-span perspective* (pp. 1–36). New York: Academic Press.

Lerner, R. M., & Lerner, J. V. (1983). *Children in their contexts: A goodness of fit model.* Paper presented at the Social Science Research Council Conference on: ''Biosocial Life-Span Approaches to Parental and Offspring Development.'' Elkridge, Maryland: Belmont Conference Center, May 22–May 25.

Lerner, R. M., Palermo, M., Spiro, A., III, & Nesselroade, J. R. (1982). Assessing the dimensions of temperamental individuality across the life-span: The Dimensions of Temperament Survey (DOTS). *Child Development, 53,* 149–159.

Palermo, M. (1982). *Child temperament and contextual demands: A test of the goodness of fit model.* Unpublished dissertation, The Pennsylvania State University.

Plomin, R., & Daniels, D. (1984). Temperament interactions. *Merrill-Palmer Quarterly, 30,* 149–162.

Radloff, L. S. (1977). The CES-D scale: A self-report depression scale for research in the general population. *Applied Psychological Measurement, 1,* 385–401.

Rosenthal, R., & Rosnow, R. L. (1984). *Essentials of behavioral research: Methods and data analysis.* New York: McGraw Hill.

Scarr, S., & McCartney, K. (1983). How people make their own environments: A theory of genotype → environment effects. *Child Development, 54,* 424–435.

Schenirla, T. C. (1957). The concept of development in comparative psychology. In D. B. Harris (Ed.), *The concept of development* (pp. 78–108). Minneapolis: University of Minnesota Press.

Seligman, M. E. P. (1975). *Helplessness: On depression, development and death.* San Francisco: Freeman.

Sorell, G. T., & Nowak, C. A. (1981). The role of physical attractiveness as a contributor to individual development. In R. M. Lerner & N. A. Busch-Rossnagel (Eds.), *Individuals as producers of their development: A life-span perspective* (pp. 389–446).   New York: Academic Press.

Super, C. M., & Harkness, S. (1981). Figure, ground, and gestalt: The cultural context of the active individual. In R. M. Lerner & N. A. Busch-Rossnagel (Eds.), *Individuals as producers of their development: A life-span perspective* (pp. 69–86). New York: Academic Press.

Super, C., & Harkness, S. (1982). *Constitutional amendments.* Presentation at the 1982 Occasional Temperament Conference, Salem, MA., October, 28–29.

Thomas, A., & Chess, S. (1977). *Temperament and development.* New York: Brunner/Mazel.

Windle, M. (1984). *The factor structure of the Revised Dimensions of Temperament Survey (DOTS-R): A cross-sectional study of measurement equivalence.* Unpublished doctoral dissertation, The Pennsylvania State University.

Windle, M., Hooker, K., Lenerz, K., East, P. L., & Lerner, R. M. (1985). *Temperament, perceived competence, and depression in late adolescents: A test of a goodness of fit model.* Unpublished manuscript, The Pennsylvania State University.

Windle, M., & Lerner, R. M. (1984). The role of temperament in dating relationships among young adults. *Merrill-Palmer Quarterly, 30,* 163–175.

9 Changes in Associations Between Characteristics and Interactions

Joan Stevenson-Hinde
Robert A. Hinde
*Medical Research Council Unit on the Development and Integration
of Behaviour, Cambridge University, Madingley, Cambridge*

That links can be found between children's temperamental characteristics and interactions with particular others is now reasonably well established. For example, "difficult" scores of infants have been shown to be related to maternal unresponsiveness (Campbell, 1979; Milliones, 1978) and to negative maternal responses (Kelly, 1976). With preschool children, meaningful associations have been found between temperamental characteristics and behavioral interactions at home (e.g., Dunn & Kendrick, 1980; Graham, Rutter, & George, 1973; Hinde, Easton, Mellor, & Tamplin, 1982; Stevenson-Hinde & Simpson, 1982) and school (Billman & McDevitt, 1980, Hinde, Stevenson-Hinde, & Tamplin, 1985). Yet the findings are not wholly consistent. Vaughn, Taraldson, Crichton and Egeland (1981) and Bates, Olson, Pettit and Bayles (1982) found few relations between infants' difficult temperament and mother/child interactions, and in the preschool studies the correlations were at best modest. Such a situation, in which correlations are more than ephemeral yet tantalizingly far from ubiquitous, demands further understanding of the dynamics of the interactions involved. Our aim here is to take some initial steps in that direction.

INITIAL CONSIDERATIONS

Behavioral Style

"Temperament can be equated to the term *behavioral style*. Each refers to the *how* rather than the *what* (abilities and content) or the *why* (motivations) of behavior" (Thomas & Chess, 1977, p. 9). However, even within the Thomas

115

and Chess framework, some dimensions of temperament are somewhat related to behavioral content. Furthermore, other workers (Campos, Barrett, Lamb, Goldsmith, & Stenberg, 1983) suggest that temperament is related to particular aspects of content, namely discrete emotions, and that differences in parameters of style (e.g., threshold) are not necessarily correlated across emotional dimensions (e.g., Goldsmith & Campos, 1982; Rothbart, 1981). They define temperament as referring to "individual differences in the intensive and temporal parameters of behavioral expressions of emotionality and arousal" and point out that Rothbart's (1981) dimensions of temperament relate fairly directly to different emotions (or affects), whilst those of Buss and Plomin (1975, 1984) are only very broadly related to specific affects and those of Thomas and Chess (1977) are largely unrelated. Now emotions are loosely, and to different degrees, related to behavioral content. Thus the several temperament dimensions reflect style (or quality), content and affect to different extents. On these grounds alone we must expect associations between temperamental characteristics and particular aspects of behavior to be far from ubiquitous and correlations not necessarily to be high. (We may note in passing that this raises the issue of what it is that the different dimensions of temperament have in common. An act of faith that they have something in common provided the basis for this symposium, but we would do well to remember that it is little more.)

Multiple Determinants

A second issue relates to the discussion of continuity vs. discontinuity. The overtones of biological determinism, which accompanied earlier approaches to temperament, have given way to a more flexible approach, and we must bear constantly in mind that the concept of psychological structures more or less isomorphic with behavior (e.g., Kagan, 1980) is misleading. We are concerned not with static entities whose effects appear as invariant action, but with propensities whose interactions with each other depend on a variety of conditions operating at the moment (Hinde & Bateson, 1984; Plomin, 1983). That being the case, correlations are unlikely to be high. If a behavioral item is equally affected by only four independent variables, each having separate effects, its correlation with any one cannot be higher than 0.50.

Social Behavior

Third, temperamental characteristics are inferred from behavior, and most of the behavior with which we are concerned is social behavior, influenced by one or more interactants. Now the study of social behavior involves several levels, each with qualities not relevant to the level below. What we actually observe are usually interactions—A does P to B, B does Q to A, A does R to B, and so on. Of course P, Q, R etc. may overlap in time, and there are many other possible complications, but it is useful to apply the term interaction to exchanges that are limited in time. A convenient level for describing interactions involves specifying the content (i.e., what the individuals are doing together—fighting, playing, conversing, etc.) and its quality or style (are they playing affectionately or competitively, gently or vigorously, etc.). Interactions may involve properties not relevant to the behavior of individuals on their own—for instance an isolated individual can talk but cannot converse, and "well-meshed" applies only to the behavior of a dyad.

The next level, that of the relationship, involves a series of interactions in time between individuals known to each other. Again, relationships have properties that are not relevant to isolated interactions: these may depend, for instance, on the relative frequency and patterning of the constituent interactions. Clearly the concept of temperament is relevant to only some of the properties of interactions and relationships: thus, according to the definition (see above) it may have little relevance to the content of interactions, but be highly relevant to their quality, and indirectly relevant to other properties such as intimacy and interpersonal perception (see Hinde, 1979).

The behavior of each individual in an interaction will depend in part on the behavior of the other, and indeed on the expectations each has of the other—the role of expectations being even more important in interactions that take place in the context of a longer-term relationship. But at the same time the behavior of individuals depends on other relationships they have experienced in the past. Thus, the nature of an interaction or relationship depends on the natures of the participants, and the natures of the participants depend in part on the nature of the current relationship and past relationships they have experienced. At the same time each interaction and relationship is affected by the social nexus in which the participants are embedded (A's relationship with B is affected by B's relationship with C) and by the social norms and expectations that each participant brings to the relationship. In turn the social nexus is constituted by the dyadic (and higher order) relationships within it, and social norms are transmitted and transmuted by the agency of interactions and relationships. It is thus helpful to think of the properties of interactions and relationships as depending dynamically on two dialectics—one with the natures of the individuals and the other with the nature of the social situation.

Thus, what we assess is seldom a property of one of the individuals. Indeed, measures of social behavior may be viewed along a continuum, with the two end points never found in practice: Towards one end lie aspects of behavior that depend very largely on a characteristic of one partner or the other, such as certain features of the behavior of a very anxious mother with her baby, and towards the other, aspects of behavior that depend on characteristics of both partners in interaction, such as joint play. We may hope that behavior reflected in scales of temperamental characteristics falls towards the "individual" end, but how close it does is an empirical issue.

That children do in fact behave differently according to whom they are with and/or where they are was amply demonstrated in some of our own data, concerning interactions observed at home or in preschool. Eleven home behavioral items with the focal child as subject were comparable with 16 school items (e.g., child friendly to mother with child friendly to adults and child friendly to peers in school), yielding 20 correlation coefficients. Of these, none was significant at 42 months, and three at 50 months. That this was not due merely to inadequacies in the data is shown by the fact that there were meaningful *patterns* of correlations between home and school behavioral data: For instance, the proportion of interactions with peers in school that involved active hostility was associated with infrequent positive and neutral interactions with the mother at home, and also with maternal permissiveness (at 42 months) or hostility (at 50 months) (see Hinde & Tamplin, 1983).

Again, when behavior to teachers and behavior to peers in the classroom were compared, only 3 out of 20 correlations were significant at 42 months, and 7 out of 20 at 50 months (Hinde, Easton, Mellor, & Tamplin, 1983). And finally there were also small but significant differences between the behavior shown to friends and to nonfriends in school (Hinde, Titmus, Easton, & Tamplin, 1985).

Other Factors

In addition to the social context, we must expect the physical situation (e.g., home vs. school, classroom vs. playground) to affect the relations between temperament and behavior. The preceding discussion also implies that the dialectic between individual characteristics and relationships may change as cognitive factors become more important (see Hinde, Perret-Clermont, & Stevenson-Hinde, 1985). Finally, the associations between temperamental characteristics and interactions may be affected by other aspects of the individual concerned, such as sex and temperamental characteristics other than the one under consideration.

Summary

Thus, temperamental characteristics cannot be viewed purely as aspects of the behavioral style of an individual. They may vary, at least to some extent, with the content of behavior. And they are affected by the social and physical situation, cognitive development, and by other aspects of the individual.

Of course, we must continue to study temperamental characteristics in their own right, building on existing scales of measurement (reviewed in Hubert, Wachs, Peters-Martin, & Gandour, 1982) and knowledge of changes during development (McDevitt, this volume). Yet it is time to seek also a higher-order level of analysis. Thus in what follows we are concerned not with changes in temperamental characteristics themselves, nor with changes in social interactions, but rather with changes in the associations between the two. The parameters for which we could find data, and which we shall consider here are: context (e.g., home vs. school), age, sex, and other temperamental characteristics. Much of the material is taken from a study of children's behavior and interactions at home and preschool.[1]

EFFECTS OF CONTEXT ON ASSOCIATIONS

Similar Associations at Home and School

In our own study, dimensions of temperament assessed at home were significantly correlated with items of behavior both at home and at school. Our present concern is with whether the behavior associated with the temperamental characteristics was similar in home and in school. Often it was. For instance, moody scores of 42-month-old girls were associated with high attention seeking at home (interview, +.58**) and with a high frequency of interactions with adults at

---

[1]Children of two-child families were observed at home and in preschool when they were 3½-years-old (n = 24 boys, 21 girls) and again 8 months later (n = 21 boys, 16 girls). In addition, mothers were interviewed at home at the earlier age (n = 26 boys, 21 girls) and again at the later age (n = 24 boys, 17 girls).

Temperamental characteristics. These were assessed by a maternal interview, developed by Garside et al. (1975). For present purposes we have selected only those dimensions that involved at least four items. These were: *active* (always on the move, 5 items), *moody* (inequable, irritable, sulky, 6 items), *intense* (over-intense expression of feelings, 4 items) and *shy* (initial withdrawal, 3 items; plus not settling in, 3 items). Spearman correlation coefficients over 8 months were: .73 for active, .50 for moody, .53 for intense, and .61 for shy (n=41, $p<.001$, two-tailed). No sex differences arose at either age for these four characteristics, except for intense at 42 months, where boys were slightly higher than girls ($p<.05$, Mann-Whitney U test, two-tailed).

The remaining measures, collected within the same period (2–4 weeks) as the temperamental characteristics, formed three sets:

Home ratings. These were based on a semistructured maternal interview given at home prior to the visit for the temperament interview. Twenty-two ratings are considered here: 5 of mother/child interactions, 4 of father/child, 2 of sibling/child, 2 of peer/child and 9 of problem behavior (for further detail, see Simpson & Stevenson-Hinde, 1985). In addition, a mood questionnaire provided four assessments, of maternal outward irritability, inward irritability, depression and anxiety (see Snaith et al., 1978).

Home observations. These were made by spoken commentary onto magnetic tape and coded by a modification of Lytton (1973) and Caldwell's (1969) coding schemes. This provided 49 measures of mother/child interactions (for further detail, see Hinde & Tamplin, 1983).

School observations. These were made by the same method as used in the home observations, to provide 31 measures of child/peer and child/adult interactions in a preschool playgroup (for further detail, see Hinde et al. 1983).

school (observation, +.43*). Similarly, the more negative mood shown by 50-month-old boys, the more inwardly and outwardly irritable were the mothers (self-ratings, +.49*, +.57**) and the more reactively hostile were teachers at school (observation, +.43*). (All correlations reported here are Spearman rank-order coefficients: *$p<.05$, **$p<.01$, two-tailed.)

Such similarities sometimes involved not similar measures, but measures of a similar type. For instance the interactions of active 50-month-old girls with their mothers tended to contain low proportions of a variety of positive and neutral items, and a high occurrence of tantrums: With peers at school, they had low relative frequencies of friendly behavior and high relative frequencies of hostile behavior.

More Associations at Home or School

One expects that if characteristics are rated at home, they should associate more strongly with other behavior at home than at school; and vice-versa. This seems to be the case. For example, Billman and McDevitt (1980), who used temperament ratings from home and from school, found stronger links between school ratings and school behavior than between home ratings and school behavior. In our study in which temperament was assessed only at home but behavior was observed at both home and school, stronger links were found between some temperamental characteristics and home observations than between the characteristics and school observations (Table 9.1). However, this finding was not ubiquitous (see moody), but did occur for active boys and girls, intense girls, and shy girls. Further investigation is necessary if we are to assess degrees of specificity or generality across situations. The outcome will no doubt depend on age, sex, and the characteristic in question.

Different Associations Between Home and School

The characteristic shy was based on reports of interactions with individuals other than the mother, and it is thus not surprising that it related differently to behavior with the mother at home and with others at school. Whereas shy 42-month-old boys tended to initiate joint activities with their mothers (+.43*) they tended to interact less than nonshy boys with peers in school (−.43*). At 50 months, the more shy the boy, the more physically friendly he was to the mother (+.50*), but the less (verbally) friendly with teachers in school (−.44*). Similarly, the more shy 50-month-old girls, the less passive they were with the mother at home (−.54*) but the more passive at school (+.54*). The data suggest that high shy ratings are associated with frequent interactions at home and infrequent ones at school, and are in harmony with the finding that children who had much warm interchange with their mothers tended to interact less with peers in school (Hinde & Tamplin, 1983).

TABLE 9.1
The Percentage of Significant Correlations Between Each
Characteristic and Interactions at Home and School

	42 Months		50 Months	
	Boys	Girls	Boys	Girls
Active				
home ratings (26 measures)	12%	12%	4% ____	15%
home observations (36 measures)	14% ----	4%	4% ____	14%
school observations (31 measures)	3% ----	0%	3% ____	8%
Intense				
home ratings	19% ____	23%	19% ____	31%
home observations	0% ____	12%	0% ____	14%
school observations	3% ----	0%	0% ____	6%
Shy				
home ratings	8%	8%	15% ____	23%
home observations	4% ____	10%	4% ____	18%
school observations	3% ____	6%	10% ____	16%
Moody				
home ratings	12% ____	19%	31% ----	15%
home observations	0%	0%	4% ____	8%
school observations	6%	6%	13% ----	3%

---- boys more than girls
____ girls more than boys

EFFECTS OF TIME ON ASSOCIATIONS

Associations between characteristics and behavior might change with time in sign, from positive to negative or vice-versa, or in strength. The former is likely to occur only with long time intervals, or to be mediated by a particular event, such as the advent or removal of a stressor. Thus, the association between "difficult" infants and "placating" mothers (Bates et al., 1982) might conceivably change to one involving less placating mothers if the mother had an additional responsibility, such as another child.

Turning to changes in strength, there is some evidence that links become tighter from infancy to preschool. In our study, where family circumstances did not change much over the 8 months between assessments, several sets of data nevertheless showed stronger correlations with temperamental characteristics at the later age. For example, correlations (sexes together) between the characteristic active and the five aggressive items in preschool (themselves at most moderately intercorrelated) varied from $-.12$ to $+.09$ at 42 months, but from $.32*$ to $.48**$ at 50 months. Such a tightening could result from adaptation to school and/or a decreased tolerance by school adults.

Looking at boys and girls separately (Table 9.1), tightening over time at both home and school occurred for active girls (from 5 significant correlations at 42 months to 14 at 50 months), shy girls (from 9 to 20) and moody boys (from 5 to 14). The more active or moody the child, the more negative and the fewer positive interactions. For example, the more active the girl at 50 months, the more tantrums (.62**) and the less mother enjoyed the child (−.61**) (home ratings), the less mother verbally friendly (−.60*) and express pleasure (−.53*) (home observations), and the less child friendly to peers (−.60*) and the more adult reactive hostile to child (.56*) (school observations). On the other hand, the more shy the girl, the more positive and fewer negative interactions. For example, the more shy the 50-month-old girl, the fewer tantrums (−.56*) and more joint activities with mother (.62**) and father (.70**) (home ratings), the fewer inhibitory controls by mother (−.54*) and more mother solicitous (+.53*) (home observations), and the less adult reactive hostile (−.56*) and peers disconfirm (−.70**) (school observations). A possible explanation for these correlations, which differ from those for shy boys, is offered in the next section.

In addition, several mundane explanations for such changes should be considered. Where the correlations involved direct observations, one possibility is that the data were less reliable at the earlier age. However, although the school data were based on shorter observation times at 42 months, split halves reliabilities were not markedly different between the two data sets. And the possibility that the temperamental characteristics were based on questions more appropriate at the later age is rendered unlikely by the fact that the instrument was a semistructured interview about what the child actually did, with ratings made by the interviewer. In the case of the school data novelty might have produced a damping of the behavior, or a ''floor'' effect at the earlier age, but this explanation could not apply to the home data.

EFFECTS OF SEX ON ASSOCIATIONS

More Associations for One Sex than the Other

Cameron (1978) and Keating and Manning (1974) have suggested that characteristics of girls are more closely related to mother/infant interactions than characteristics of boys. Such a trend was not clearly present in our data at 42 months, but was strongly suggested at 50 months. Of the four characteristics considered here, there were more significant correlations for girls than boys at 50 months for active, intense, and shy, but not for moody (Table 9.1). School interactions were involved as well, so that stronger links for girls are not restricted to mother/child interactions.

Different Associations between Sexes

Different links between activity and interactions have been found for boys vs. girls by Buss (1981). He correlated actometer readings when the child was 3- 4-

years-old with parent/child interactions as the child attempted to complete cognitive tasks. Activity was associated with positive interactions between fathers and sons, but negative interactions between fathers and daughters. With mothers, activity was correlated with negative interactions for both sons and daughters.

Our findings agree with Buss's insofar as active 50-month-old boys had a positive sibling relationship (interview, $+.20$), while active girls did not ($-.55*$); and at preschool, active girls were often disconfirmed by adults (observation, $+.35$), while active boys were not ($-.50*$). However, these were the only large differences ($\geq.70$). Similarly, for moody and intense there were only one or two large differences at either age (out of a total of 106 possible at each age, see footnote 1). However, for shy, there were four large differences at 42 months and 12 at 50 months (Table 9.2). Furthermore, the differences formed a consistent pattern: Shyness in boys was correlated with fewer positive and more negative interactions, while the opposite held for girls. In addition, the interactions involved all possible participants: mother, father, sibling, teachers, and peers. The interviews provided a clue as to why such differences were more common at the later age. Some mothers complained that their boys should have grown out of their shyness by this age, when they had passed their fourth birthday and had been in nursery school for a year, while others commented with approval that their girls still preferred being at home with mother. It may be that mothers become less accepting of shy boys but more accepting of shy girls as they get older (see also Kagan & Reznick, this volume; Simpson & Stevenson-Hinde, 1985). In a different study mothers rated shy as a feminine characteristic, while assertive was rated as masculine (Maccoby & Sants, 1984). Thus, the data are compatible with the view that parental values may be mediating the differences observed. Mothers may prefer girls to be shy, and boys to be assertive.

However in other cases, alternative possible explanations of such differences must not be forgotten. Thus, correlations could appear to differ between the sexes for the relatively trivial reason that extreme behavior is more common in one sex than the other. Or, a given characteristic may relate to behavioral items which, though different for boys and girls, represent mother/child relationships that are in some respects similar. Nor must we lose sight of the possibility that the behavioral categories may have subtly different qualities in boys and girls. To take an example from a comparison between behavioral items in the two situations, child hostility to the mother at home was associated with frequent girl-peer interactions but infrequent boy-peer interactions in school. One possibility is that the home hostility involved "assertiveness" in girls which was displayed also in school but "uncooperativeness" in boys (Hinde & Tamplin, 1983).

EFFECTS OF OTHER CHARACTERISTICS ON ASSOCIATIONS

Thus far, we have been considering links involving only one characteristic at a time. Now we are in fact dealing with a whole individual, so that it would seem

TABLE 9.2

Spearman Correlations Between the Characteristic Shy and Interactions at Home and School Which Showed Large Differences (>.70 Points) Between Boys and Girls

	42 Months				50 Months	
	Boys	Girls			Boys	Girls
Home Ratings (26 measures)	+.28	-.67**	squabble/sib	M sensitive to C	-.51**	+.35
				M enjoys C	-.52**	+.50*
				Joint activities/M	-.23	+.62**
				Joint activities/F	-.11	+.70**
				Relationship/sib	-.38	+.45
Home Observations (49 measures)				C conversational questions M	-.43	+.56*
				C active hostile M	+.50*	-.33
				C passive	+.35	-.54*
				M/C activity changes	+.40	-.67**
School Observations (31 measures)	+.30	-.49*	C initiates to adult	C reactive hostile peers	+.26	-.50*
	+.15	-.77**	peers disconfirm C	peers disconfirm C	+.15	-.70**
	+.32	-.38	adult disconfirms C	adult disconfirms C	+.38	-.37

*$p < .05$; **$p < .01$, 2-tailed

that the more characteristics one can deal with at once, the better prediction one might get, providing each characteristic is relevant to the interaction in question. We have not space here to explore all possible combinations of characteristics, so will select an example, using the nursery school observations taken when children were 50-months-old (Table 9.3). At school, adults tended to disconfirm (ignore, change subject) boys who were shy (.38), but not boys who were intense ($-.37$). Furthermore, shy and intense were not intercorrelated (.14). Nevertheless, when the intense scores were subtracted from shy scores, the correlation of "shy-minus-intense" with disconfirm rose to .56**. Similarly, shy-minus-intense correlated more strongly with adult reactive hostile to boys ($-.42$) than with either shy ($-.12$) or intense (.27) alone.

On the other hand for girls, a single characteristic was a better predictor than shy-minus-intense, although intense and shy were intercorrelated ($-.46$). Thus, adding two intercorrelated characteristics (i.e., for the girls), did *not* provide better prediction to school, but adding two unrelated characteristics did (i.e., for the boys). Nevertheless, adding does make the point that adults disconfirmed shy-minus-intense boys ($+.56$**), but not shy-minus-intense girls ($-.58$*, see previous section).

SUMMARY

We have focused on some factors that may affect correlations between temperamental characteristics and social interactions, and Table 9.4 provides a summary. Section A of the table shows that temperamental characteristics are somewhat situation dependent, in that some associations between temperament ratings and interactions were stronger when the ratings were made in the same context as that in which the interactions were observed. Furthermore, for at least one characteristic, shy, the *direction* of the association changed with context. As the child gets older (section B), there tends to be a tightening of associations. Although this was not ubiquitous, there was little evidence of the converse, namely a

TABLE 9.3
Spearman Correlations Between Two Characteristics
(Alone and in Combination) and Two Negative Adult-to-Child
Interactions in Preschool, at 50 Months

	Adult Disconfirms Child		Adult is Reactive Hostile to Child	
	Boys	Girls	Boys	Girls
	(n=21)	(n=16)	(n=21)	(n=16)
Shy	+.38	-.37	-.12	-.56*
Intense	-.37	+.66**	.27	.09
Shy-Intense	+.56**	-.58*	-.42	-.33

*$p < .05$; **$p < .01$, 2 tailed

TABLE 9.4

Differences in Correlations Between Temperamental Characteristics v. Interactions, depending on
(A) Context, (B) Age, (C) Sex, and (D) Other Characteristics

Differences	
In Strength	In Direction

A. Context

Active v. home observations > active v. school observations (boys, girls)

Intense v. home observations > intense v. school observations (girls)

Shy v. home observations > shy v. school observations (girls)

School behavior v. school temperamental characteristics > school behavior v. home temperamental characteristics (Billman & McDevitt, 1980)

Shy v. more activities etc. at home but less activities etc. at school (Boys, 42 and 50 mos; girls 50 mos)

B. Age

Active v. aggressive school interactions at 42 mos < at 50 mos (sexes together)

Active v. home and school interactions at 42 mos < at 50 mos (girls)

Shy v. home and school interactions at 42 mos < at 50 mos (girls)

Moody v. home and school interactions at 42 mos < at 50 mos (boys)

C. Sex

Active v. home or school interactions of girls > of boys (50 mos)

Intense v. home or school interactions of girls > of boys (50 mos)

Shy v. home or school interactions of girls > of boys (50 mos)

Temperamental characteristics v. home interactions of girls > of boys (Cameron, 1978; Keating & Manning, 1974)

Shy v. positive interactions at home and school for girls but negative interactions for boys (50 mos)

Active v. positive father/child interactions for boys but negative interactions for girls (Buss, 1981)

D. Other Characteristics

Shy or intense alone v. negative interactions from adults at school < shy-intense together (Boys, 50 mos) weakening of associations with age. Considering sex (section C), girls sometimes produced stronger associations than boys, especially in the context of the mother/child relationship. In addition, the direction of some correlations differed between the sexes. While shy was associated with more positive and fewer negative interactions for girls, the opposite held for boys. This difference occurred not only in interactions with mother, but also with father, sibling, teachers, and peers (Table 9.2). On the other hand, for active, the differences in direction occurred only in the context of father/child, and not mother/child, interactions. Whereas active boys had positive interactions with fathers, active girls had negative ones (Buss, 1981). Finally, it is possible for a combination of characteristics to produce stronger associations than any single characteristic (section D), although we have no rule as yet for deciding which combination will be a good predictor for which sex. Indeed, in no section of Table 9.4 does an effect hold for all possible cases. For example, differences in associations due to sex of the child occurred only for some characteristics.

To improve prediction, of when strong associations between temperamental characteristics and interactions will arise and when they will change, more data are needed. The paucity of results to fit such a framework is undoubtedly due to the rarity of studies in which the relation of temperamental characteristics to interactions has not only been assessed, but also assessed separately for individuals who differ in other ways (age, sex, etc.) and/or who are observed in different contexts. Only when such data are available will further understanding of the dynamics of individual development be within our reach.

ACKNOWLEDGMENT

This work was supported by the Medical Research Council and the Royal Society.

REFERENCES

Bates, J. E., Olson, S. L., Pettit, G. S., & Bayles, K. (1982). Dimensions of individuality in the mother-infant relationships at six months of age. *Child Development, 52,* 446–461.

Billman, J., & McDevitt, S. C. (1980). Convergence of parent and observer ratings of temperament with observations of peer interaction in nursery school. *Child Development, 51,* 395–400.

Buss, D. M. (1981). Predicting parent-child interactions from children's activity level. *Developmental Psychology, 17,* 59–65.

Buss, A. H., & Plomin, R. (1975). *A temperament theory of personality development.* New York: Wiley.

Buss, A. H. , & Plomin, R. (1984). *Temperament: Early developing personality traits.* Hillsdale, NJ: Lawrence Erlbaum Associates.

Caldwell, B. M. (1969). A new "APPROACH" to behavioral ecology. In I. P. Hill (Ed.), *Minnesota symposia on child psychology, Vol. 2.* Minneapolis: University of Minnesota Press.

Cameron, J. R. (1978). Parental treatment, children's temperament, and the risk of childhood behavioral problems: 2. Initial temperament, parental attitudes, and the incidence and form of behavioral problems. *American Journal of Orthopsychiatry, 48,* 140–147.

Campbell, S. B. G. (1979). Mother-infant interaction as a function of maternal ratings of temperament. *Child Psychiatry and Human Development, 10,* 67–76.

Campos, J. J., Barrett, K. C., Lamb, M. E., Goldsmith, H. H., & Stenberg, C. (1983). Socioemotional development. In P. H. Mussen (Ed.), *Handbook of child psychology.* New York: Wiley.

Dunn, J., & Kendrick, C. (1980). Studying temperament and parent-child interaction: Comparison of interview and direct observation. *Developmental Medicine and Child Neurology, 22,* 484–496.

Garside, R. F., Birch, H., Scott, D., Chambers, S., Kolvin, I., Tweddle, E. G., & Barber, L. M. (1975). Dimensions of temperament in infant school children. *Journal of Child Psychology and Psychiatry, 16,* 219–231.

Goldsmith, H. H., & Campos, J. J. (1982). Toward a theory of infant temperament. In R. N. Emde & R. J. Harmon (Eds.), *The development of attachment and affiliative systems: Psychobiological aspects.* New York: Plenum.

Graham, P., Rutter, M., & George, S. (1973). Temperamental characteristics as predictors of behavior disorders in children. *American Journal of Orthopsychiatry, 43,* 328–339.

Hinde, R. A. (1979). *Towards understanding relationships.* London: Academic Press.

Hinde, R. A., & Bateson, P. (1984). Discontinuities versus continuities in behavioural development and the neglect of process. *International Journal of Behavioural Development, 7,* 129–143.

Hinde, R. A., Easton, D. F., Mellor, R. E., & Tamplin, A. M. (1982). Temperamental characteristics of 3–4 year-olds and mother-child interaction. In *Temperamental differences in infants and young children.* Ciba Foundation Symposium 89, London: Pitman.

Hinde, R. A., Easton, D. F., Mellor, R. E., & Tamplin, A. (1983). Nature and determinants of preschoolers' differential behaviour to adults and peers. *British Journal of Developmental Psychology, 1,* 3–19.

Hinde, R. A., Perret-Clermont, A. N., & Stevenson-Hinde, J. (Eds.). (1985). *Relationships & Cognitive development.* Oxford: Oxford University Press.

Hinde, R. A., Stevenson-Hinde, J., & Tamplin, A. (1985). Characteristics of 3–4 year olds assessed at home and interactions in preschool. *Developmental Psychology, 21.*

Hinde, R. A., & Tamplin, A. (1983). Relations between mother-child interaction and behaviour in preschool. *British Journal of Developmental Psychology, 1,* 231–257.

Hinde, R. A., Titmus, G., Easton, D. F., & Tamplin, A. (1985). Incidence of "Friendship" and behaviour to strong associates vs. non-associates in preschoolers. *Child Development, 56,* 234–245.

Hubert, N., Wachs, T. D., Peters-Martin, P., & Gandour, M. (1982). The study of early temperament: Measurement and conceptual issues. *Child Development, 53,* 571–600.

Kagan, J. (1980). Four questions in psychological development. *International Journal of Behavioral Development, 3,* 231–241.

Keating, G. W., & Manning, T. M. (1974). Infant temperament and sex of infant: Effects on maternal behavior. In P. M. Shereshefsky & L. J. Yarrow (Eds.), *Psychological aspects of a first pregnancy and early postnatal adaptation.* New York: Raven Press.

Kelly, P. (1976). The relation of infant's temperament and mother's psychopathology to interaction in early infancy. In K. F. Riegal & J. A. Meachant (Eds.), *The developing individual in a changing world* (Vol. 11). Chicago: Aldine.

Lytton, H. (1973). Three approaches to the study of parent-child interaction: Ethological, interview and experimental. *Journal of Child Psychology & Psychiatry, 14,* 1–17.

Maccoby, E., & Sants, H. K. A. (1984, Feb.). Personal Communication.

Milliones, J. (1978). Relationship between perceived child temperament and maternal behavior. *Child Development, 49,* 1255–1257.

Plomin, R. (1983). Childhood temperament. In B. Lahey & A. Kazdin (Eds.), *Advances in clinical child psychology* (Vol. 6). New York: Academic Press.

Rothbart, M. K. (1981). Measurement of temperament in infancy. *Child Development, 52,* 569–578.

Simpson, A. E., & Stevenson-Hinde, J. (1985). Temperamental characteristics of three- to four-year-old boys and girls and child-family interactions. *Journal of Child Psychology and Psychiatry, 26,* 43–53.

Snaith, R. P., Constantopoulos, A. A., Jardine, M. Y., & McGuffin, P. (1978). A clinical scale for the self-assessment of irritability. *British Journal of Psychiatry, 132,* 164–171.

Stevenson-Hinde, J., & Simpson, A. E. (1982). Temperament and relationships. In *Temperamental differences in infants and young children.* Ciba Foundation Symposium 89, London: Pitman.

Thomas, A., & Chess, S. (1977). *Temperament and development.* New York: Brunner/Mazel.

Vaughn, B., Taraldson, B., Crichton, L., & Egeland, B. (1981). The assessment of infant temperament: a critique of the Carey Infant Temperament Questionnaire. *Infant Behavior and Development, 4,* 1–18.

10 Temperament, Development, and Culture

Charles M. Super
Sara Harkness
Judge Baker Guidance Center and
Harvard School of Public Health

Psychology and psychiatry, central disciplines in the quest for understanding individual behavioral dispositions, have never had an easy time with group differences. Without major exception, dimensions of variation that can be useful in theory and practice concerning individuals have become awkward, confusing, and invidious when they are used to characterize sets of individuals. Race differences in intelligence, sex differences in field-dependence, cultural differences in personality, these and other extensions of individual psychology to natural group differences repeat a pattern of error that, while possibly as necessary for growth as falling off the bicycle while learning to ride, can be seen now as wasteful and injurious. It gives one pause at the threshold of research on culture and temperament.

The flaw that organizes this pattern of failure is rooted in the way the social and behavioral sciences divide epistomological questions among themselves— what pieces of reality one tries to explain and how one goes about it. We believe that efforts in the past decade to integrate concepts from the social and the behavioral disciplines, centered on the developing individual, offer an appropriate way to approach the issues of temperament, development, and culture, and in this chapter we attempt to demonstrate both the need and the promise. The first section outlines the problem of development-environment systems and their importance to the comparison of naturally occurring groups of individuals. Selected reports of cultural differences in temperament-like behaviors are reviewed in the second section. Finally, we outline four questions that need further exploration before comparative studies of temperament can be sensibly interpreted, exploration that will, in turn, contribute to our understanding of development in each culture.

ENVIRONMENTS ARE ORGANIZED AND THEY ORGANIZE DEVELOPMENT

Psychology in general has taken as its focus the individual as an organized entity. Its paradigm of investigation, beyond the correlation of individual differences, is the isolation and study of features of the environment as they impinge on the individual. Psychology and related disciplines have therefore tended to overlook the significance of environmental *organization* as a regulator of development. This is true in developmental traditions that, inspired by Gesell, Piaget, Freud, and Erikson, emphasize internally regulated stages or sequences of development, and those, like social learning theory, that focus on discrete interactions with the environment. Single features of the psychosocial environment, we are now learning, have little importance for development by themselves, even for relatively gross outcomes; it is the interaction of environmental features, and of environmental features with individual characteristcs, that influence growth (Sameroff & Chandler, 1975). The same is no doubt true for less visible features of development, where the personal construction of reality depends on a large complex of sustained meaning, and it is exactly the organization of sustained meaning, of integrated symbols and relations, that cultures provide.

Anthropology and sociology, in complement to psychology, do take the environmental system as the primary focus of study. They have formulated concepts such as socioeconomic status that are useful in studying populations, and they have addressed questions such as why socioeconomic status makes sense as an analytic concept in some cultures and not in others. In other words, the environmental disciplines work with theories of the structure and functioning of social orders. They tend to neglect, in turn, the constraints imposed by the nature of individuals and individual development.

The complementarity of the individual and environmental disciplines is striking and would seem to offer an opportunity for important synthesis. But how the individual and environmental systems interface to regulate development is not a question easily addressed by the traditional tools of either kind of discipline, for the figure of one perspective is ground for the other, and the full Gestalt invokes new rules of organization (Super & Harkness, 1981). Nevertheless, the comparative study of temperament necessarily invokes this larger system. To some degree, in fact, the interface of individual and environment is already central to the temperament literature. Clinical and developmental considerations, especially as they are derived from the founding work of Thomas and Chess (e.g., 1977), rest as much on the conept of "goodness of fit" (between temperament type and environmental demands) as they do on the premise of relatively stable, innately disposed behavioral style. Temperament theory in this sense is more easily abstracted to the model addressed here than most theories born of psychology and psychiatry. The critical point to be elaborated, however, is that the organization of environments may influence the organization, expression, and function of temperament. Classical theories of societal functioning provide a background in how customs, values, institutions and roles co-evolve; what remains to be constructed is a framework for linking theory at this level with the more immediate factors influencing development and temperament.

The "developmental niche" has been proposed as a way of linking psychological and behavioral theories of development with general theories of societies and cultures (Harkness & Super, 1983; Super, 1985; Super & Harkness, 1981, 1982, in press a). Briefly, the niche consists of the physical and social setting children are found in; the culturally regulated customs for child care, socialization, and behavior management; and the psychology of the caretakers, including beliefs and values about the nature of development. Each of these three dimensions of the developmental niche has its own set of ties to other cultural features, such as physical ecology, methods of economic production, marriage patterns, political organization, and ethics. There is a psychological dynamic, as well, to keep the three dimensions of the niche in some harmony, that is, for example, customarily to place children in settings that are believed to be good for them. Of particular importance to the study of temperament is the sequence of developmental niches that a culture creates for its children at different stages of development, stages which are themselves defined in part by the culture.

A concept such as the developmental niche allows theory to recognize that environments can not only affect the average value of individual attributes (as traditional psychological theory permits), but also that they can influence the organization of development and indeed the environment-development relationship. The theoretical failure to see relationships as variable occurs, and is occasionally noted (e.g., Posner, 1978), in many branches of psychology. There are few examples in the developmental literature that focus on this issue, but one from the area of cognition is provided by the Bogota Study of Malnutrition and Development (Super, 1984; see also Herrera et al., 1980). The intercorrelation of environmental features thought to promote cognitive growth is different there from that found in American samples. For example, Bogota mothers who use multiple caretakers for their 3-year-olds tend to teach their children the names for colors, etc., while the opposite relationship holds in urban America: *not* having multiple caretakers is associated with greater maternal teaching. Similarly, the relationship of home environment to child development differs in the American and Colombian samples: provision of a toy chest for the child, for example, is correlated with cognitive evaluations in the former but not the latter. In short, both the structure of the environment and the relationship of specific environmental features to individual development are to some degree cultural constructions.

This observation suggests that the meaning of behaviors taken to reflect temperament is derived in part from their place in the environment-development system. Culturally comparative research on temperament, therefore, will be most illuminating when it uses group similarities and differences as tools to investigate the interaction of individual dispositions and the developmental niche.

CURRENT RESEARCH ON GROUP DIFFERENCES IN
TEMPERAMENT

There are two research traditions in the general field of temperament that are now being expanded to the comparative arena. The largest by far obtains multiple indices of hypothetical dimensions of temperament, then searches for their cohesion as indices, for validating concurrent measures, or for predictable consequences. The temperament measures are most often questionnaire or interview items; the correlates are usually behavioral observations or clinical or educational outcomes (Chess & Thomas, 1984). The second tradition measures directly behaviors that sample a less abstract temperament construct, usually involving only a single dimension such as autonomic reactivity (Eliasz, 1979) or behavioral inhibition (Garcia-Coll, Kagan, & Reznick, 1984; Kagan et al., 1984). Infant behavioral examinations such as the Newborn Behavioral Assessment Scales (Brazelton, 1973), although usually multidimensional, belong in this category as well when they focus directly on response differences.

The two traditions face related but distinct problems when they are applied without elaboration in cross-cultural work. The more common approach of using ratings must deal with the meaning of target behaviors; approaches that elicit responses, on the other hand, must be concerned with stimulus equivalence. More generally, construct validity in both approaches needs reexamination with traditional and specifically comparative tools, and this requires going considerably beyond the examination of mean differences in the behavioral measures of interest. One can observe that as other domains of developmental research have entered the cross-cultural arena they, too, have usually started by seeking variation in dependent measures; indeed for a period that appeared to be a promising strategy for opening up the field to a world perspective (LeVine, 1970). More recently, however, with greater sophistication in both developmental and comparative theory, it is clear that greater attention to causal, mediating, and consequential variables is needed (LeVine, 1977; Super, 1980). Without such effort in temperament research, we will be vulnerable to serious, if innocent, misinterpretation of the comparative data and, in turn, pass up the opportunity to ask some fundamental questions about the nature of temperament and development.

The importance of looking beyond mean differences in dependent variables can be illustrated by the work of Freedman (1974; Freedman & Freedman, 1969) and Hsu, Soong, Stigler, Hong, and Liang (1981). Their work is used here to illustrate the problems not because they are poorly done; on the contrary, they reveal the issues clearly because they are highly competent applications of the limited paradigm. They appear to make a compelling case for group differences in temperament, but in the next section we outline neglected issues that prevent such an easy conclusion.

Freedman and Freedman (1969) examined Chinese-American and Euro-American newborns with a preliminary version of the Newborn Behavioral Assessment Scales. Despite small differences in the samples in parity and maternal medication, the two groups were found to be similar in sensory development, central nervous system maturity, motor development, and social responsivity. The Chinese-American infants, however, scored lower on several items characterized as excitability or irritability. They were less likely to change their state of arousal during the exam, they were physically less active, and they were less upset in response to slight facial obstruction. They were also more consolable and better at self-quieting when upset. Freedman (1974) reports similar findings among other genetically related samples (Japanese, Hawaiian, and Navajo) and attributes them to differences between European and Oriental gene pools.

Hsu et al. report the mean ratings given by 349 Taiwanese mothers to their 4 to 8 month old infants on a translation of the Carey and McDevitt (1978) Infant Temperament Questionnaire (ITQ). Back-translation methods were used to assure accuracy of the instrument, while maternal comments and item distributions supported its face validity. Reliable differences from the American means (Carey & McDevitt, 1978) were found on 8 of the 9 dimensions. Chinese infants were, for example, significantly less active, less distractible, more withdrawn, and more intense. The authors conclude that because of the care in translation and the apparent face validity, the differences must be due to "response biases, racial differences, or a combination of these two factors" (p. 1337).

The dilemma of both studies is a classic one in comparative research: Two samples differ on some standard measure and the only specified correlate, in the n of 2, is a confound of race and culture as they are popularly conceived in Western society. We are thus apparently faced with two possible explanations: genetic differences to account for the behaviors, or, when ratings are compared, response bias that derives somehow from the culture. One outcome—so far avoided in temperament research—is a scientific barbarism such as "African Infant Precocity," in which the observed difference is conceptualized as a characteristic of the less familiar group. Such global constructs, it seems, are too easily taken as answers about the nature of the individuals of that race or culture (Super, 1980; Warren, 1972), rather than opportunities to pursue fruitful questions of origin, meaning, validity, and function.

FOUR NEW QUESTIONS

The behavioral sciences' relative inexperience in conceptualizing and measuring the broad environment, along with the emphasis in temperament research on structure and outcome (to the relative neglect of causal pathways) combine to leave the nascent field of temperament and culture cut short, as above, at empirical reports of differences. Beyond the guidance of existing theory, four issues seem important for future research on culture and temperament. First, the present literature raises questions about the origins of temperament which are not addressed in the mainstream of research but which appear promising. Second, individual questionnaire items in the rating approach warrant qualitative examination for their relationship to the everyday lives of infants and children. Third, construct validity should be examined through examination of the correlational structure of the items, within and across time. Finally, comparative studies will make the greatest contribution as they explore the functional value of behavioral dimensions in the developmental niche and, in particular, in the sequence of niches that a culture offers.

Origins. Perhaps because the recent origin of temperament theory was in response to a professional *zeitgeist* of overbearing environmentalism (Thomas & Chess, 1977), the major work has been to define and demonstrate the importance of relatively stable constitutional dispositions. The basis of temperament within a general notion of "constitution" received only secondary attention. More recently, the field of behavioral genetics has made progress in organizing evidence on its side of the traditional "nature/nuture" debate, even while arguing that the ancient dialectic is wanting (Buss & Plomin, 1984). In addition, however, there is a growing appreciation that "biological" and "constitutional" differences are not only reflections of genetic DNA. Of particular importance here is the fact that early environment can influence the physiological responsiveness or organization of the maturing nervous system in ways that have long-term consequences on behavioral disposition.

Chisholm and Heath (in press) have presented a general model for prenatal influences on development and point to several routes by which maternal responses to her environment, particularly stress responses, may be transmitted to the fetus. The most relevant models for the study of infant temperament are circulating maternal adrenocortical stress hormones that pass through the placenta; vigorous vestibular stimulation that may elicit the fetal stress response; and maternal catecholamine responses to stress that may reduce the flow of oxygen and nutrients to the fetus. Several independent studies have used maternal blood pressure to index such processes and report a significant relationship with infant irritability (e.g., Richards, 1979; Woodson et al., 1979). Of particular note are Chisholm's reports (1981, 1983; Chisholm, Woodson, & da Costa, 1978) that Anglo-Navajo and Anglo-Australian Aboriginal differences similar to those reported by Freedman (1974) can be accounted for by variation, within normal range, of maternal blood pressure during pregnancy. The infant physiological mechanisms involved have not been extensively explored although there has been speculation about hippocampal and hypothalamic sensitivity to hypoxia (see Chisholm & Heath, in press).

A separate body of research on the relationship of early postnatal stress and later responsiveness to stress offers a strong model of constitutional disposition as the outcome of early environment. Numerous studies with animals indicate that early stress sets a threshold for pituitary-adrenocortical reactivity later in life. Outcome measures include inhibition in response to novelty as well as physical growth (see Dennenberg, 1969). The direction of effect, it should be noted, is opposite to the prenatal picture, namely, early postnatal stress is associated with lowered reactivity later. There are several lines of evidence for a related phenomenon in humans, although in this literature the temperament outcomes have not been a major focus (see Landauer & Whiting, 1964, 1980).

The amount and kinds of stress on mother, fetus, and infant are in a general sense regulated by the culture (Super & Harkness, in press b). There are, as well, other aspects of the developmental niche early in life that might affect biological dispositions for behavioral style. Diet is one. Yogman and Zeisel (1983) have demonstrated that the balance of serotonin precursors (amino acids that can be used to make the neurotransmitter serotonin) in infant formula affects patterns of sleep. The demonstrated effect appears to be transient, but long-term consequences of routine diet on mood or activity level, for example, might exist. In any case, chronic features of infant and child diet could maintain transient, constitutionally mediated dispositions.

Cultures also differ in the number of children typically born to a family, and hence in typical birth order. About half the children of the present cohort in North America are first-born, while in many rural Third World settings the figure is under 20%. It has been suggested (Super, 1980) that in cross-cultural studies of early infancy the usual confounding of group and parity should not be ignored, because parity has known effects on maternal hormone production (see Bell, 1963) and infant autonomic functioning (Weller & Bell, 1965), as well as early infant behavior (Thoman, Turner, Leiderman, & Barnett, 1970; Waldrop & Bell, 1966). If such effects are universal (and not due to confounding in Western samples with medication, length of labor, etc.) and if they are associated with infant temperament, parity would thus be an additional route of cultural influence on group differences.

The data on first- vs. later born differences in temperament, however, are equivocal. Three reports found scattered differences in Swedish and American samples (Persson-Blennow & McNeil, 1981; Carey, 1970; Sameroff, Seifer, & Elias, 1982) but the specific contrasts are not consistent from one sample to the next, and Carey's finding was not statistically significant. Bates (1980), working in the USA, and Kohnstamm (1982), in Holland, report that first-born babies are rated higher than later borns on Bates' difficulty measure. That scale includes global judgments about "difficultness," whereas the measures used in the other studies focus entirely on specific behaviors. Carey (1981) does report that mothers in his sample rate their first-borns as globally more "difficult." Thus the clearest reports of a birth-order effect might only signal the mother's relative unfamiliarity or unease with her first-born. It may still be wise, however, for comparative studies of temperament to attend to parity as a possible confound of culture.

The studies reviewed here do not by any means form a definitive explanation of group differences in temperament. They do demonstrate, however, several ways culturally constructed reality, independent of gene pool, might influence constitutional dispositions ordinarily considered to reflect temperament.

The Meaning of Test Items.   In our use of the Carey's (1970) original infant temperament questionnaire (ITQ) in a rural African community of Kipsigis people (Super & Harkness, 1981, 1982), we were puzzled by mothers' responses to the item that asks if the baby can entertain him/herself when left alone for one-half hour. We had followed standard procedures for translation and back-translation to confirm the meaning of the question in the local language. The question was asked as part of an interview with ample opportunity for clarification. Yet many of the mothers answered "yes" even though we knew from informal observation, as residents of the community, that infants were almost never left alone, certainly not for that length of time. Our questioning became more aggressive: "How is it," we asked, "that you tell me your baby can be happy when left alone for half an hour, when I know that no mother would do that? I have seen that when you leave for the river you give the baby to his sister, she carries the baby and plays with him until you return."

"When you say 'alone,'" replied the mother, "do you mean with no one at all? Of course the baby would not be happy to be left with no one. I thought you meant when the baby was alone with his sisters and brothers."

The literal meaning of our words, although technically accurate, simply made no sense in the context of normal child care, and the mothers made a reasonable inference about what we wanted to know. Such misunderstanding is not response bias in the usual sense, and the anecdote illustrates that ratings of children are made in the context of broad and unspoken assumptions about behavior.

A more profound and probably more common bias in the meaning of questions—contextual bias, it might be called—can be illustrated by cultural variation in children's distress at maternal departure, comparable measures having been collected by Kagan and his associates (see Kagan, 1976). In samples of working-class Americans, Ladino and Mayan Guatemalans, !Kung San in the Kalahari Desert, and Israeli infants in a kibbutz, it was found that very few infants cried when the mother departed until the age of about 7 or 8 months. The likelihood rises steeply to a peak shortly after the first birthday in all samples, and then declines. There are group differences in the maximum proportion of children showing distress at the peak, however, ranging from about 70 to 100%, as well as substantial variation in the rate of decline in distress following the peak. Qualitative comparison of the infant's niche in each of these samples (Super, 1980) as well as related studies by Kagan et al. (1979) and Lester et al. (1974) suggest that the peak and duration of distress at maternal departure are related to the frequency of nonmaternal caretakers in the infants' routine daily care. Similarly, it has been argued (Chisholm, 1983; Super & Harkness, 1982), that the frequency and decline of fear of strangers in a population is related to the infants' exposure to them. If this hypothesis is correct, group differences in social experience will result in divergent scores on Approach, Intensity, and Adaptability on the ITQ, because reaction to strangers is used as a frequent point of reference on the questionnaire.

At the core of contextual bias in comparative research is the fact that the specific behaviors used as markers for underlying constructs vary in their meaning, in their experiential and functional significance, across cultures. This holds true for babies' baths, childrens' reactions to pain, and family routines at mealtime as it does for experience with strangers. Ironically, the more successful questionnaires are in eliciting accurate ratings for *specific* behaviors and settings, a goal of most temperament surveys, the more susceptible they are to contextual bias in comparative applications. The more they become sampling instruments (compared to attitude surveys) the more limiting is the varying representativeness of sample items for the cultural universe. Psychology's insistence on "holding the stimulus constant" is logical only within the experimental paradigm, and as the meaning of the stimulus becomes defined by its context the comparative paradigm requires other avenues to truth.

Intercorrelations and Construct Validity. Examination of the intercorrelation of items thought to tap the same underlying construct (e.g., Activity Level) is a standard procedure for establishing construct validity. Perhaps because of the personological bias in behavioral sciences (Harkness, 1980), the examination of structure is too rarely undertaken in comparative research. If, as suggested above, the structure of behavior is influenced by the structure of the environment, then it is important to ask if the same dimensions of temperament exist in foreign settings, even though questions about the most appropriate dimensions to draw in the American setting are by no means resolved.

The little information available about intergroup similarity in the correlational structure of temperament indices serves at this point mostly to indicate the possible rewards of more careful research; fragile though the evidence is, it does suggest robustness in the factor structure of temperament questionnaires in a wide range of contexts. Let us note, to start, that the coherence of temperament *scales* (e.g., Thomas and Chess's nine) should be examined through the intercorrelation of questionnaire *items*, that is, the kind of psychometric analysis that has been carried out by Carey and McDevitt (1978), for example. One ought to be satisfied with the comparable coherence and meaning of each scale in two samples before proceeding to compare the intercorrelation among scales. With multiscale questionnaires, this level of analysis is not available, with a few exceptions that do not permit easy comparison (e.g., Laosa, 1982). There is some consolation in that the scale scores, being more reliable (in the technical sense) than individual items, should yield more stable factor structures.

Three comparisons of structure within Western groups are available. Kohnstamm (1982) administered a translation of Bates' Infant Characteristics Questionnaire to a very large and diverse Dutch sample and found a factor structure of the items similar to that reported for the original American group. Maziade (1982; Maziade et al., 1984), using a French translation of Carey and McDevitt's ITQ also reports a factor structure of the nine scales similar to what is found in US samples. Finally, Laosa (1982) reports on use of the Behavioral Style Questionnaire (McDevitt & Carey, 1978) with a Chicano, largely working class sample. On the basis of scale intercorrelations he reports, a factor analysis with varimax rotation of 4 factors was carried out and the results proved comparable to McDevitt's (1976) results from an Anglo-American sample. At 4 years, both data sets yield 4 dimensions: activity, rhythmicity, and persistence; distractability and threshold; intensity and mood; and approach and adaptability. In the same sample 6 months earlier, Laosa's data give the same results except that mood and rhythmicity change places, that is, intensity and rhythmicity (negative) constitute one factor; and activity, persistence, and mood, another.

Two other reports concern African studies. DeVries and Sameroff (1984) used a modified version of the ITQ in three diverse Kenyan groups (peri-urban Gikuyu, seminomadic Masai, and agricultural Digo) and report, without elaboration that "the first two factors in each of the (groups) contained the same" scales. The first factor contained adaptability, approach, mood, and distractibility; the second loaded on intensity and threshold. Super (1985) also modified the ITQ for use in Kokwet, a rural farming community of Kipsigis people in Kenya. The original ITQ was also given to a sample of middle and upper-middle class mothers in metropolitan Boston. The nine summary scales were modified, by the omission of unique items, to be as comparable as possible in the two groups. Even though the number of subjects is excessively small for a robust factor solution, the results in the two samples are fairly similar. In both cases one factor contained rhythmicity, approach, and adaptability, and the second factor contained activity, intensity, threshold, and distractability. Mood and persistence, paired in both cases, went onto the first factor in Kokwet and the second in Boston. Although deVries and Sameroff's two factors did not include all nine scales, their results and Super's are related for the common scales.

In summary, it seems that a core of temperament markers are interrelated in similar ways in several samples from the urban West and rural Africa. Children who are rated as adaptable are also rated as approaching; those who have low thresholds for response tend also to be intense in their reactions. Mood, rhythmicity, distractability, and persistence seem less stable across samples in their intercorrelations but it is not possible to know whether this reflects true sample differences, measurement error, or method variance. Only further studies designed for confirmatory factor analysis will be able to provide greater understanding.

At a more general level, the intercorrelation of measures across time and context is an important index of construct validity. The latter question—whether children who appear a certain way in one context behave similarly, relative to their peers, in another—has occupied much careful attention recently for it has been seen to a central aspect in the idea of temperament. The issue remains open even for the restricted populations that form the core of Western science. The comparative literature, for a variety of reasons, is generally thin at the levels of construct validity, so "a few discrete behaviors too quickly become an index of a much larger, unvalidated concept of temperament, cognitive ability, or attachment" (Super, 1980, p. 246). This is certainly true for comparative studies of temperament. To return to the examples used earlier, the findings of Hsu et al. (1981) and Freedman (1974) both suggest lower levels of activity and responsivity in Oriental infants than Caucasian ones, a picture further supported by Caudill and Weinstein's (1969) classic observations on the lower rates of activity and vocalization in Japanese, compared to American, infants. There is also, however, substantial contradictory evidence (see Super, 1980). Rosenblith and Anderson-Huntington (1975) and Shand, Lin, & Kosawa (1984), for example, report *higher* irritability and activity levels among Japanese than Caucasian newborns.

The appearance of coherence to the Oriental-Caucasian temperament literature draws to some degree on the Western stereotype of the reserved, serene, even inscrutable Easterner, an image that is reinforced by anecdotal reports of quiet, attentive school children. Yet Earls (in press) cites evidence that attention deficit disorder, or hyperactivity, is as common in Chinese school children as in the West. It should be evident that cultures play a substantial role in the socialization of expressive behaviors relevant to several dimensions of temperament, not only in childhood but in infancy as well (Harkness & Kilbride, 1983; Harkness & Super, 1985). Miyake and his associates (Miyake, Campos, & Kagan, 1982/83; Miyake, Campos, & Svejda, 1985), to cite one relevant example, have demonstrated that by 11 months Japanese infants respond differently than American infants to maternal vocal signals of anger, but not to signals of joy or fear. "Because the differences in inhibition were not found following the expression of fear by the mother, the findings cannot be attributed to *temperamental* differences between the Japanese and American babies. Rather, it suggests that the vocal expression of anger has already assumed much greater behavior regulatory control among the Japanese infants." (Miyake, Campos, & Kagan, 1982/83, p. 8, emphasis in the original).

The contradictory data and contrasting evidence do not invalidate each other, of course, but they do suggest cautious looks before conceptual leaps. If there is a population difference that is not primarily cultural, the present, very limited evidence suggests it is not the standard picture of temperament writ large. Indeed, we may find a warning in the demise of the "culture and personality" school of anthropology, a demise due in part to the realization that progress could not be made under the presumption that, in Benedict's phrase, culture is personality writ large. Group variation is not simply individual variation on a grander scale, and the stability of behavior across contexts within a culture says nothing about the results between cultures or, indeed, within another culture.

The inclusion of stability over time in the usual definition of temperament comes not only from the theory of stable personalities that "temperament" was trying to counter, but also from the implications of "constitutional." The degree of stability in personality or cognitive measures is of course very much in debate now (Brim & Kagan, 1980; McCall, this volume), and it is evident as well that biologically regulated functions need not be developmentally smooth (Wilson, 1978). The special emphasis on stability in temperament theory may turn out to be problematic and unnecessary. In any case, to the degree that environmental factors influence behavior, the continuity of developmental niches will contribute to the continuity of measured temperament. This observation is discussed more in the next section, and it is only necessary to point out here that comparative study of temperament over time would be an invaluable source of information, but none is presently available.

The Functional Value of Temperament.   The purpose of temperament theories, whatever their exact content, is to acknowledge individual differences in shaping and responding to the environment, differences that are relatively independent of interpersonal experience and, perhaps, relatively generalizable over time and situation. For temperament theory to draw conclusions about the functional value of dispositions for normal and abnormal development, however, it requires a picture of the environment in which temperament operates.

The variety of environments in which humans exist may produce some surprises, and deVries' (1984) study stands as a stark example. Returning after 3 months of drought and famine to Masai families in southern Kenya whom he had studied earlier, when the infants were 4- to 6-months-old, deVries found that many babies had died of malnutrition and its complications. Most of those who at initial contact fit the classic definition of "difficult"—fussy and irregular, not adapting or approaching, and intense in their responses—had survived (5 of 6 cases). Most of their more quiet, positive, accepting peers did not (2 of 7 cases). Thus the cluster of traits that is associated with relative freedom from behavioral pathology in one setting is associated in another with death.

DeVries is appropriately cautious in his conclusion that temperament is a causal factor, for even though the effect is large, the number of subjects is small and the statistical significance of the difference is marginal ($p = .07$). Nevertheless the "squeaky wheel" hypothesis, that fussy babies are more likely to be fed and survive under such conditions is more reasonable than it may first appear to the "innocently Western" reader (Warren, 1980, p. xiii). First, deVries was able to examine for, and rule out, a number of alternative explanations, such as prior health status and family variables. Second, it is supported by the observation that the "difficult" infants were, at first encounter, larger than the "easy" ones, which would follow if the former were nursed more frequently. Third, the result is consistent with ethnographic observation by deVries, and many others in similar settings, that infant crying is always responded to, usually with the breast. Mothers in traditional societies often suggest that if an infant does not cry she is not hungry. Finally, there is good theoretical reason to expect a functional relationship between demanding behavior and survival in an environment of limited resources. Chisholm and Heath (in press) hypothesize that such facultative adaptation lies behind the observed relationship between maternal blood pressure and infant irritability. "A concrete prediction of this evolutionarily-based hypothesis," they write, "is that when mothers experience at least some kinds of stress or anxiety during pregnancy and have relatively more irritable infants as a consequence, then this relatively irritable temperament of the infant should somehow be adaptive in the larger postnatal environment which caused the maternal anxiety in the first place."

Maternal values in such situations are also consistent with the hypothesis, as our comments on coherence of the developmental niche would suggest. Scheper-Hughes (in press) interviewed mothers in a shanty-town in Northeast Brazil where pregnancy wastage and infant mortality were extraordinarily high: Of 686 reported pregnancies in her sample, nearly one-seventh did not yield a live birth. Of the 588 children born alive, 43% died before 5-years-of-age. In this setting physical survival requires stamina and enterprise, and the mothers decidedly preferred "fighters."

"I prefer," reported one mother, "a more active child, because when they are intelligent and lively they will never be *parada* (stopped or stumped) wherever they live. The worst temperament in a child is one who is *morte de espiritu* (spiritless), a child so calm that he sits there without any energy. When they grow up they're good for nothing. The child who wants to run outdoors all day long, who wants to be out on the street playing soccer from the crack of dawn, that's the same child who is out hustling in the street by 10 o'clock looking for whatever work or scraps or leftovers there are. Now that's a child with good temperament!" (Scheper-Hughes, in press).

Placidity and ennervation can reflect malnutrition and disease as well as temperament, of course, and the "temperament" mothers look for may be as much a result as a cause of the "survivability." Nevertheless, it is evident that intensity, threshold, and activity, at least, play a developmental role in such settings that is different from that observed in middle-class USA.

There are two other studies, with less tragic outcome variables, that have examined how environments determine the functional value of temperamental dispositions, and both of them report important differences from the mainstream of American findings. The first is an extension of the New York Longitudinal Study to a working-class Puerto Rican sample living in New York City (Thomas & Chess, 1977). Unlike the case in the middle-class, largely Jewish group, the Puerto-Rican parents did not enforce regular times for their preschool children to go to bed and get up, and only one child developed sleep problems during this time (Thomas, Chess, Sillen, & Mendez, 1974). When the time came to attend school, however, the demands for regularity suddenly increased, and five families faced temper tantrums at bedtime and related problems. In a related analysis, Korn and Gannon (1983) found that behavioral adjustment at 5 years, indexed by a symptom checklist from parental interviews, was independent of difficult temperament in the working-class Puerto Rican sample, whereas among the middle-class group, for whom the "difficult" concept was developed, the correlation of temperament with symptomatology was significant. Among children under 9 years, half of the clinical cases in the Puerto Rican sample involved excessive motor activity; a syndrome completely absent (with the exception of one brain-damaged child) in the original middle-class sample. Although other factors of health and nutrition might be involved, this outcome is consistent with the fact that the working-class families were less able to accommodate the highly active child in their small, crowded apartments—the niche, in this case, was not adaptable to the child's disposition.

A further variation in the "goodness of fit" was found in Kokwet, a rural African farming community by Super and Harkness (1981, 1982; Super, 1984). Functional features of the infant's niche, particularly with regard to the structuring of sleep, were delineated by ethnographic methods, and it was found that individual differences in rhythmicity were not of great significance in that context. In addition, some developmental changes that reinforce the salience of differences in the American case (notably the increase in length of sleep episode) do not take place for an extended period in Kokwet. Adaptability to multiple caretakers, on the other hand, and willingness to be soothed by back-carrying and other techniques available to sibling caretakers are critical components in being an "easy" baby in Kokwet. Until recent years, with the advent of infant day care centers and "Snugli" pouches for carrying babies, this expression of infant variation was not even discernible in the American context.

The African study also raises more explicitly a concern latent in the NYLS discussion of their two samples, namely the importance of continuities and discontinuities in the sequence of niches for development provided by cultures (and subcultures). We have argued (Harkness & Super, 1983) that cultures vary in the definition of both the content and the timing of developmental stages, and further that the sequence of stages corresponds to the sequence of developmental niches. The functional requirements of the stages, that is, the disposition and adaptability of the niches, may be discontinuous, as proved to be the case for rhythmicity in the New York Longitudinal Study Puerto Rican sample. The same point has been made regarding other aspects of social and cognitive development among minority children in the USA (Laosa, 1979). In these cases the individual must change and reintegrate lessons from the past.

On the other hand, there may also be continuities in the niche. The continuities may be simple continuations (one still has to get up on time), and they may be more abstract similarities of the sort developmentalists refer to when speaking of hierarchical integration of old content into new structures. Thus one can note, in our African study, that the Boston infant was learning to accept impersonal, externally imposed regularity, whereas the Kipsigis baby was required to adapt to the needs and behaviors of a small number of particular people. The same lessons are relearned, in new contexts, throughout childhood. They are also reflected in the social regulation of adult functioning. In Kokwet, the difficult deviant refuses to cooperate with family and neighbors and defies the personal mediation involved in local dispute settlement (Harkness, Edwards, & Super, 1981). In America, the adult who is never on time, misses appointments, or chafes at schedules is the troublesome one. Environmental continuity in the functional value of temperamental traits, in short, may contribute to the pattern of continuity and discontinuity in temperament, and indeed to the construction of personality from the interaction of temperament and experience.

CULTURAL DIFFERENCES IN TEMPERAMENT

The central point of this discussion is that the comparative study of culture and temperament raises issues that have not been critical in the monocultural research to date. In general, there are sources of between-group variation in the behaviors commonly used to index temperament that are not major sources of within-group variance, or at least that have not been well investigated within samples because they lack visibility and do not fit easily in the traditional dialectic between nature and nurture.

It will be moot in the end, but at the moment it seems worthwhile as a way to organize thinking in the area, to consider what kinds of between-group results would truly qualify as cultural differences in temperament. At one end of the spectrum, response and item bias in questionnaire and interview data are clearly artifacts to exclude. Systematic differences in the settings that elicit behavior, another possibility, although true effects of culture, would not qualify as dispositions of the individual. Similarly, differences in response hierarchy that result directly from culturally organized experience (such as use of nonmaternal caretakers) might satisfy the generality and stability concerns of temperament theory, but would not depend in a relevant way on biological dispositions. If the pattern and timing of experience alter the biological substrates that regulate later behavior, on the other hand, as might be the case regarding stress and reactivity, the theoretical considerations would be met. Continuing one step further, some of the existing findings, and future ones too, may reflect true differences in gene pools. In that case, the relatively arbitrary covariation of culture and gene pool will have been useful as an intermediate device to point us in the right direction; culture, however, will have no role in regulation of temperament.

The study of temperament and development in a variety of cultural contexts promises more than the isolation of pathways to group differences. It leads us instead to fundamental questions about the organization, function, and development of behavior that are difficult to answer—even to ask—in a single environment. Exploration of the issues raised by comparative research will contribute much to our understanding of human temperament.

ACKNOWLEDGMENT

The preparation of this work was supported in part by the Carnegie Corporation of New York. The authors are indebted to William Carey and Luis Laosa for helpful comments on an earlier version. All statements made and opinions expressed are the sole responsibility of the authors.

REFERENCES

Bates, J. E. (1980). The concept of difficult temperament. *Merrill-Palmer Quarterly, 26*(4), 299–319.

Bell, R. Q. (1963). Some factors to be controlled in studies of the behavior of newborns. *Biologia Neonatorum, 5,* 200–214.

Brazelton, T. B. (1973). *Neonatal behavioral assessment scale.* London: Spastics International Medical Publications.

Brim, O. G., & Kagan, J. (Eds.). (1980). *Constancy and change in human development.* Cambridge, MA: Harvard University Press.

Buss, A. H., & Plomin, R. (1984). *Temperament: Early developing personality traits.* Hillsdale, NJ: Lawrence Erlbaum Associates.

Carey, W. B. (1970). A simplified method for measuring infant temperament. *Journal of Pediatrics, 77*(2), 188–194.

Carey, W. B., & McDevitt, S. C. (1978). Revision of the infant temperament questionnaire. *Pediatrics, 61*(5), 735–739.

Carey, W. B. (1981). The importance of temperament-environment interaction for child health and development. In M. Lewis & L. Rosenblum (Eds.), *The uncommon child* (pp. 31–55). New York: Plenum Press.

Caudill, W., & Weinstein, H. (1969). Maternal care and infant behavior in Japan and America. *Psychiatry, 32,* 12–43.

Chess, S., & Thomas, A. (1984). *Origins and evolution of behavior disorders.* New York: Brunner/Mazel.

Chisholm, J. S. (1981). Prenatal influences on aboriginal-white Australian differences in neonatal irritability. *Ethology and Sociobiology, 2,* 67–73.

Chisholm, J. S. (1983). *Navajo infancy.* Chicago: Aldine.

Chisholm, J. S., & Heath, G. (in press). Evolution and pregnancy: A biosocial view of prenatal influences. In C. M. Super & S. Harkness (Eds.), *Studies in comparative human development, Vol. 1: The role of culture in developmental dysfunction.* New York: Academic Press.

Chisholm, J. S., Woodson, R. H., & da Costa, E. (1978). Maternal blood pressure in pregnancy and newborn irritability. *Early Human Development, 2*(2), 171–178.

Dennenberg, V. H. (1969). Animal studies of early experience: Some principles which have implications for human development. In J. P. Hill (Ed.), *Minnesota Symposia on Child Psychology* (Vol. 3). Minneapolis: University of Minnesota Press.

deVries, M. W. (1984). Temperament and infant mortality among the Masai of East Africa. *American Journal of Psychiatry, 141*(10), 1189–1194.

deVries, M. W., & Sameroff, A. J. (1984). Culture and temperament: Influences on infant temperament in three East African societies. *American Journal of Orthopsychiatry, 54*(1), 83–96.

Earls, F. (in press). Child mental health in an international context. In C. M. Super & S. Harkness (Eds.), *Studies in comparative human development, Vol I: The role of culture in developmental dysfunction.* New York: Academic Press.

Eliasz, A. (1979). Temporal stability of reactivity. *Polish Psychological Bulletin, 10*(3), 187–198.

Freedman, D. G. (1974). *Human infancy: An evolutionary perspective.* Hillsdale, NJ: Lawrence Erlbaum Associates.

Freedman, D. G., & Freedman, N. C. (1969). Behavioral differences between Chinese-American and European-American newborns. *Nature, 244,* 1227.

Garcia-Coll, C., Kagan, J., & Reznick, J. S. (1984). Behavioral inhibition in young children. *Child Development, 55,* 1005–1019.

Harkness, S. (1980). The cultural context of child development. In C. M. Super & S. Harkness (Eds.), Anthropological perspectives on child development, *New Directions for Child Development, 8,* 7–13.

Harkness, S., Edwards, C. P., & Super, C. M. (1981). Social roles and moral reasoning: A case study in a rural African community. *Developmental Psychology, 17,* 595–603.

Harkness, S., & Kilbride, P. L., (Eds.). (1983). The socialization of affect. Special issue of *Ethos, 11*(4).

Harkness, S., & Super, C. M. (1983). The cultural construction of child development: A framework for the socialization of affect. *Ethos, 11*(4), 221–231.

Harkness, S., & Super, C. M. (1985). Child-environment transactions in the socialization of affect. In M. Lewis & C. Saarni (Eds.), *The socialization of affect* (pp. 21–36). New York: Plenum.

Herrera, M. G., Mora, J. O., Christianse, N., Ortiz, N., Clement, J., Vuori, L., Waber, D., de Paredes, B., & Wagner, M. (1980). Effects of nutritional supplementation and early education on physical development. In R. R. Turner & H. W. Reese (Eds.), *Life-span developmental psychology: Intervention.* New York: Academic Press.

Hsu, C.-c., Soong, W.-t., Stigler, J. W., Hong, C.-w., & Liang, C.-c. (1981). The temperamental characteristics of Chinese babies. *Child Development, 52,* 1337–1340.

Kagan, J. (1976). Emergent themes in human development. *American Scientist, 64,* 186–196.

Kagan, J., Klein, R. E., Finley, G., Rogoff, B., & Nolan, E. (1979). A cross-cultural study of cognitive development. *Monographs of the Society for Research in Child Development, 44*(5, Serial No. 180).

Kagan, J., Reznick, J. S., Clarke, C., Snidman, N., & Garcia-Coll, C. (1984). Behavioral inhibition to the unfamiliar. *Child Development, 55,* 2212–2225.

Kohnstamm, G. A. (1982, October). Bates' ICQ in the Netherlands. Paper presented at the Fourth Occasional Temperament Conference, Salem, MA.

Korn, S. J., & Gannon, S. (1983). Temperament, cultural variation and behavior disorder in preschool children. *Child Psychiatry and Human Development, 13*(4), 203–212.

Landauer, T. K., & Whiting, J. W. M. (1964). Infantile stimulation and adult stature of human males. *American Anthropologist, 66,* 1007–1028.

Landauer, T. K., & Whiting, J. W. M. (1980). Correlates and consequences of stress in infancy. In R. H. Munroe, R. L. Munroe, & B. B. Whiting (Eds.), *Handbook of cross-cultural human development.* New York: Garland.

Laosa, L. (1979). Social competence in childhood: Toward a developmental, socioculturally relativistic paradigm. In M. W. Kent & J. E. Rolf (Eds.), *Primary prevention of psychopathology, Vol. III: Social competence in children* (pp. 253–278). New Hampshire: University Press of New England.

Laosa, L. (1982, October). *Temperament in childhood: Its construct validity and population generalizability.* Paper presented at the Fourth Occasional Temperament Conference, Salem, MA.

Lester, B. M., Kotelchuck, M., Spelke, E., Sellers, M. J., & Klein, R. E. (1974). Separation protest in Guatemalan infants: Cross-cultural and cognitive findings. *Developmental Psychology, 10,* 79–85.

LeVine, R. A. (1970). Cross-cultural study in child psychology. In P. Mussen (Ed.), *Carmichael's manual of child psychology* (3rd ed., Vol. 2). New York: Wiley.

LeVine, R. A. (1977). Child rearing as cultural adaptation. In P. H. Leiderman, S. R. Tulkin, & A. Rosenfeld (Eds.), *Culture and infancy: Variations in the human experience.* New York: Academic Press.

Maziade, M. (October, 1982). *Questionnaire assessment of NYLS dimensions in school children in Montreal.* Paper presented at the Fourth Occasional Temperament Conference, Salem, Massachusetts.

Maziade, M., Boudreault, M., Thivierge, J., Caperaa, P., & Cote, R. (1984). Infant temperament: SES and gender differences and reliability of measurement in a large Quebec sample. *Merrill-Palmer Quarterly, 30,* 213–226.

McDevitt, S. C. (1976). *A longitudinal assessment of continuity and stability in temperamental characteristics from infancy to early childhood.* Unpublished doctoral dissertation, Temple University.

McDevitt, S. C., & Carey, W. B. (1978). The measurement of temperament in 3–7 year old children. *Journal of Child Psychology and Psychiatry, 17,* 223–228.

Miyake, K., Campos, J. J., & Kagan, J. (1982/83). Issues in socio-emotional development. In *Annual report* of the Research and Clinical Center for Child Development, Faculty of Education, Hokkaido University, Sapporo, Japan.

Miyake, K., Campos, J., & Svejda, M. (1985, April). *Maternal emotional expression as a determinant of social reactivity in Japanese and American infants.* Paper presented at the biannual meetings of the Society for Research in Child Development, Toronto.

Persson-Blennow, I., & McNeil, T. F. (1981). Temperament characteristics of children in relation to gender, birth order, and social class. *American Journal of Orthopsychiatry, 51*(4), 710–714.

Posner, M. I. (1978). *Chronometric explorations of the mind.* Hillsdale, NJ: Lawrence Erlbaum Associates.

Richards, M. P. M. (1979). Conception, pregnancy, and birth—a perspective from developmental psychology. In L. Carenza & L. Zichella (Eds.), *Emotion and reproduction—Proceedings of the Serono Conference* (Vol. 20). New York: Academic Press.

Rosenblith, J. F., & Anderson-Huntington, R. B. (1975). Defensive reactions to stimulation of the nasal and oral regions in newborns: Relations to state. In J. F. Bosma & J. Showacre (Eds.), *Development of upper respiratory anatomy and function: Implications for sudden infant death syndrome.* Bethesda, MD: Department of Health, Education and Welfare Publication NIH 75-941.

Sameroff, A. J., & Chandler, M. J. (1975). Reproductive risk and the continuum of caretaking casualty. In F. D. Horowitz (Ed.), *Review of child development research* (Vol. 4). Chicago: University of Chicago Press.

Sameroff, A. J., Seifer, R., & Elias, P. K. (1982). Sociocultural variability in infant temperament ratings. *Child Development, 53,* 164–173.

Scheper-Hughes, N. (in press). Basic strangeness: Maternal detachment and infant survival in a Brazilian shantytown. In C. M. Super & S. Harkness (Eds.), *Studies in comparative human development, Vol. I: The role of culture in developmental dysfunction.* New York: Academic Press.

Shand, N., Lin, P., & Kosawa, Y. (1984). *Asian and Caucasian differences in spontaneous motor activity from birth through three months.* Unpublished manuscript.

Super, C. M. (1980). Behavioral development in infancy. In R. H. Munroe, R. L. Munroe, & B. B. Whiting (Eds.), *Handbook of cross-cultural human development.* New York: Garland Press.

Super, C. M. (1981). Cross-cultural studies of infancy. In H. Triandis, A. Heron, & E. Kroeger (Eds.), *Handbook of cross-cultural psychology* (Vol. 4). Boston: Allyn & Bacon.

Super, C. M. (1984). Models of development and models of assessment. In J. Brozek & B. Schurch

(Eds.), *Critical assessment of key behaviors in research on malnutrition and behavior.* Geneva: Nestle Foundation.

Super, C. M. (1985). *The cultural construction of behavior problems in infancy.* Unpublished manuscript.

Super, C. M., & Harkness, S. (1981). Figure, ground, and Gestalt: The cultural context of the active individual. In R. M. Lerner & N. A. Busch-Rossnagel (Eds.), *Individuals as producers of their development: A life-span perspective.* New York: Academic Press.

Super, C. M., & Harkness, S. (1982). The infant's niche in rural Kenya and metropolitan America. In L. L. Adler (Ed.), *Cross-cultural research at issue.* New York: Academic Press.

Super, C. M., & Harkness, S. (in press a). Looking across at growing up: The expressions of cognitive growth in middle childhood. In E. Gollin (Ed.), *Developmental plasticity: The social context of development.* New York: Academic Press.

Super, C. M., & Harkness, S. (in press b). The role of culture in developmental dysfunction. In C. M. Super & S. Harkness (Eds.), *Studies in comparative human development, Vol. I: The role of culture in developmental dysfunction.* New York: Academic Press.

Thoman, E. B., Turner, A. M., Leiderman, P. H., & Barnett, C. R. (1970). Neonate-mother interaction: Effects of parity on feeding behavior. *Child Development, 41,* 1103–1111.

Thomas, A., & Chess, S. (1977). *Temperament and development.* New York: Brunner/Mazel.

Thomas, A., Chess, S., & Birch, H. G. (1968). *Temperament and behavior disorders in children.* New York: New York University Press.

Thomas, A., Chess, S., Sillen, J., & Mendez, O. (1974). Cross-cultural study of behavior in children with special vulnerabilities to stress. In D. Ricks, A. Thomas, & M. Roff (Eds.), *Life history research in psychopathology* (Vol. 3, pp. 53–67). Minneapolis: University of Minnesota Press.

Waldrop, M. F., & Bell, R. Q. (1966). Effects of family size and density on newborn characteristics. *American Journal of Orthopsychiatry, 36,* 544–550.

Warren, N. (1972). African infant precocity. *Psychological Bulletin, 78,* 353–367.

Warren, N. (1980). *Studies in cross-cultural psychology* (Vol. 2). London: Academic Press.

Weller, G. M., & Bell, R. Q. (1965). Basal skin conductance and neonatal state. *Child Development, 36,* 647–657.

Wilson, R. (1978). Synchronies in mental development: An epigenetic perspective. *Science, 202,* 939–948.

Woodson, R. H. (1983). Newborn behavior and the transition to intrauterine life. *Infant Behavior and Development, 6,* 139–145.

Woodson, R. H., Blurton Jones, N. G., da Costa Woodson, E., Pollack, S., & Evans, M. (1979). Fetal mediators of the relationship between increased pregnancy and labour blood pressure and newborn irritability. *Early Human Development, 3,* 127–139.

Yogman, M. W., & Zeisel, S. (1983). Short term modification of sleep patterns in neonates by diet. *New England Journal of Medicine, 309,* 1147–1149.

11 Clinical Interactions of Temperament: Transitions from Infancy to Childhood

William B. Carey
University of Pennsylvania Medical School and
The Children's Hospital of Philadelphia

INTRODUCTION

Although other reviews in this volume have touched on practical aspects of temperament research, this one is primarily concerned with these clinical interactions. Those of us who are clinicians feel an understandable enthusiasm for this aspect of the field and an inclination to regard it as the ultimate purpose of more theoretical investigations.

The term "clinical conditions," as employed here, is intended to include the broad range of variations and deviations from the norms of physical health, development, and behavior that concern parents and bring infants and children to the attention of primary care clinicians, especially pediatricians.

Interactions of temperament and clinical conditions can be viewed in two principal ways, temperament as an *outcome* of various clinical conditions and as a factor *predisposing* to them. A third major category, mentioned briefly, is that in which the effects are bidirectional or uncertain.

The plan of this chapter is to consider these two principal sorts of interactions separately, first, temperament as an outcome and then as a predisposing factor. After a brief synopsis of the range of clinical conditions involved in each, some general conclusions are presented, and finally, we proceed to an examination of the transitions observed as children pass from infancy to early childhood. The chapter concludes with some exhortatory remarks about the importance of clinical research.

This chapter will not attempt to cite individually all of the more than 140 research studies considered. More detailed review articles may be consulted for the rest of these references (Carey, 1981, 1985a).

TEMPERAMENT AS AN OUTCOME OF CLINICAL CONDITIONS

Specific Conditions Possibly Affecting Temperament

Table 11.1 displays the considerable variety of clinical conditions evaluated so far as possibly having an impact on children's temperament. It should be pointed out that factors in the psychosocial environment have been deliberately excluded from this table. There is no question that they are extremely important. They are eliminated here simply because they are outside the limits of this presentation.

Two levels of clinical conditions are listed in Table 11.1. The first is biological insults or "risk" factors, such as prematurity or toxemia, in which organic pathology may or may not be documented in the child. The other is established organic disease such as malnutrition or cerebral palsy. These two levels of clinical involvement are treated together because studies performed so far often do not permit a clear separation.

The specific conditions range from genetic, chromosomal, and other congenital anomalies through complications of the pregnancy and perinatal period to postnatal insults to the central nervous system and a variety of neurological and general physical conditions. Most of these conditions are the same ones that may also threaten children's physical health and development.

General Comments

Any conclusions based on the data accumulated so far must be tentative since the studies are few, the number of subjects usually is small, the findings often are inconclusive and inconsistent, and the behaviors rated vary from one investiga-

TABLE 11.1
Temperament as an Outcome of Clinical Conditions:
Specific Conditions Possibly Affecting Temperament

1. Prenatal conditions
   (a) genetic abnormalities--e.g., inborn errors of metabolism like phenylketonuria
   (b) chromosomal abnormalities--e.g., Down syndrome, XXY
   (c) other congential anomalies--e.g., minor physical anomalies

2. Pregnancy and perinatal stress
   (a) obstetrical complications--prematurity (respiratory distress syndrome), intrauterine growth retardation, asphyxia, medication, trauma
   (b) medical complications of pregnancy--nutrition, toxins, drugs, infections, medical illness, emotions
   (c) other medical complications of newborn--hyperbilirubinemia, phototherapy

3. Postnatal insults to central nervous system--nutrition, toxins, infections, other trauma

4. Handicapping conditions of central nervous system--retardation, cerebral palsy, seizure disorders, information processing deficits

5. General medical illness--allergy (asthma), endocrine (adreno-genital syndrome, hypothyroidism), serous otitis, anemia

tion to another. Nevertheless, the most convincing evidence to date of effects on temperament seems to be the chronic conditions affecting the central nervous system, such as malnutrition (Chavez, Martinez, & Yaschine, 1979) or toxins (Kolata, 1978), rather than the more transient ones like abnormal delivery or head trauma.

There is enough evidence from this review, however, to suggest strongly that the current model of the psychosocial environment interacting with genetically determined behaviors is far too simple. The model must be expanded to include as participants in the interaction the child's general physical, neurological, and developmental condition and the nonhuman environment. Although developmental behavioral genetics has made impressive strides in recent years, it is possible that failure to consider this additional set of factors has been an impediment to progress.

As research projects studying these phenomena continue to increase, several points might prove helpful. One should expect that initial studies by behavioral scientists in the relatively unfamiliar terrain of clinical conditions would run into problems. Investigators have had to realize that meaningful data require careful attention to such matters as sample selection. All children with a certain condition such as deafness, retardation, or serous otitis are not the same as to etiology, duration, and severity. Moreover, specialty clinic samples may be skewed by various factors including social class, clinical manifestations, or the treatment modality offered by the facility. "Risk factors" have often been treated as if they were uniform influences. Interdisciplinary collaboration between behavioral scientists and medical clinicians is one way of minimizing such errors.

Transitions

This volume is concerned in particular with the issue of transitions from infancy to early childhood. Let us pose the questions we should like to answer.

As the child gets older, is there a change as to which clinical conditions affect temperament? Are there differences in the temperament patterns produced? The questions are presented without much difficulty but must remain largely unanswered at present. The only hypothesis possible now is that there may be a wearing off of the effects induced by various influences during pregnancy. Just as premature babies undergo a catching up in their growth and perhaps in their development, we may expect that any similar effects on behavioral style would decrease with time. The same may be true also of other prenatal influences such as maternal malnutrition or drug use. Proof of these assumptions is awaited.

TEMPERAMENT AS A FACTOR PREDISPOSING TO CLINICAL CONDITIONS

Before describing the clinical conditions in which various temperamental characteristics appear to play a contributing role in their *incidence,* we should reflect briefly on the way the child's *response* to an illness and its outcome may be affected by the child's temperament. Although it has not been well documented yet, children tend to have typical illness styles that are a part of their general behavioral styles. Those who have low sensory thresholds and tend to react negatively and intensely to discomfort are likely to be more easily identifiable as ill by their parents. This may enable caretakers and physicians to diagnose the problem and initiate appropriate treatment earlier in the course of this illness. However, it is also likely to mean that caretakers have a more onerous task in management of an irritable child. No studies are available to support the possibility, but clinical impressions suggest that these more "difficult" children are more likely to experience excessive diagnostic and therapeutic procedures.

On the other hand, the easier child is not necessarily better or worse off. The more mild and positive child may be pleasanter for his parents to manage when sick and may evoke warmer, more sympathetic care, but this child also runs the risk of not complaining enough and misleading caretakers and physicians into underestimating the gravity of the illness.

Specific Conditions With Possible or Probable Relationships

Table 11.2 demonstrates the extent to which the original focus of the New York Longitudinal Study on behavior problems has been broadened in the last 2 decades to include all the major aspects of children: physical health, development, and behavior.

TABLE 11.2
Temperament as a Factor Predisposing to Clinical Conditions:
Specific Conditions With Possible or Probable Relationships to Temperament

1. Physical health
   (a) organic--accidents, child abuse, morbidity in adults
   (b) functional--"colic," functional abdominal pain, sleep problems, enuresis, constipation and encopresis
   (c) nutrition and growth--failure to thrive, obesity, survival in famine

2. Neurological status--confusion of temperament with central nervous system malfunction: "hyperactivity," "m.b.d.," "a.d.d."

3. Development--influence of activity and difficult/easy

4. Behavioral adjustment
   (a) social competence--certain characteristics (esp. difficult) predispose to "poor fit," stress, and reactive behavior problems; also secondary effects by changes induced in parental behavior
   (b) task performance--several characteristics (esp. adaptability and persistence/attention span) affect school work; direct effect on performance and indirect one via reaction of teacher
   (c) other--self-direction, care, esteem; coping style ("defenses") anxiety, depression, etc.--no data. Effects on motivation?

The only aspect of children not included in the outline as an outcome variable is temperament itself. This is, of course, the same as the question of stability, which is dealt with elsewhere in this volume. The main clinical issue here is how and why temperament changes or remains stable when such traits as high activity and inattentiveness are involved in some clinical problem and caretakers and clinicians seek to modify them.

1. Physical Health.   (a) Organic—Higher accident rates have been reported among infants who are more difficult or more active (Carey, 1972; Matheny, Brown, & Wilson, 1971). Many clinicians believe difficult temperament predisposes to child abuse, but this has been hard to confirm because of the methodological requirement of assessing the child shortly before the abuse occurs. A cohort of medical students rated as having Gesell's gamma temperament type (uneven and irregular) experienced more premature illness and death than did their classmates in the following 30 years (Betz & Thomas, 1979).

(b) Functional—Temperamental traits have been found to be related to "colic" in young infants (Carey, 1972), functional abdominal pain in the preschool period (Huttunen & Nyman, 1982), and sleep disturbances in infants (Carey, 1974). A role in enuresis and constipation has been suspected but is not well documented yet.

(c) Nutrition and growth—A participation of behavioral style in failure to thrive is regarded as likely by many clinicians but, as with child abuse, clear confirmation calls for the very demanding requirement of temperament determinations shortly before the clinical problem emerges. Obese children may be less active than their leaner peers, but no data are available to clarify whether this or other traits are present before the onset of excess weight. The survival of most of a group of difficult infants, while the easy ones largely perished in a famine in East Africa, raises questions about the possible "survival value" of difficult temperament (deVries, 1984). It may be that irritable infants are fed more and thereby gain more (Carey, 1985b).

2. Neurological Status.   No study has claimed to show that temperament in any way affects the child's neurological status, nor does it seem likely that any such evidence will be forthcoming. However, with our present diagnostic confusion over the phenomena referred to by the nebulous terms of "hyperactivity," "minimal brain dysfunction," or "attention deficit disorder," many children with certain behavioral style characteristics like low adaptability, low attention span, and high activity have been assumed to have something wrong with their nervous systems despite objective evidence to the contrary (Carey & McDevitt, 1980). Thus, temperament seems not to predispose to clinical problems with the nervous system but is sometimes mistaken as evidence of malfunction.

3. Development.   Although the rate of development of various skills and capacities appears to be largely a result of innate potential and stimulation from the psychosocial environment, two types of temperamental characteristics have been shown to influence it. More active infants (Carey, 1972; Escalona, 1968) tend to reach various developmental milestones earlier, and easier infants (Wachs & Gandour, 1983) and children (Moller, 1983) seem more able than difficult ones to utilize environmental stimuli that promote development. These phenomena may become clinical problems if the low activity or difficult temperament results in a level of development that arouses concern about the potential for development.

4. Behavioral Adjustment.   (a) Social competence—The original New York Longitudinal Study (NYLS; Thomas, Chess, & Birch, 1968) has been followed by at least eight comparable but smaller, briefer ones (e.g., Earls, 1981). Although different populations and methods have been employed, conclusions all have a common theme: Certain temperament characteristics, especially the "difficult" ones, predispose children to a "poor fit" with the values and expectations of their caretakers, to stressful interactions with them, and thus to reactive behavior problems. Furthermore, there may be secondary effects on the child via altered interactions due to changes, such as low self-esteem and depression, induced in the caretakers by the child's temperament. The stressful interactions and consequent behavior problems are more likely to be generated at times of transitions and change such as the birth of a sibling or a new teacher at school than when the affairs of life are running smoothly without adaptational challenges (Thomas et al., 1968).

(b) Task performance—While the earlier work on behavioral problems was more concerned with general social adjustment, some more recent studies have concentrated on this other major aspect of adjustment, task performance, particularly at school. A similar number of studies, also with varied measures, subject groups, and findings, have converged toward the conclusion that several temperamental characteristics, especially adaptability and persistence/attention span, affect school work (see especially: Keogh, 1982; Martin, Nagel, & Paget, 1983). There appears to be both a direct effect on how the child undertakes and pursues his work and an indirect one via the reaction of the teacher. More sociable and diligent children seem more likely to evoke positive support from their teachers and this, in turn, probably enhances the school performance.

(c) Other—Clinical impressions notwithstanding, available data are too meager to demonstrate a link between temperament and self-relationships, coping style or "defenses," and other adjustment measures such as anxiety and depression. The possibility that temperament helps to shape motivation in adults has been suggested by Burks and Rubenstein (1979) but not yet explored to a sufficient extent in children.

General Comments

A review of the preceding paragraphs should make clear that data are somewhat more plentiful from studies of temperament as a predisposing factor than as an outcome of clinical conditions. The volume of evidence is greater in the area of behavioral adjustment than in the physical and developmental outcomes. Yet, there is room for replication and clarification in all areas.

A major conclusion to be derived from this review is that the temperamental characteristics that predispose to clinical conditions are not just the original cluster of "difficult" ones described by the NYLS (Thomas et al., 1968). They found that low rhythmicity, approach, and adaptability; negative mood; and intensity made children more likely to develop behavior problems. A secondary role was seen for three of the other characteristics—activity, persistence/attention span, and distractibility—and none for sensory threshold. The subsequent studies have established a primary clinical importance for these other four traits as well, especially persistence/attention span in the older child.

Although the focus of this section is on temperament traits as predisposing factors for clinical conditions, we gain a useful perspective if we recognize that for each characteristic that makes a problem more likely, there is the opposite one that makes it less likely. If a low sensory threshold makes a young infant more vulnerable to the physiological disruption called "colic," then a high sensory threshold can be viewed as a factor tending to prevent it. Furthermore, what makes a characteristic predispose to a problem or buffer against it in one situation may be quite different in another. High activity may stimulate development in one environment but encourage accidents in another.

Transitions

As the child grows from infancy to early childhood, are there changes in the temperament characteristics conducive to clinical problems? Are there changes in the clinical conditions produced due to shifts in the interactions of temperament with other factors? These are the questions this section attempts to answer. In brief, we conclude that there are some similarities and some changes in clinical conditions related to temperament. Changes appear to be due primarily to shifts in factors interacting with temperament rather than alteration of the temperament itself.

1. Shifting impact of temperament. We may reasonably assume that, if an individual child's temperament changes as he grows older, he may consequently experience differing interactions and outcomes. We know that such changes can occur but that there can also be substantial continuity of the reaction patterns. This issue of stability is discussed elsewhere in this volume and is not our primary concern here. We are rather engaged with the issue of how the other elements in the interactions do or do not change as the child grows older.

One clear change occurring in the impact of temperament is the increased general perceptions (but not specific ratings) of difficult temperament as the child grows older. While only 3.7% of mothers judged their 4- to 8-month-old infants "more difficult than average" in the standardization sample of the Infant Temperament Questionnaire, 12.5% of practically the same population of mothers judged them thus at 1- to 3-years-of-age in the standardization of the Toddler Temperament Scale (McDevitt & Carey, 1981). This over three-fold increase, which was similar to that observed in the NYLS (Thomas et al., 1968), establishes that, however parents may rate their children's specific behavior, they become less accepting of inflexible, negative children when they are no longer young infants.

Furthermore, as infants develop into young children, there are some changes in the specific characteristics regarded as difficult. Low persistence/attention span seems to present few problems in managing infants but assumes increasing importance as the characteristic interferes with task performance in young children (Carey, McDevitt, & Baker, 1979). A distractible infant, one who is easily soothed, tends to be regarded as easy to handle, but the distractible child, who has trouble staying with tasks, is the reverse (Carey & McDevitt, 1978). Low sensory threshold can predispose to functional problems in infants (Carey 1972, 1974) but has not yet been found to be of consequence in children. However, adaptability and mood retain their same importance as difficult characteristics throughout infancy and childhood (Hegvik, McDevitt, & Carey, 1982).

The studies reported in Table 11.2 and the findings about changes in the characteristics predisposing to clinical problems lead inevitably to the conclusion that the definition of difficult temperament must be revised. We have noted how the original NYLS definition included the cluster of five characteristics, as measured in the first 5 years, that inclined their urban, middle-class study population to behavior disorders by the age of 10 (Thomas et al., 1968). However, their study did not consider clinical problems in the children's physical health and development, and did not examine school performance as closely as later studies have. Moreover, if being "difficult" enables an infant to survive in a famine or being "easy" predisposes to failure to thrive (Carey, 1985b), the meaning of the terms has become seemingly contradictory. The current definition is definitely less appropriate in infancy and middle childhood and of uncertain utility in other social settings.

Two possible approaches may solve this diagnostic classification problem. The concept of temperamental difficulty could be defined either in more general or more specific terms. A more general one would be: Any behavioral style characteristic or cluster of characteristics that make a child or group of children hard for their caretakers to manage and are thereby conducive to interpersonal stress and reactive clinical problems in the child. On the other hand, we might particularize into specific problem areas such as social difficulty, educational difficulty, temperamental predisposition to child abuse, abdominal pain, etc. It would have to be understood that the strength of the predispositions would vary and that their impact would be determined in large measure by the milieu. In any case, parents and clinicians would have to manage such children with special care because of the narrower range of settings in which they would be likely to achieve satisfactory adjustment.

Efforts at mathematical simplification of the complex phenomenon of difficult temperament are hazardous and must be derived from and make sense in the clinical setting.

2. Changes in clinical conditions with shifts in psychosocial environment rather than due to alterations in temperament.   (a) Increased expectations and controls—Although increased demands from the psychosocial environment as the child grows older are required to promote social competence, they also inevitably are a factor in creating organism-environment dissonance, stress, and reactive behavior problems. In the NYLS, which began evaluating infants shortly after birth, 42 out of 136 developed behavior problems by the age of 10 (Thomas et al., 1968). The fact that the earliest symptoms of these clinical cases did not begin until age 2 years might give the impression that there was no conflict before that time. A better interpretation is that, as the infants became young children, the parents exerted more pressure toward socialization, were less likely to be tolerant of difficult temperament and the ensuing deviations of behavior, and were more prone to seek psychiatric consultation for them.

(b) Increased requirement for task orientation—As children grow older, more is expected of them in domestic responsibilities and in work at school. This anticipation of increasing levels of performance promotes scholastic achievement for most children but creates substantial problems in school for some. Those with a low attention span or low adaptability in particular will be more likely to have trouble with academic performance and to earn the currently familiar diagnoses of ''hyperactive,'' ''minimal brain dysfunction,'' or ''attention deficit disorder'' (Carey et al., 1979).

(c) Increasing parental encouragement of self-care and self-regulation, although a necessary basis for children's achievement of personal autonomy, may be stressful for some children. If the quality or timing is not right for the child, enuresis or constipation may possibly be a consequence.

(d) Decreased parental controls in some other areas such as selection of the child's diet allows more self-regulation and may uncover a tendency to obesity.

3. Shifts in other factors.   (a) Physical, neurological, and developmental status—Whatever the child's temperament and environment, ''colic'' usually stops by 3 or 4 months due to unknown factors but possibly a maturation of the central nervous system (Carey, 1984). Failure to thrive has mostly been detected by 18 months and decreases thereafter (Bithoney & Rathbun, 1983), the reason being uncertain but probably having to do with increased size and developmental level rather than change in temperament. Child abuse reaches a peak around 2- or 3-years-of-age and then declines (Snyder, Hampton, & Newberger, 1983), probably due to factors other than shifts in the child's behavioral style.

(b) Changes in the nonhuman environment—This theoretical possibility is largely unexplored but must include phenomena such as increased opportunity for accidents as the child's world expands.

BIDIRECTIONAL EFFECTS OR UNCERTAIN ONES

One must acknowledge that the direction of effects in preceding sections of this chapter may be different from those suggested. For example, the decreased activity associated with obesity may be the result rather than a cause of the problem. In other cases there may be complex bidirectional effects. For example, a malnourished child may become apathetic (less active and intense), which may elicit less stimulation from his caretaker and jeopardize his development further (Rossetti-Ferreira, 1978). In yet other instances the nature of the relationship may still be obscure. The report of an association between chronic non-specific diarrhea and high activity, irritability, and intensity was unable to determine whether the behavioral style caused the overactivity of the bowel, the discomfort of the abdominal cramping affected the behavior, or both were the consequence of some common disturbance of autonomic function (Wender, Palmer, Herbst, & Wender, 1978).

CONCLUSION: A PLEA FOR MORE CLINICAL RESEARCH

An earlier review stated that, "At this early stage, all that the field of temperament can offer with confidence to the clinician is its emphasis on individuality" (Plomin, 1983, p. 82). To be sure, the suggested clinical strategies have been presented mostly in broad outlines (Carey, 1982), but meaningful clinical applications of temperament concepts exist and are increasing. The rate of this growth depends entirely on the direction and extent of research efforts.

This reviewer, although impressed by the recent upsurge of interest in the field, cannot leave this presentation without some expression of hope that a greater portion of available resources be invested in clinical research. As we clinicians struggle to help parents deal with the variety of clinical problems related to temperament, we find little help in more elegant tables of factor structures or debates over whether difficult temperament is "real" or just a parental perception. These discussions bring to mind the reports of tedious arguments by the obstetricians of the last century over the question of whether labor pains are "real" when many practical problems like high maternal and infant mortality were begging for solution.

As clinical investigations increase, the best results will certainly emerge where there is close cooperation between behavioral scientists and clinicians. Such associations are not just mutually enriching, they are absolutely essential for dealing with these complex matters.

SUMMARY

This chapter explores temperament both as an outcome of clinical conditions and as a predisposing factor, and considers the degree to which both sorts of interactions change as the child moves from infancy into early childhood. Temperament appears to be affected by a considerable variety of clinical conditions, although present data are so sparse as to prohibit firm conclusions. However, it is reasonable to suggest that the current model of genetic factors interacting with psychosocial factors be broadened to include these other elements of the child's physical and developmental status and the nonhuman environment. As to transitions, one can do no more than speculate about the wearing off of pregnancy effects. On the other hand, more data are available to demonstrate a wide range of clinical conditions in physical health, development and behavior with temperament as a predisposing factor. As infants become young children, there are some similarities and some changes in the temperamental factors involved and in the resulting clinical conditions, but changes in outcome appear to be due mainly to shifts in the psychosocial environment and other factors rather than to alterations of temperament itself. The need for a revised definition of difficult temperament is stressed, and a plea is issued for the investment of a larger proportion of research efforts in these clinical matters.

REFERENCES

Betz, B. J., & Thomas, C. B. (1979). Individual temperament as a predictor of health or premature disease. *Johns Hopkins Medical Journal, 144,* 81–89.

Bithoney, W. G., & Rathbun, J. M. (1983). Failure to thrive. In M. D. Levine, W. B. Carey, A. C. Crocker, & R. T. Gross (Eds.), *Developmental-behavioral pediatrics*. Philadelphia: W. B. Saunders.

Burks, J., & Rubenstein, M. (1979). *Temperamental styles in adult interaction: Applications in psychotherapy*. New York: Brunner/Mazel.

Carey, W. B. (1972). Clinical applications of infant temperament measurements. *Journal of Pediatrics, 81,* 823–828.

Carey, W. B. (1974). Night waking and temperament in infancy. *Journal of Pediatrics, 84,* 756–758.

Carey, W. B. (1981). The importance of temperament-environment interaction for child health and development. In M. Lewis & L. Rosenblum (Eds.), *The uncommon child*. New York: Plenum.

Carey, W. B. (1982). Clinical use of temperament data in pediatrics. In R. Porter & G. M. Collins (Eds.), *Temperamental differences in infants and young children* (Ciba Foundation Symposium 89). London, Pitman.

Carey, W. B. (1984). ''Colic''—Primary excessive crying as an infant-environment interaction. *Pediatric Clinics of North America, 31,* 993–1005.

Carey, W. B. (1985a). Interactions of temperament and clinical conditions. In M. Wolraich & D. H. Routh (Eds.), *Advances in developmental and behavioral pediatrics* (Vol. 6). Greenwich, CT: JAI Press.

Carey, W. B. (1985b). Temperament and increased weight gain in infants. *Journal of Developmental and Behavioral Pediatrics, 6,* 128–131.

Carey, W. B., & McDevitt, S. C. (1978). Revision of the Infant Temperament Questionnaire. *Pediatrics, 61,* 735–739.

Carey, W. B., & McDevitt, S. C. (1980). Minimal brain dysfunction and hyperkinesis. A clinical viewpoint. *American Journal of Diseases of Children, 134,* 926–929.

Carey, W. B., McDevitt, S. C., & Baker, D. (1979). Differentiating minimal brain dysfunction and temperament. *Developmental Medicine and Child Neurology, 21,* 765–772.

Chavez, A., Martinez, C., & Yaschine, T. (1979). The importance of nutrition and stimuli in child mental and social development. In J. Cravioto, L. Hambraeus, & B. Valquist (Eds.), *Early malnutrition and mental development,* Uppsala: Almquist & Wiksell.

deVries, M. W. (1984). Temperament and infant mortality among the Masai of East Africa. *American Journal of Psychiatry, 141,* 1189–1194.

Earls, F. (1981). Temperament characteristics and behavior problems in three-year-old children. *Journal of Nervous and Mental Diseases, 169,* 367–373.

Escalona, S. (1968). *The roots of individuality.* Chicago: Aldine.

Hegvik, R., McDevitt, S. C., & Carey, W. B. (1982). The Middle Childhood Temperament Questionnaire. *Journal of Developmental and Behavioral Pediatrics, 3,* 197–200.

Huttunen, M. O., & Nyman, G. (1982). On continuity, change and clinical value of infant temperament in a prospective epidemiological study. In R. Porter & G. Collins (Eds.), *Temperamental differences in infants and young children.* London: Pitman.

Keogh, B. K. (1982). Children's temperament and teachers' decisions. In R. Porter & G. Collins (Eds.), *Temperamental differences in infants and young children.* London:Pitman.

Kolata, G. B. (1978). Behavioral teratology: Birth defects of the mind. *Science, 202,* 732–734.

Martin, R. P., Nagle, R., & Paget, K. (1983). Relationships between temperament and classroom behavior, teacher attitudes and academic achievement. *Journal of Psychoeducational Assessment, 1,* 377–386.

Matheny, A. P., Jr., Brown, A. M., & Wilson, R. S. (1971). Behavioral antecedents of accidental injuries in early childhood. A study of twins. *Journal of Pediatrics, 79,* 122–124.

McDevitt, S. C., & Carey, W. B. (1981). Stability of ratings versus perceptions of temperament from early infancy to 1–3 years. *American Journal of Orthopsychiatry, 51,* 342–345.

Moller, J. S. (1983). Relationships between temperament and development in preschool children. *Research in nursing and health, 6,* 25–32.

Plomin, R. (1983). Childhood temperament. In B. Lahey & A. Kazdin (Eds.), *Advances in clinical child psychology* (Vol. 6). New York: Plenum.

Rossetti-Ferreira, M. C. (1978). Malnutrition and mother-infant asynchrony: Slow mental development. *International Journal of Behavioral Development, 1,* 207–219.

Snyder, J. C., Hampton, R., & Newberger, E. H. (1983). Family dysfunction: Violence, neglect and sexual misuse. In M. D. Levine, W. B. Carey, A. C. Crocker, & R. T. Gross (Eds.), *Developmental-behavioral pediatrics,* Philadelphia: W. B. Saunders.

Thomas, A., Chess, S., & Birch, H. G. (1968). *Temperament and behavior disorders in children.* New York: New York University Press.

Wachs, T. D., & Gandour, M. J. (1983). Temperament, environment, and six-month cognitive-intellectual development: A test of the organismic specificity hypothesis. *International Journal of Behavioral Development, 6,* 135–152.

Wender, E. H., Palmer, F. B., Herbst, J. J., & Wender, P. H. (1976). Behavioral characteristics of children with chronic non-specific diarrhea. *American Journal of Psychiatry, 133,* 20–25.

12 Commentary: Issues for Future Research

Judith Dunn
Medical Research Council Unit on the Development and Integration of Behaviour, Cambridge University, Madingley, Cambridge

An interest in temperamental differences among children brings together people of widely differing scientific concerns—a heterogeneous group of people pursuing very different questions, looking for different kinds of answers, satisfied with different levels of precision in those answers. It is important to keep in mind that different levels of precision may indeed be appropriate for the varied questions which are at issue. A clinician faced with a series of distraught and difficult toddlers looks for a very different order of precision in his attempts to suggest strategies of management than does the researcher concerned with, say, the details of stability in measures of heart rate over time. The point was clearly made by Aristotle (1959):

> It is the mark of the educated man to look for precision in each class of things just so far as the nature of the subject admits; it is evidently equally foolish to accept probable reasoning from a mathematician and to demand from a rhetorician logical proof.

In his contribution to this volume Bates shows how important the issue of the different "constituencies" in temperament research is for our evaluation of the usefulness, stability, and methodological respectability of temperament measures. Our assessment of a particular temperament measure will, as he points out, crucially depend on our particular interests—our "constituency."

In spite of the diversity of interests among temperament researchers, and the parallel diversity in their scientific approaches and standards, it is clear from this volume that we have much to learn from each other. It is as important for developmental psychologists concerned with the precision and rigor of their

163

measures of individual differences to be aware of the urgency of the clinical issues as it is for clinicians to be aware of the problems involved in establishing the origins of individual differences between children, or in creating instruments for describing temperament that have good psychometric properties. It is clear, too, from this volume that in all the areas of research covered—pediatrics, child psychiatry, developmental psychology—that studies including assessments of temperament are increasing in frequency. Research into temperament is certainly alive and growing. But what is its future? One purpose of bringing together summaries of this research in conjunction with discussions of developmental issues by psychologists not primarily concerned with temperament was to raise some general questions about the direction of future research into temperament. What are the most pressing issues highlighted by recent research? Are there leads in the research covered in this monograph that suggest particularly useful research strategies? Do the current concerns of developmental psychologists raise issues of which temperament researchers should be aware? Where should we go from here? In this final section, I shall comment briefly on five issues that seem particularly important, setting my comments primarily in the context of the concern with *change* that is a major focus of this volume.

1. DEVELOPMENTAL CHANGE AND ITS RELATION TO TEMPERAMENT

The first issue concerns the relation of temperamental differences to developmental transitions—"developmental functions," as McCall terms the important developmental changes common to all children. McCall argues forcibly that it is important for temperament researchers not only to consider stability and change in individual differences, but also to examine developmental function. He points out that there are stages of development within which there is relative stability, but between which there is not, and shows that in the field of mental development the study of transition points between such stages informed researchers about *both* developmental function and individual differences in development. There is surely an important message for temperament research here. Take, for instance, the major changes involved in the transition from infancy to childhood. During the second year there are dramatic changes in children's emotional expressive behavior, in their cognitive powers, in their social relationships, and in their sense of self. Their social behavior is transformed: In addition to becoming language users, their powers of social manipulation develop, and they understand and anticipate others' moods and intentions. By 2 years of age they possess a grasp of the social rules and roles of their family world which makes them powerful members of that world (Dunn & Munn, 1985). How do these changes affect the expression of temperament dimensions? How do parents change in their perception of their children's temperament as the emotional and social behaviors of those children change so dramatically?

It would without question be illuminating to look sensitively at the expression of temperament dimensions over the transition points of the second year— illuminating both for our understanding of the development of individual differences in temperament, and for our theories of emotional and social behaviors more broadly considered. It would also be clinically useful: From pediatric research discussed by Carey we know that parental reports of difficult temperament increase as children reach 24 months of age, that there is a change in the perception of characteristics seen as difficult, that behavior problem symptoms appear at 24 months, and that child abuse peaks at 24 months. As McCall points out, we don't as yet have very effective conceptual methodological tools for studying change. We are presented here with a challenge rather than a recipe for how to carry out research. It's a challenge that should be taken up.

2. INDIVIDUAL AND ENVIRONMENT

The other issues that I want to discuss all concern particular aspects of a very broad topic—the question of what developmental processes are involved in the interaction between individual and environment. As the chapters by Wilson and Matheny, and by Plomin show, we are gaining a much clearer understanding of the relative genetic and environmental contributions to variance between individuals in temperament at different points in development. The question of the nature of the *processes* involved in the links between temperamental differences in individuals and environmental influence, discussed by the Lerners, Super and Harkness, and the Hindes is obviously of central developmental importance. In relation to this question, there are two important issues in current developmental theory that deserve particular attention from temperament researchers. The first issue concerns the developmental models that distinguish three different types of correlation between individual child and environmental influence—passive, active, and reactive. These developmental models are obviously centrally important to those thinking about how temperament relates to developmental processes. Yet they are at present very much *theoretical* models. It has been argued, for instance, that there are changes with age in the relative importance of the different types of genotype-environment correlation (Scarr & McCartney, 1983), a proposal that certainly deserves research attention. However, it will be very difficult to design powerful methods for distinguishing these different forms of temperament-environment or genotype-environment correlation.

The second issue concerns the question of why children who are brought up in the same family, siblings who share 50% of their genes, differ from one another in personality almost as much as do quite unrelated children brought up in different families (Rowe & Plomin, 1981). As Maccoby and Martin (1983) point out, it is a sobering reflection on how little of the variation in children's behaviour is explained by the "traditional" variables of family influence that we have presumed to be important. What can explain it? Differential treatment by parents? Direct influence of siblings upon one another? Ecological "niche-picking" within the family by the different children? To assess the relative importance of these different processes we need research strategies that include detailed study not only of the children who are the targets of research, but also of the family in which the children are growing up. This is a general theme that recurs in several chapters of this book—the need to study the child's family world as well as the individual child. Here again the recent theoretical writings of developmental psychologists and of developmental behavior geneticists present us with a major challenge, rather than with an easy route forward.

Individual Differences in the Stability of Temperament

One particular aspect of this topic of the processes of temperament-environment interaction concerns the issue of why some children change in their temperamental behavior, whereas others appear more stable. It is clearly important that, for instance, one-third of the inhibited children in the study described by Kagan, Reznick, and Snidman became "uninhibited." In every study of temperament *some* children change their classification. To begin to understand these changes we need to refine the questions that we ask about stability and change. We need to identify which factors affect which children and which dimensions of temperament, at which developmental stages, and to distinguish endogenous from exogenous sources of variation. The causes of stability may well be different for different dimensions of temperament and for different children. Do some children remain "stable" in particular temperamental dimensions because they actively "niche-pick" and seek particular kinds of social environment? Do others remain stable because their parents consistently respond to and encourage certain styles of behavior? How can we best address the question of what processes are involved in the patterns of stability and change that we find?

Certainly we need to study children's relationships within the family and with their friends. We should also note Matheny's (1983) analysis of twins in the Louisville study. He demonstrates with precision and clarity that between 6 months and 24-months-of-age there are "marked reorderings of individual differences of temperament from one age to another. . . . The profile correlations obtained from the identical and fraternal pairs are particularly instructive. The correlations show within the context of behavioral transitions, that the sequences of individual change are partially regulated by genetic influence. . ." (p. 359). The illuminating findings of this study raise the question of how family members respond to such changes in emotional and social behavior. If we pursue the example of the developmental transitions of the second year, two points are clear. First, both parents and siblings change in their behavior towards the child as he grows from 14- to 24-months (Dunn & Munn, 1985). These changes in behavior reflect a sensitivity towards the developing child's new capabilities, but they also remind us that we should not assume that such environmental changes are necessarily unimportant as contributors to the developmental changes in the child. Second, *differences* in the ways in which family members change in their behavior towards the child in the course of the second year may well be important in accounting for individual differences in how children develop over this period. The question of how parent, sibling, and child mutually adjust to the transformation of a 1-year-old into an emotionally labile, expressive, and manipulative 2-year-old clearly deserves attention.

Individual Differences in Vulnerability and Resilience

The next aspect of individual-environment interaction to be discussed is one of urgent practical importance that again highlights the need to study the family rather than solely the child. Why are some children more vulnerable than others to stressful life events, responding with increased anxiety and disturbed behavior to the same environmental experiences that other children apparently weather without difficulty? The importance of monitoring the changes in family relationships that accompany such life events, as well as considering the child's temperament as a mediating variable, is illustrated by some findings from a study of children's responses to the arrival of a sibling, a common but potentially stressful event in the life of preschool children. The results showed first that temperamental differences between the firstborn children assessed before the sibling birth were linked to differences in the children's immediate reaction—the degree of disturbance that they showed in the 2–3 weeks after the birth—and also to the incidence of fearful worrying and anxious behavior in the following year (Dunn & Kendrick, 1982). However, the results also demonstrated that there were marked changes in the interaction of the mother and firstborn following the sibling birth, and that individual differences in the mother-child and father-child relationship before and after the birth were also associated with differences in the behavior of the firstborn children over the next year.

It is not, of course, simply the parent-child relationship that must be examined. In their chapter in this book, Thomas and Chess report findings that demonstrate the predictive importance of conflict between mother and father during childhood for adult adjustment. It is a result that we should pay serious attention to, from the sole study that explores temperamental stability and change from childhood to adulthood. What the nature of the links between the marital relationship in the early childhood years, temperamental differences, and adult behavior might be remains to be clarified. It is important that we should think hard about how we can best study such a difficult issue: We need, presumably, a combination of epidemiological and observational methods applied to a longitudinal sample. The recent study by Rutter and his colleagues of women who were brought up in institutions and were studied both as children and as mothers provides a useful model (Quinton, Rutter, & Liddell, 1984).

Temperament and Attachment

Next, the relation between temperamental differences and the quality of attachment between child and mother is an issue that is very much a topic of controversy and argument at present. The dispute centers on the question of whether differences between babies in their behavior in the Ainsworth Strange Situation reflect primarily temperamental differences in the babies, or differences in the quality of the relationship between mother and child. Sroufe (in press) argues that the A-B-C classification scheme cannot be reduced to, and is to a large extent orthogonal to, temperamental variation. Children in *each* group show the entire range of behaviors on all specific dimensions of temperament frequently cited in the literature (activity, soothability, arousability, etc.). Further, the child is more than a collection of traits, and qualitative aspects of *relationships* cannot be reduced to differences on individual temperament dimensions.

Others argue that the observed differences in children's behavior in the Strange Situation are a reflection of the child's characteristic pattern of reaction to stress; that is, they reflect the child's endogenous temperament rather than the quality of the relationship between child and mother (Chess & Thomas, 1982). It certainly seems plausible that some of the variance in behavior in that situation is related to temperamental traits (Campos, Barrett, Lamb, Goldsmith, & Stenberg, 1983). Sroufe (in press) indeed does not propose that temperamental differences make no contribution to the quality of mother-child relationship, but he disputes the position that attachment classification reflects temperamental differences in children: "While not at all incompatible with studies of temperamental differences and the role of temperament in development, attachment research represents a distinct domain and attachment classifications a different level of analysis."

In fact, there appear to be distinct parallels between the arguments put forward by attachment theorists and by temperament researchers. Sroufe shows, for instance, that the attachment classification depends on the pattern of behavior across contexts—the "overall organization" of behavior—rather than upon specific behaviors such as distress at separation, and that it is this classification which provides useful prediction of the child's behavior in other settings. Some of the arguments for broad temperament dimensions have been put forward in quite similar terms, emphasizing the conceptual and predictive usefulness of relatively global overall categorizations such as "difficult" temperament.

However, two centrally important issues in the dispute remain unclear. First, the relationship of neonatal differences between babies *either* to attachment quality or to temperamental differences at 1 year is still uncertain. Thus, while it is reasonably well established that the kind of maternal care a child has received during the first year of life does indeed relate to the quality of attachment between mother and child at 12 months, it is still not certain how far early individual differences between babies—including temperamental differences— *also* contribute to the quality of attachment is assessed in the Strange Situation. Campos and colleagues conclude that:

> . . . there seems to be some evidence that C babies may be difficult babies from earliest infancy and that certain aspects of their Strange Situation performance (e.g. their threshold to cry and their passivity) may be evident long before the attachment relationship is built. However, the precise contribution of other temperamental factors to the Strange Situation performance and the specific mechanism by which temperament influences classification status awaits careful investigation (Campos et al., 1983, p. 868).

Second, a similar cloud of uncertainty hangs over the question of whether temperamental differences are related to the quality of the mother-child relationship earlier in the child's life. We do know that differences in certain temperamental traits are concurrently associated with differences in the behavior of mothers to their children, as described by Stevenson-Hinde and Hinde in this book (also, see Dunn & Kendrick, 1980). The Hindes' chapter lucidly presents the point at issue: Temperamental differences cannot be viewed as invariant psychological structures—features of an individual's behavioral style independent of his or her relationships. They are intimately connected with the particular social setting in which the child is studied, with the stage of the child's development, and with the nature of his or her relationships. We do not know what part such differences in family relationships play in the development or earlier expression of temperamental differences. Clearly these questions need further investigation.

Social Behavior and the Measurement of Temperament Differences

My final point is very much that of an outsider, visiting the field of temperament research as an extraterrestial might visit earth, with interest and considerable puzzlement. It concerns measurement. One feature of the measurement issue that apparently is rarely considered is the social and ecological relevance of the behavior that is chosen to index the temperament characteristic that is presumed on theoretical grounds to be important. Yet this appears potentially very important to an ethologically trained person from another world.

In the work of Kagan and his colleagues with 4-year-olds, the power and salience of two measures stands out: the behavior of the child with a peer, and the spontaneous talk of the child with the examiner. To a parent of a 4-year-old it would come as no surprise that if you want to pick out important individual differences in children of this age, behavior with peers and talkativeness with adults turn out to be such useful measures. The lesson is that if we choose measures of children's behavior that are of real significance to children of that particular age, we are likely to do well. The point is equally relevant to our concern with stability and change. Much of the investment of temperament researchers has been in the search for measures that will reflect the stability of individual differences over a period when the children themselves change dramatically with development—an intractable problem which has been extensively discussed. Are we really interested in the stability of the *measures*? Ultimately not. We want to know what these stable individual differences mean for children in their real life environments.

Why then do temperament researchers not invest more energy in examining children's behavior in their own worlds? There are comparatively few studies of temperament that examine how the global temperament characteristics or the detailed laboratory measures relate to children's behavior in the settings that matter to them. The Hindes' study is a notable exception. Yet this is in the end what we want to be able to predict or explain. It is often stressed that we need more validation of temperament measures. Bates, for instance, argues for more varying measures of children in different situations. Surely it is of prime importance to include in these assessments direct measures of children's social behavior in their world of family and friends. Whether our concerns are clinical or more specifically developmental, we will learn more of significance this way.

In summary, there are, on the one hand, urgent practical questions towards which temperament research can be directed—child abuse, the response of children to stressful change, traumatic experiences, or family discord—all of which require research which includes the assessment of temperament. On the other hand, some of the major issues in developmental psychology—the elucidation of the processes involved in developmental change, the different forms of individual-environment correlation, the origins of differences in children's relationships with their family and friends—may well be illuminated by studies which include careful assessments of temperamental differences in children. If we address such questions, we cannot fail to learn more about the nature and developmental implications of the variations among children which we call temperamental differences.

REFERENCES

Aristotle (1959). *Nichomachean ethics,* Book 1, Chapter 3 (Berlin Edition). Berlin: Spring-Verlag.

Campos, J. J., Barrett, K. C., Lamb, M. E., Goldsmith, H. H., & Stenberg, C. (1983). Socioemotional development. In P. H. Mussen (Ed.), *Handbook of child psychology (4th ed.): Vol. II. Infancy and developmental psychobiology* (pp. 783–915). New York: Wiley.

Chess, S., & Thomas, A. (1982). Infant bonding: Mystique and reality. *American Journal of Orthopsychiatry, 52,* 211–222.

Dunn, J., & Kendrick, C. (1980). Studying temperament and parent-child interaction: Comparison of interview and direct observation. *Developmental Medicine and Child Neurology, 22,* 484–496.

Dunn, J., & Kendrick, C. (1982). Temperamental differences, family relationships, and young children's response to change within the family. In R. Porter & G. M. Collins (Eds.), *Temperamental differences in infants and young children* (Ciba Foundation Symposium 89). London: Pitman.

Dunn, J., & Munn, P. (1985). Becoming a family member: Family conflict and the development of social understanding in the second year. *Child Development, 56,* 480–492.

Maccoby, E. E., & Martin, J. A. (1983). Socialization in the context of the family: Parent-child interaction. In P. H. Mussen (Eds.), *Handbook of child psychology (4th Ed.): Vol IV. Socialization, personality and social development* (pp. 1–101). New York: Wiley.

Matheny, A. P. (1983). A longitudinal twin study of stability of components from Bayley's Infant Behavior Record. *Child Development, 54,* 356–360.

Quinton, D., Rutter, M., & Liddell, C. (1984). Institutional rearing, parental difficulties and marital support. *Psychological Medicine, 14,* 107–124.

Rowe, D. C., & Plomin, R. (1981). The importance of non-shared (E_1) environmental influences in behavioral development. *Developmental Psychology, 17,* 517–531.

Scarr, S., & McCartney, K. (1983). How people make their own environments: A theory of genotype-environment effects. *Child Development, 54,* 424–435.

Sroufe, L. A. (in press). Attachment classification from the perspective of infant-caregiver relationships and infant temperament. *Child Development.*

Author Index

Numbers in *italics* indicate pages with complete bibliographic information.

Subject Index